Rock Band Name Origins

Rock Band Name Origins

The Stories of 240 Groups and Performers

GREG METZER

McFarland & Company, Inc., Publishers
Jefferson, North Carolina, and London

LIBRARY OF CONGRESS CATALOGUING-IN-PUBLICATION DATA

Metzer, Greg, 1960–
    Rock band name origins : the stories of 240 groups
and performers / Greg Metzer.
        p.   cm.
    Includes bibliographical references and index.

    ISBN 978-0-7864-3818-1
    softcover : 50# alkaline paper ∞

    1. Rock groups — Names — Dictionaries.
I. Title
ML102.R6M48   2008
781.6601'4 — dc22   2008012735

British Library cataloguing data are available

Cover design by Tony Roberts

Manufactured in the United States of America

*McFarland & Company, Inc., Publishers
    Box 611, Jefferson, North Carolina 28640
    www.mcfarlandpub.com*

To my children, Parke and Olivia Metzer.
May this book prove to you that anything is possible!
I love you both.

And to my father, the late, great
Jim "Captain Justice" Metzer. I'm looking
forward to the day we get the chance to
do some serious catching up.

Acknowledgments

I'd like to thank my agent and friend, Kirk Bjornsgaard, who was the first one who "got" this book and believed in it from the start.

Thanks, too, to my best friend and sounding board, Pete Brzycki, who has been my biggest fan throughout this endeavor.

Thanks to Tony Roberts for the great cover art.

Other members of my support system include Mom, Missy, Bart Borsky, my cohorts at Metzer & Austin and my old D.U. buds, all of whom have promised to buy a copy.

Finally, to all rock and roll artists for making life so much more interesting. I couldn't make this stuff up!

Table of Contents

Preface

This book reveals for the first time how some of the most famous musical acts from the sixties through today decided on their names. Some individuals are included but most of the entries deal with groups. I concentrate on the most popular and well-known acts to ensure the book is interesting to both casual music fans and so-called rock snobs.

My inspiration for the book came one morning while driving to work (to my "real" job, as an attorney). I was listening to Rick and Brad on Oklahoma City's KATT-FM who were discussing the origin of the name Nickelback. I was embarrassed to admit that I did not know the story. People often tell me I possess vast pop music knowledge but I realized that I really didn't know the full story behind the names of most bands. Oh sure, I can spout off the year of release or peak chart position of most songs released in the last 45 years, but what average person really cares about that? How the great pop acts came upon their names— that is far more interesting!

I therefore set out to learn these stories for myself and, in the process, I realized there exists no book in which that information is compiled in story form. There are many web sites and a few books (*Rock Formations, What's in a Name, Rock Names*) in which authors mention thousands of obscure bands and explain their names in a sentence or two, but none that tell all the sordid details. And there are stories that beg to be told.

Rather than providing a quick explanation of each band's name, I relate a fleshed-out account of each act's name. For background, I include the year the group was formed, the names of all relevant members of the group, and the group's best known hit. Most significantly, each entry lists the name(s) by which the group or solo performer had been called previously, names the act considered using but then discarded, the meaning of the name ultimately chosen, and the mechanics of settling on the name. I use direct quotations whenever possible to lend credence to the story and help bring it to life. By the end of each entry, the reader will have a real sense of the story behind the name that he or she can share with others. I consider myself an authority on rock/pop music history, but I learned something new in every story I researched.

Many materials were used as research sources for this book, including books, the Internet, and interviews with parties of interest. There were some sources used numerous times, without which my research would have been infinitely more difficult. The following books and website are excellent reference guides and I would strongly encourage anyone who enjoys my book to buy these as well:

Bogdanov, Vladimir, Chris Woodstra, and Stephen Thomas Erlewine. *All Music Guide to Rock. The Definitive Guide to Rock, Pop and Soul.* San Francisco: Backbeat Books, 2002.

Buckley, Jonathan, Orla Duane, Mark Ellington, and Al Spicer. *Rock, the Rough Guide.* London: Rough Guides, 1999.

Whitburn, Joel. *Top Pop Singles, 1955–1999.* Menomonee, WI: Record Research, 2000.

Wikipedia, The Free Encyclopedia. www.en.wikipedia.org.

The book you are about to read lists all acts alphabetically to give the casual reader the opportunity to open it to any page and read at leisure, the historian the ability to easily pinpoint the subject of his or her research, or the die-hard rock fan the chance to learn from A to Z the origin of names of the biggest acts in rock and pop music history. Enjoy!

Greg Metzer
Edmond, Oklahoma
Spring 2008

Introduction

So what *is* in a name anyway? A rock and roll name is really only a conglomeration of words. That is, until life is given to the words by the group. The words may evoke an image of the musical style of the band or the personalities of the members. After the name acquires an identity based on the artist's work, it is very difficult to separate the name from that image. The mere mention of that name immediately means something to the listener. This is true no matter how far-fetched or meaningless the name was when it was chosen. Before you can say (or smell) teen spirit, the word "Nirvana" means something very different from what it ever meant before.

So we can only wonder, given the ever-increasing absurdity of band and individual stage names, "What *were* they thinking?" Well, sometimes all sorts of things. Other times, nothing at all. But since the band "makes the name" after it chooses the name, any name is fair game if you have the goods to bring it to life.

Sometimes a name describes the band (Beach Boys), its origins (Blues Traveler), or its music (Metallica). Sometimes it names members of the band (Crosby, Stills, Nash & Young). Sometimes it's chosen for shock value (Sex Pistols). Other names are selected to mean nothing at all in order to avoid labeling the band as playing a certain style of music (R.E.M.).

With all this in mind, an interesting exercise would be to discuss bands and their musicians and names considered but not chosen, or names they originally had but later changed. So try wrapping your mind around this banter:

"Did you catch the Rock and Roll Hall of Fame inductions last night? The highlight of the night was the induction speech of that lead singer from Mookie Blaylock when honoring Cans of Piss for their outstanding career. They were one of the few bright spots to come out of the 1980s when such bands as The Vegetables, Morris and the Minor, and Sex Gang Children were all over the radio."

"With the way pop music has evolved, I often find myself looking back nostalgically for those great songs from the 1960s. That was an innocent time when we thought Johnny & the Moondogs, the Pendletones, and the Four Lovers would last forever. Of course, Mythical Ethical Icicle Tricycle almost did, as we well know. If it wasn't for them Naked Pilgrims wouldn't have had the inspiration they needed to hit it big."

That's probably as odd for you to read as it is for me to write. How many of those groups did you know? Read this book to find out who was who.

Here is a cross-choice exercise to see how much more you know. Try to match the group on the left with their former name:

1. Alice In Chains	A. Mabel Greer's Toy Shop
2. Cheap Trick	B. Shrinky Dinx
3. Goo Goo Dolls	C. Nameless
4. Green Day	D. Tea Set
5. Heart	E. The One Percent
6. Lynyrd Skynyrd	F. Hocus Pocus
7. Pink Floyd	G. Sweet Children
8. Scorpions	H. Sex Maggots
9. Sugar Ray	I. Sick Man of Europe
10. Yes	J. Diamond Lie

Answers: The left column matches up with the *opposite* of the right column (1/J, 2/I, and so forth). How much different would the music of the groups have been with the different names? None at all. But wouldn't it be weird holding up your lighter at a concert of The One Percent anxiously awaiting the encore of "Freebird"?

In this book I have concentrated on only the *most well-known* groups and solo performers in pop and rock music history from the 1960s through today. Even casual music fans will know almost all of the acts discussed. There are a few one-hit wonders included simply because their name is so unusual that everyone knows them (Mungo Jerry, for example), although their music may be all but forgotten.

Choosing a name is a watershed event in the career of every music act. When the act is a group, there is a dynamic involved requiring the consent of the group members. Reaching agreement on a name can be contentious, humorous, or frustrating for the members. For better or worse, every story is an interesting one! Well, nearly every story.

Years after the group has lost its relevance, there may still be disagreement about who should receive credit for the name or what it really meant (Blood, Sweat & Tears). Even the Rolling Stones can't agree on the origin of the name. But you know, memory can be one of the casualties of old age.

Suppose you overhear someone at a cocktail party spouting off his trivia (trivial?) knowledge about such subjects as the origin of the name of certain music acts. Your contempt for this individual is almost palpable. Just think—after reading this book you can *be* this person! But you should not hold this person in contempt, just because he maintains this information in the dark recesses of his brain. Instead, this person is to be respected for one simple reason: he has purchased this book and, in the process, is helping to put (my) two children through college. As far as being the know-it-all of the party, it's still okay to hate him.

So read on and enjoy each story. The 240 acts covered here truly are the greatest *names* in rock music history. Go find out what in the world they mean!

ABBA

GROUP FORMED IN: 1970
ORIGINAL MEMBERS: Agnetha Faltskog, Bjorn Ulvaeus,
Benny Andersson, Anna-Frid "Frida" Lyngstad
LATER MEMBERS OF NOTE: None
BEST KNOWN SONG: Dancing Queen (#1, 1977)

The history of Sweden's ABBA is well documented. When the group became an international sensation, Bjorn and Agnetha were married. Benny and Frida were also romantically involved, though not wed. Together they perfected the art of the pop song, in the process becoming the most commercially successful group of the 1970s. Ultimately, however, the couples split and the group was unable to maintain its chemistry beyond 1982. Numerous attempts by promoters to bring the group back together 20 years later failed, despite their tremendous return to popularity through covers by other artists and use of their songs in movies and on Broadway.

ABBA is an acronym of the first letters of the group members' names, (Frida's true first name is Anna-Frid). Their first single, "People Need Love," was released in Sweden in June 1972 under the unwieldy name of Bjorn & Benny, Agnetha and Anna-Frid. It was later credited when released in the United States to Bjorn & Benny with Svenska Flicka (Swedish girl).

Although their manager, Stig Anderson, resisted any name which gave the girls equal billing with Bjorn and Benny, he preferred brevity and marketability. He toyed with the name ABBA, but there was already a Swedish canned herring company of the same name. A contest was held by the Gothenburg (Sweden) newspaper to name the group. Among the entries were Flower Power, Black Devils, Golden Diamonds, Baba, Alibaba, and Friends & Neighbours. ABBA, however, was the most mentioned name, so Stig decided to follow his first instinct. After Stig cleared the legal hurdles and convinced Bjorn and Benny, the name stuck. Anders Ekstrom, managing director of the canning company, has noted it was the best publicity his company ever received.

Palm, Carl Magnus. Bright Lights & Dark Shadows. *London: Omnibus Press, 2002; Potiez, Jean-Marie.* ABBA. The Book. *London: Aurum Press, 2000.*

AC/DC

GROUP FORMED In: 1973
ORIGINAL MEMBERS: Angus Young, Malcom Young,
Dave Evans, Larry Van Knedt, Colin Burgess
LATER MEMBERS OF NOTE: Phil Rudd, Ron Belford "Bon" Scott,
Cliff Williams, Brian Johnson, Rob Bailey, Peter Clark,
Chris Slade, Mark Evans, Simon Wright
BEST KNOWN SONG: You Shook Me All Night Long (#35, 1980)

One of music's standard bearers and pioneers for hard rock 'n' roll is AC/DC, which was started by brothers Angus and Malcom Young. The brothers were born in Scotland and emigrated to Australia at an early age. Many have labeled the music created by AC/DC as heavy metal but the band has routinely preferred the term "hard rock" and the members find the heavy metal description offensive.

AC/DC was originally called Third World War. The genesis for the band's current name came from a sewing machine. Or was it a vacuum cleaner? Angus claims he first got the idea after seeing AC/DC on the back of their sister Margaret's sewing machine. Malcolm says it was the vacuum cleaner of his sister-in-law Sandra. The acronym means alternating current/direct current, indicating that a device can be powered by either type of energy source. The Young brothers liked the way the name symbolized the band's raw energy and power-driven performances.

Rumors have abounded that the name is a reference in some cultures to bisexuality. Others claim a more sinister motive, suggesting it stands for Anti-Christ/Death to Christ or similar satanic references. Neither is true. The band members have said they were not aware of the sexual connotation of the name until it was brought to their attention. Likewise, the religious connotation is denied and Malcom has been quoted as saying, "Me mum would kill me for that!"

Masino, Susan. The Story of AC/DC. Let There Be Rock. *London: Omnibus Press, 2006.*

Ace of Base

GROUP FORMED IN: 1990
ORIGINAL MEMBERS: Jenny Berggren, Linn Berggren,
Jonas "Joker" Berggren, Ulf "Buddha" Ekberg

LATER MEMBERS OF NOTE: None
BEST KNOWN SONG: The Sign (#1, 1994)

Sweden's Ace of Base is comprised of the three Berggren siblings— Jenny, Linn, and Jonas— and Ulf Ekberg. Initially, however, the Berggrens were in Tech-Noir with bandmates Johnny Linden and Nicklas Trank (the group was named after a nightclub in the Arnold Schwarzenegger movie *The Terminator*). The style of this group could best be categorized as techno or house music.

After Linden and Trank left the group in 1989 and 1990, respectively, Ekberg was brought in to complete the lineup. Tech-Noir was an unpopular name among the group because, according to Linn, "No one could pronounce the name of the group and nobody could remember it."

In trying to determine a more descriptive and fitting name the members looked inward and created Ace of Base. The meaning is twofold: "Ace" refers to being masters of the studio, and "Base" refers to the studio as their "military" base of operations. The studio was, coincidentally, in the *base*ment of a car repair shop.

Along with its new name, the group also changed to a more radio friendly Euro-pop sound, which led to their first single to hit the U.S. charts, "All That She Wants" on the album entitled *The Sign*. After the first hit peaked at #2, the title cut zoomed to #1 and stayed there for six weeks. The album also spawned a third top five single and was one of the highest selling debut albums in history, selling in excess of 9 million copies worldwide. Although the follow-up album *The Bridge* went platinum, it could not match the phenomenal success of the group's debut effort.

Auty, Dan, Justin Cawthorne, Chris Barrett, and Peter Dodd. 100 Best Selling Albums of the 90s. *New York: Barnes & Noble Books, 2004; www.aceofbase.co.uk; www.virginradio.co.uk; www.arts.enotes.com.*

Aerosmith

GROUP FORMED IN: 1970
ORIGINAL MEMBERS: Steven Tyler (born Steven Tallarico), Brad Whitford, Joey Kramer, Tom Hamilton, Joe Perry
LATER MEMBERS OF NOTE: Jimmy Crespo, Rick Dufay
BEST KNOWN SONG: Walk This Way (#10, 1977)

Aerosmith *is* America's rock band. With a seemingly endless shelf life, a strutting, big-lipped front man, a hard-living, hard-playing lead guitarist, and a largely unchanged lineup for going on four decades, the Boston-based band is also America's version of the Rolling Stones (although none of Aerosmith's members are actually from Boston — nor are the Stones, for that matter).

The first name considered by the band was Spike Jones and the Hookers. This wasn't really acceptable since "spike" was junkie slang for a syringe and a "jones" was an addiction. The drug references were too obvious. Tyler liked simply The Hookers but he was the only one.

They needed something that matched the power of the band and gave fans the sense of *lift* they got when playing together. Joey Kramer, the newest member of the band, suggested Aerosmith. Tom Hamilton objected, "Oh, no, it's that book they made you read in high school. That's too sophisticated," referring to the Sinclair Lewis novel *Arrowsmith*. But when it was spelled out to them "A-e-r-o...," Hamilton and the group realized Kramer had suggested the perfect name.

According to Hamilton, "One of the first things we did with the name was have it stamped on packs of generic rolling papers. We were always driving around Boston in Mark Lehman's van, giving these Aerosmith rolling papers to hitchhikers as a primitive merchandising tool and expression of our general philosophy of life. Those papers are my first memories of seeing the name of the group in print."

Aerosmith, with Stephen Davis. Walk This Way: The Autobiography of Aerosmith. *New York: HarperCollins, 1997.*

a-ha

GROUP FORMED IN: 1982
ORIGINAL MEMBERS: Morten Harket,
Pal Waaktaar, Magne "Mags" Furuholmen
LATER MEMBERS OF NOTE: None
BEST KNOWN SONG: Take On Me (#1, 1985)

Originally from Norway, the members of a-ha relocated to London in 1982 to enhance their chances of succeeding in the music business. As with many undiscovered acts, they lived in poverty for a time in what was called the "legendary London flat" for its state of disrepair. The group chose their recording studio because it had a Space Invaders video game. This was the studio of musician and producer John Radcliff, who would later become their manager.

The group was looking for a name with positive connotations. Since the group members were raised speaking a language not spoken by the music-buying public of England and the United States, they were in need of an English name or phrase that would be easily recognized and remembered. After checking dictionaries (obviously only a few pages in) they noticed "a-ha" which is defined as "Used to express surprise, pleasure or triumph." This enthusiastic definition matched the upbeat vibe the group wished to portray to the public. Additionally, the name was short, easy to say, and unusual.

Their persistence in striving to succeed in the music business paid off when "Take On Me" became a worldwide smash hit in 1985, due in large part to the exposure of its stunning video on MTV, which fused animation with real-life action. The song and its album sold millions of copies. As a result, a-ha became the best known Norwegian band of all time in the United States, allowing them to move into significantly better quarters.

Alice in Chains

GROUP FORMED IN: 1987
ORIGINAL MEMBERS: Layne Staley, Jerry Cantrell,
Mike Starr, Sean Kinney
LATER MEMBERS OF NOTE: Mike Inez,
William DuVall, Pat Lachman (guest vocalist)
BEST KNOWN SONG: No Excuses
(#48-Hot 100 airplay, 1994)

Some would say Seattle's Alice in Chains was the consummate heavy metal band during the height of the grunge movement. But to pigeon-hole the group under any genre label is difficult and narrow-minded. Alice in Chains was not purely grunge, alternative, hard rock, post-punk, or glam, but it was certainly a little of each.

Diamond Lie was the name of Jerry Cantrell's band when, in 1987, he invited Layne Staley to join. Bass player Mike Starr was added as was drummer Sean Kinney (who was dating Starr's sister at the time), which completed the initial lineup. They actually began calling the band Fuck. "We weren't getting work anyway, so we thought it wouldn't hurt us," said Staley. They went so far as to hand out condoms embossed with "Fuck The Band" as a publicity stunt.

Realizing such a racy moniker couldn't be used if the band was to break out on the national stage, the name was changed to Alice in Chains, which was a derivation of one of Staley's former bands, Alice N' Chainz. Staley's vision for his new band was that they would dress in drag and play speed metal, not unlike Pantera in its early years.

Shortly thereafter the music landscape was changing. Hair bands were out and grunge bands were in. Alice in Chains chose to abandon any pretense of glam-rock and became straight-ahead rockers, balancing grinding hard rock with subtly textured acoustic numbers. Their first official release was the EP entitled *We Die Young*, which presaged the group's premature demise as well as Staley's untimely death in April 2002 of a cocaine and heroin overdose.

Ressner, Jeffrey. "Alice through the Looking Glass: The Dark Brooding Side of the Seattle Scene." Rolling Stone 644, (November 26, 1992).

The All-American Rejects

GROUP FORMED IN: 1998
ORIGINAL MEMBERS: Tyson Ritter, Nick Wheeler,
Mike Kennerty, Chris Gaylor
LATER MEMBERS OF NOTE: Tim Campbell
BEST KNOWN SONG: Swing Swing (#60, 2002)

Tyson Ritter and Nick Wheeler formed their playing and songwriting team while both were in high school in Oklahoma. The duo added Mike Kennerty and Chris Gaylor to the fold in 2002 to fill out the quartet. Their teeth were cut in much the normal way, playing bars and clubs in and around their hometown. Their power pop music style resonated with the youth of the new millennium, making The All-American Rejects an instant success following the release of its eponymous debut CD on independent Doghouse Records.

Wheeler doesn't seem too certain where the name originated, saying, "I think that was a lyric on one of our songs." Actually the full name of the group resulted from two factions coming together. Wheeler was thinking, "The All-American..." somethings, but was at a loss for the second part.

Ritter made a suggestion to call the band simply The Rejects. When the two parts were combined, it eventually stuck. "By the time we were writing this [debut] album, we were like, 'all right, this is for real ... what's our name?'" Wheeler remembers asking. "The All-American Rejects" sounded more and more natural after repeating the entire phrase several times, so the band decided that was it.

The band built upon its initial success with the second full-length CD, *Move Along*, which was certified platinum shortly after its release. No longer on the independent label, the band was finally receiving the marketing support it lacked with its debut effort, catapulting the members from small-town Oklahoma to big-time players on the pop music scene.

www.andpop.com; www.tv.com.

The Amboy Dukes

GROUP FORMED IN: 1966
ORIGINAL MEMBERS: Ted Nugent, John Drake,
Gary Hicks, Dick Treat, Gail Uptadale
LATER MEMBERS OF NOTE: Steve Farmer, Rick Lober,
Bill White, Dave Palmer, Andy Solomon,
Greg Arama, Rusty Day
BEST KNOWN SONG: Journey to the
Center of the Mind (#16, 1968)

This may be a group you know by name only casually, but it merits discussion in this book for three reasons: (1) the group was the starting point in the career of Ted Nugent; (2) their one hit, "Journey to the Center of the Mind," is considered one of the defining songs of the psychedelic era; and, most importantly, (3) the colorful origin of the group's name.

Nugent joined The Detroit Amboy Dukes at the age of 17. The band later shortened its name to The Amboy Dukes. Their style combined psychedelic and garage music with classic pop hooks. While their tenure was short and their influence limited, The Amboy Dukes developed an underground following that sustained the band until internal bickering led to its implosion in 1975.

The source of the name comes from a real-life Brooklyn street gang called Amboy Dukes, to which notorious mobster Louis "Lepke" Buchalter once belonged. Lepke's criminal record began at age 18 and blossomed into a career in the mob. He has been called the bloodiest Jewish gangster of all time. He controlled Murder, Incorporated, the portion of the National Crime Syndicate in charge of performing murders for hire for the major crime bosses across the country and the Five Families of New York.

During his years in Murder, Incorporated, Lepke oversaw no less than

85 murders. He was ultimately convicted on one specific murder and sentenced to die in the electric chair, which ultimately took place at Sing Sing Prison on March 4, 1944. He became the first and only mob boss ever to be executed.

www.paperlessarchives.com.

Ambrosia

GROUP FORMED IN: 1970
ORIGINAL MEMBERS: David Pack, Joe Puerta,
Christopher North, Burleigh Drummond
LATER MEMBERS OF NOTE: Ken Stacey,
David Lewis, Doug Jackson
BEST KNOWN SONG: How Much I Feel (#3, 1978)

Ambrosia was an American band formed in the Los Angeles area that was influenced by British prog-rock bands such as Yes, Pink Floyd, and Genesis. Unlike those from whom they drew inspiration, Ambrosia created a more commercial sound for the 1970s, sounding much more like straight pop music than the ethereal sounds of the true progressive rock bands that confined those acts to AOR stations.

David Pack and Joe Puerta joined forces when they were 15 years old in a band called The Sentries. Inspired by the advent of rock supergroups such as Cream, Pack and Puerta left The Sentries and set out to handpick the best keyboard player and drummer in southern California.

According to Pack, they "heard about this wild, wacky keyboard player, Chris North, who is the baddest blues keyboard player in San Pedro, California. We coerced him into coming into the band. Then we met Burleigh [Drummond] through the Musicians Contact just because we thought, out of 100 drummers, he had the coolest name. We were surprised that he was also a great drummer."

Their first name for the group was Ambergris Might, a strange name considering ambergris is a waxy material formed in the intestines of sperm whales. It is sometimes found floating at sea and is often added to perfumes to slow down the rate of evaporation. Unbelievably, another group also decided to use the name (do they know something I don't know?). Pack and Puerta decided to go to the dictionary for another name. According to Pack, "The next name underneath ambergris was ambrosia," so the group opted for this much more palatable moniker.

www.kaos2000.net; www.classicrockrevisited.com.

America

GROUP FORMED IN: 1969
ORIGINAL MEMBERS: Gerry Beckley, Dewey Bunnell, Dan Peek
OTHERS INVOLVED IN THE BAND: David Dickey, Willie Leacox, Michael
Woods, Rich Campbell, Joe Osborn, Hal Blaine,
Jim Calire, Tom Walsh, Tony Garofolo, Brad Palmer
BEST KNOWN SONG: A Horse with No Name (#1, 1972)

America was a soft rock trio of Americans living in England. Gerry Beckley and Dan Peek were born in the United States but moved to England where their air force fathers were stationed. Dewey Bunnell was born in England. All three had American fathers and British mothers.

The band explains the band name choice: "Dan and Dewey were working in a cafeteria on the [Air Force] base and there was a jukebox called 'The Americana' in the corner. That's where we got the idea and the more we thought about it the better it seemed to explain our origins. It did get a little confusing when we finally did come to the States to perform and the ads said 'Live from England ... America!'"

The group's style was acoustic folk-rock using three-part harmonies similar to Crosby, Stills & Nash, making this trio of half-British lads sound quite American indeed. After the bulk of their commercial success, including two #1s ("A Horse with No Name" and "Sister Golden Hair"), as well as four other top-10 hits, Peek left the group to become a Contemporary Christian artist. Beckley and Bunnell have continued on as a duo, with the studio and road assistance of many others to fill out the sound.

The group developed an unusual idiosyncrasy with their albums. After the first eponymous album, the next seven albums all started with the letter "H." According to the group, it started by accident. After the second and third albums began with "H" (*Homecoming* and *Hat Trick*), the record company started printing *Horse with No Name* on the first album, and from then on a conscious effort to keep the string going was afoot.

www.venturahighway.com.

The Animals

GROUP FORMED IN: 1962
ORIGINAL MEMBERS: Alan Price, Hilton Valentine,
Bryan "Chas" Chandler, John Steel, Eric Burdon
LATER MEMBERS OF NOTE: Dave Rowberry, Barry Jenkins, Vic Briggs,
John Wieder, Danny McCulloch, Zoot Money, Andy Summers
BEST KNOWN SONG: House of the Rising Sun (#1, 1964)

In terms of R&B bands of the British Invasion, The Animals were second only to the Rolling Stones. Led by gritty, deep-voiced Eric Burdon, this act of enormously talented musicians had fourteen top-40 hits in the United States from 1964 to 1968, ultimately landing them in the Rock and Roll Hall of Fame.

However, the Newcastle quintet would never have made it into the congeniality Hall of Fame. Burdon and group founder Alan Price had a tension-filled relationship before Price left the band in 1965. Burdon's on- and off-stage antics could best be described as frenetic. He would throw himself into his songs, whip the band into overdrive, and incite the audience into a frenzy.

The group had a number of early names, such as the wonderfully descriptive Alan Price Combo. Later names included The Pagan Jazzmen, and later simply the Pagans. Eventually the band became less into jazz and more consumed in R&B music as it began utilizing Burdon's vocal ability to the fullest. This new emphasis on the developing style and grit of Burdon and the band led to a renaming of the group. History has shown that the new name, The Animals, was an incredibly appropriate moniker.

The name came courtesy of Ronan O'Reilly, but the group took to it immediately. "Animals? Sure. We're really Animals!" said Burdon. "I like it because our music is raw, uninhibited material. It's untamed and wild—exactly the type of basic emotional appeal which can be described as Animalistic."

Burdon, Eric, with J. Marshall Craig. Don't Let Me Be Misunderstood. *New York: Thunder's Mouth Press, 2001. Altham, Keith.* Animals: Sure, We're Really Animals! *NME Summer Special, 1966. www.rocksbackpages.com and www.rollingstone.com/artists/theanimals/biography.*

Art of Noise

GROUP FORMED IN: 1983
ORIGINAL MEMBERS: Anne Dudley, Gary Langan,

J.J. Jeczalik, Trevor Horn, Paul Morley
LATER MEMBERS OF NOTE: Lol Creme
BEST KNOWN SONG: Paranoimia (#34, 1986)

Rarely has a band been more aptly named than Art of Noise. The music created by this group was a combination of synthesizer, tape splicing, and studio gimmickry. The group employed the assistance of some formerly great artists, including Duane Eddy on their remake of the "Peter Gunn Theme" and Tom Jones on their version of Prince's "Kiss." The band was equally groundbreaking in its videos, using a computer-enhanced man known as Max Headroom to perform a dialogue on "Paranoimia."

The group's name was taken from a 1913 essay by Italian futurist Luigi Russolo. In his manifesto *The Art of Noises*, Russolo championed a rosy if abrasive future, liberated by technology, and he was vehemently opposed to nostalgia and romanticism.

Paul Morley is credited with naming the group. His story is as follows: "When I heard the kind of sounds and noises this team could create, inventing new textures to fill out the shape of songs so that the songs resembled songs—but as if reassembled in the way that Picasso reassembled facial features—I knew exactly what to call the group. They played me a piece of music that was made up of a computer-generated drum that sounded as big as the sky, the sound of a car ignition starting up an engine, the recording of a tennis match, and a bassline that was a machine's hopeful idea of boogie-woogie. I named them the The Art of Noises."

The name underwent a slight alteration. Groups beginning with "The" were out of favor at the time, and "Noises" was shortened to "Noise" to ultimately arrive at Art of Noise.

www.guardian.co.uk.

Asia

GROUP FORMED IN: 1981
ORIGINAL MEMBERS: Steve Howe, Carl Palmer,
John Wetton, Geoff Downes
LATER MEMBERS OF NOTE: Mandy Meyer, Pat Thrall,
John Payne, Guthrie Govan, Jay Schellen, Greg Lake,
Michael Sturgis, Al Pitrelli, Vinny Burns, Trevor Thornton,
Aziz Ibrahim, Elliot Randall, Chris Slade
BEST KNOWN SONG: Heat of the Moment (#4, 1982)

Asia is the marriage of two concepts of pop music, the supergroup and progressive rock. The four original members represented former members of Yes, ELP, King Crimson, and the Buggles. However, the Asia heard on the radio was much more like the arena-rock bands Journey, REO Speedwagon, and Styx than the prog-rock sound of the members' progenitors.

The band name was unusual, considering that the British band members had no connection to the largest continent. John Wetton recalls a meeting at the Sun Artists office: "The name subject was on the agenda, and there were several names that flew around that afternoon, and Asia was dismissed fairly rapidly. Brian Lane (group manager) did suggest it, but there seemed to be no interest. I don't mention this for any other reason than it stuck with me, and the more I thought about it, the more it made sense.

"I liked the geometry of the A — A, four letters for four people, and Brian Lane liked the 'SI' in the middle standing for 'YES' (in Spanish)," continued Wetton. "He thought that would be a good omen. Little did I know then, but the rest of the letters would also be a great omen for me, too."

Asia took the pop music scene by storm in 1982 with their eponymous debut album and took full advantage of a relatively short MTV video rotation with their evocative music videos. A second album gave the group its second top-10 single, "Don't Cry," but diminishing returns followed and Asia was gone in 1985, for all intents and purposes.

www.drmusic.org.

The B-52's

GROUP FORMED IN: 1976
ORIGINAL MEMBERS: Kate Pierson, Cindy Wilson, Ricky
Wilson, Fred Schneider, Keith Strickland
LATER MEMBERS OF NOTE: Sara Lee, Pat Irwin, Zachary Alford
BEST KNOWN SONG: Love Shack (#3, 1989)

The B-52's are the quintessential party band, and they would have it no other way. Cutting their teeth in New York after originating in Athens, Georgia, the band got their first break at Max's Kansas City and CBGB's. The B-52's, together with Talking Heads and Blondie, are considered among the seminal new wave bands in America. Ever quirky, campy, and eclectic, The B-52's have kept fans on their feet and on their toes simultaneously for more than three decades.

In more recent years the band has become more socially conscious, primarily in the areas of the environment, animal rights, and AIDS. The latter cause is close to the heart of the group since original member Ricky Wilson (older brother of Cindy) died from AIDS-related complications in 1985. Following his death, the group took a three-year hiatus and contemplated its future. As they soldiered on, Keith Strickland moved from drums to guitar and the group hired Don Was and Nile Rogers to produce their huge breakthrough album *Cosmic Thing*. To fill out their sound, Sara Lee, Pat Irwin, and Zachary Alford were added for the studio and concerts.

The origin of the group name is twofold: (1) the Boeing B-52 Stratofortress was an eight-engine strategic bomber used by the U.S. Air Force, and (2) B-52 is a southern slang nickname for a beehive hairdo (so called because it resembled the bulbous nose of the airplane). Kate Pierson and Cindy Wilson wore bouffant wigs in the band's early days, which featured this hair style and which, as much as their sound, became a signature of the band.

www.theb52s.com.

The Babys

GROUP FORMED IN: 1976
ORIGINAL MEMBERS: John Waite, Walt Stocker,
Mike Corby, Tony Brock
LATER MEMBERS OF NOTE: Jonathan Cain, Ricky Phillips
BEST KNOWN SONG: Isn't It Time (#13, 1977)

The Babys were a British pop/rock group led by John Waite, later to have a notable if not stellar solo career, after which he formed Bad English with former Babys bandmates Cain and Phillips. In its four-year chart life, The Babys produced eight top 100 hits in the United States, but only three made the top 40. However, all three ("Isn't It Time," "Every Time I Think of You," and "Back on My Feet Again") still garner substantial airplay on stations playing hits of the '70s, attesting to the catchiness of the tunes.

The group name was more marketing ploy than anything. Clearly not attuned to the punk tremors already rumbling, the group knew many record companies were looking for nonthreatening images in their clients, similar to Abba or the Bay City Rollers.

According to Waite, the name "was meant to be a joke. We took the name simply because the record companies wouldn't listen to any band they thought were rock & roll. I mean, they wanted sure-fire teen bands, pre-teen bands. We

couldn't get anybody down to hear us to get a record deal, so we called ourselves The Babys.

"We thought we'd keep the name just for two weeks. Then, the word got
around London that there was a band playing rock & roll called The Babys and
it seemed so off the wall, so completely crazy, that it was worth taking a shot
with. It really appealed to everyone's sense of humor. I liked the name very
much. It's backfired occasionally and I think it's definitely harmed us, but there
you go. It sort of makes it more interesting. I mean, people [didn't] know what
to expect."

www.netwaite.com.

Backstreet Boys

GROUP FORMED IN: 1992
ORIGINAL MEMBERS: Nick Carter, Howie Dorough, Alex
James "AJ" McLean, Charles Edwards, Sam Licata
LATER MEMBERS OF NOTE: Kevin Richardson, Brian Littrell
BEST KNOWN SONG: Everybody (Backstreet's Back) (#4, 1998)

Backstreet Boys were a band manufactured by their manager, Lou Pearlman, who desired to create a boys band for the '90s like New Kids on the Block
had been almost a decade earlier. With ages ranging from 12 (Nick Carter) to
21 (Kevin Richardson) when they joined, the group members were able to lure
pre-teens, post-teens, and every teen in between into their screaming group of
female fans.

The group spent countless hours working on voice and dance training
along with learning songs and choreography. At one of the group's traditional
dinners with Pearlman at T.G.I. Friday's in Orlando, Lou brought up the subject of naming the group. Pearlman recalls the evening going as follows, "We
came up with loads of names that night, but we didn't like any of them. We
were sitting in a booth by a window and I looked out. Across the street was a
flea market called Backstreet Market where a lot of the local kids used to hang
out. AJ, Nick and Howie used to go there sometimes. I said to the guys, 'What
about Backstreet?'"

"We all thought about it for a while," Pearlman continued, "and said the
word a few times. Everyone liked the sound of it. Then we started trying to
think of another word to go with it and we all more or less said 'Boys' at the
same time." This was a natural choice for the obvious reason that they *were* a

group of boys, but, more appropriately, prior to the group having a name they were always being collectively referred to as "the boys," as if they were five brothers.

McGibbon, Rob. *Backstreet Boys — Official Biography*. London: Boxtree, 1997.

Bad Company

GROUP FORMED IN: 1973
ORIGINAL MEMBERS: Paul Rodgers, Simon Kirke,
Mick Ralphs, Raymone "Boz" Burrell
LATER MEMBERS OF NOTE: Brian Howe, Dave "Bucket"
Colwell, Rick Wills, Robert Hart, Steve Price,
Felix Krish, Jaz Lochrie, Mark Wolfe
BEST KNOWN SONG: Feel Like Makin' Love (#10, 1975)

Following the lead of Cream and Buffalo Springfield, Bad Company formed from a collection of all-star musicians from various groups. This supergroup came from members of Free, Mott the Hoople, and King Crimson. They also borrowed from Led Zeppelin by sharing their manager (Peter Grant) and label (Swan Song). This hard rock, blues-based band was driven by the strong vocals of Paul Rodgers and power chords of Mick Ralphs. Bad Company was instrumental in establishing arena rock by knocking out rock music that could be danced to.

The name chosen by the group was culled from the 1972 Robert Benton movie entitled *Bad Company* starring Jeff Bridges and Barry Brown. The movie is set during the American Civil War. A young man is sent by his family to the untamed West to avoid being drafted into the war. He drifts throughout the land with a loose confederation of young vagrants to survive, ergo the "bad company."

Rodgers was adamant about using this title for the band name. Peter Grant was less enthusiastic and the record company "thought it was a terrible name," according to Rodgers. A meeting was scheduled to discuss the issue with the label and the band met in advance to devise their strategy. Rodgers "had been through this before with Free as Island Records had wanted to call us the Heavy Metal Kids. We agreed to go in and tell them we were going to be called Bad Company and that was the end of the story. As soon as Peter heard how strongly I felt about the name, he became very supportive and turned the record company around."

www.badcompany.com; www.bestprices.com.

Bad English

GROUP FORMED IN: 1988
ORIGINAL MEMBERS: John Waite, Jonathan Cain,
Ricky Phillips, Neal Schon, Deen Castronovo
LATER MEMBERS OF NOTE: none
BEST KNOWN SONG: When I See You Smile (#1, 1989)

Bad English is another example of a supergroup, hand-picked and made up of notable members of other bands. The band was comprised of John Waite (formerly of the Babys), Neil Schon (Santana, Journey), Jonathan Cain (the Babys, Journey), Ricky Phillips (the Babys), and Deen Castronovo, an acclaimed session drummer who also had been with some lesser known groups.

With a name like Bad English, one might infer the group must have been English and/or really bad. In fact the former was barely true and the latter was most certainly not. There was one Brit, John Waite. And while the band broke up before a distinguished legacy could be left, they did have a good run for two years, placing one song at #1, another in the top 10, and four other singles of varying success in the top 100.

The name comes not from nationality but from the game of pool. Jonathan Cain was reading a book on pool strategies. Among the shots he was learning were methods of spinning the cue ball, called putting "english" on it. This included spinning the ball right (right english) and spinning the ball left (you guessed it, left english). Memories are fuzzy, but either Neal Schon or John Waite spun the ball in the completely wrong direction and Cain coined the phrase "Bad English." This was the moment the band realized they had their name.

The band broke up in 1991 because, as Ricky Phillips noted, "Too many cooks. Nobody wanted to bend anymore." Power struggles over whose songs made the albums ruined Bad English as it had so many other bands before.

www.netwaite.com.

Badfinger

GROUP FORMED IN: 1968
ORIGINAL MEMBERS: Pete Ham, Tom Evans, Joey Molland, Mike Gibbins

LATER MEMBERS OF NOTE: Ronald Griffiths, Bob Jackson,
Joe Tansin, Glen Sherba, Tony Kaye, Richard Bryan
BEST KNOWN SONG: Day After Day (#4, 1972)

Badfinger was blessed and cursed by their association with the Beatles. A supremely talented act, they were never taken seriously by critics who saw them as nothing more than pawns or clones of the Beatles despite the emerging song-writing talents of Pete Ham together with the musicianship and harmonies the quartet produced.

In a sense, Badfinger were themselves partly to blame. They were signed to the Beatles Apple label and worked closely with all four Beatles, recording the Paul McCartney song "Come and Get It" (which McCartney also produced). Later they played on George Harrison's *All Things Must Pass*, provided vocals on Ringo Starr's "It Don't Come Easy" and performed on John Lennon's *Imagine* album.

Badfinger started out as "The Panthers," later changing their name to The Iveys in 1968, so named after a street in their hometown of Swansea, Wales (and also a pun on The Hollies). After signing with Apple the group recorded and released its first single, "Maybe Tomorrow," which peaked at only number 67 on the American hot 100.

In late 1969 the group felt a change of image and name were in order. Their style was becoming edgier and The Iveys a name too reminiscent of the British Invasion. Again the Beatles figured prominently in their decision. McCartney suggested Home and The Glass Onion while Lennon suggested (predictably) The Prix. Instead the band borrowed Badfinger from "Bad Finger Boogie," the working title of the Beatles's "With a Little Help from My Friends."

www.bbc.co.uk.

Bananarama

GROUP FORMED IN: 1981
ORIGINAL MEMBERS: Keren Woodward, Sara Dallin, Siobhan Fahey
LATER MEMBERS OF NOTE: Jacquie O'Sullivan
BEST KNOWN SONG: Venus (#1, 1986)

Before there were the Spice Girls there was Bananarama, the erstwhile most successful British girl group in pop history. The group consisted of Keren Woodward and Sara Dallin (who were friends from school), and Siobhan Fahey who met Dallin at the London College of Fashion. After singing for fun at parties and nightclubs, they came to the attention of Paul Cook, formerly of the Sex Pistols, who produced their first song called "Aie A Mwana," which they sung phonetically in Swahili.

The girls' ska roots brought them to the attention of up-and-coming British ska artists Fun Boy Three, who backed the girls on *Really Saying Something*. This musical leaning also provided part of the group's name. They took the word "banana" and merged it with the Roxy Music song *Pyjama-rama* to create Bananarama. Stories abound that the first half of the name was taken from the Hanna-Barbera Saturday morning children's show *The Banana Splits Adventure Hour* but Woodward debunked this by explaining that "The bananas thing just came from the fact that our first single was sung in Swahili and we thought it was kind of tropical. Sara is responsible for the name, bless her."

Not until 1986 did Bananarama achieve the same success in the United States they had enjoyed in England when, with the production help of Stock, Aitman, and Waterman, they hit #1 with a remake of Shocking Blues's "Venus." Two years later, Fahey split from the group (after having married Eurythmics's Dave Stewart a year earlier). She was replaced that year by Jacquie O'Sullivan, who then left the group in 1991. Since that time, Woodward and Dallin carried on as a duo but failed to crack the U.S. top-100 chart again.

MadPod.com interview by Shadoe Steele- www.mefeedia.com; www.biggeststars.com; www.planetgeorge.org.

The Bangles

GROUP FORMED IN: 1981
ORIGINAL MEMBERS: Susanna Hoffs, Vicki Peterson,
Debbi Peterson, Annette Zalinkas
LATER MEMBERS OF NOTE: Michael "Micki" Steele, Abby Travis
BEST KNOWN SONG: Walk Like an Egyptian (#1, 1986)

The Bangles were formed after sisters Vicki and Debbi Peterson responded to an ad placed by Susanna Hoffs in the Los Angeles weekly *The Recycler*, asking for potential band members who were into the Beatles, the Byrds, and Buffalo Springfield. Later Annette Zalinkas was added and the Colours were born, the name owing to the colorful psychedelic era of the 1960s by which the band members were influenced.

The band practiced in Hoffs's garage and developed a vocal style owing as much to The Beach Boys and The Hollies as to the bands listed in the ad. In an effort to improve the name and image of the band they changed it to The Supersonic Bangs and later shortened the name to just The Bangs.

It was at this point Michael Steele (formerly of The Runaways) replaced Zalinkas at bass. CBS, their record label, was looking to further develop the group's music, image, and, of course, popularity. This involved a more mature look and sound with assistance of established songwriters, including Prince (or "Christopher" as he was credited).

But before the makeover took place, The Bangs received notice that a group of the same name from New Jersey was threatening legal action if the conflicting group name wasn't changed. This led to the slightly longer name of The Bangles, which refers to a bracelet slipped over the hand or ankle. The imagery created by this name suited the band and did not require a substantial modification from the former name. The Bangles went on under the new moniker to achieve superstar status in becoming (with the Go Go's) one of the first two all-girl bands that played their own instruments.

www.vocalgroup.org; www.nndb.com.

Barenaked Ladies

GROUP FORMED IN: 1988
ORIGINAL MEMBERS: Steven Page, Ed Robertson (born Lloyd Edward Elwyn Robertson), Jim Creeggan, Andy Creeggan
LATER MEMBERS OF NOTE: Tyler Stewart, Kevin Hearn
BEST KNOWN SONG: One Week (#1, 1998)

As Mike Myers's Saturday Night Live character Linda Richman might say on *Coffee Talk*, "I'll give you a discussion topic: The Barenaked Ladies are neither barenaked nor ladies. Discuss. Twok amongst yourselves." The Barenaked Ladies (BNL) are actually a Canadian alternative rock band begun by Steve Page and Ed Robertson. The two went through school together and knew of each other but were not well acquainted.

The genesis of the band came in 1988. Page picks up the story: "When we were teens Ed and I were at a Bob Dylan concert bored out of our minds and we started making fun of bands that did not exist. One was Barenaked Ladies. It made us laugh and reminded us of when we were eight years old, and would look at the women's underwear section of the Sears catalog."

At the time Robertson was in a band that was booked to play a benefit show. Prior to the show the band broke up. When Robertson received a call to confirm his band's participation he affirmed the commitment, but he said the name of the band had been changed to Barenaked Ladies. The next call Robertson made was to Page about forming a duo. He agreed and they decided to keep the joke name "because if we changed our name, how would the seven people that were there find us again," joked Page.

The band was once banned from playing at Toronto City Hall by city officials because they felt the name was sexist. Robertson explained they meant no disrespect. "We wanted to remind people about being little kids and the name, for us, really reflected that. It's supposed to be a kid's term."

www.rockitoldschool.com.

Bay City Rollers

GROUP FORMED IN: 1967
ORIGINAL MEMBERS: Les McKeown, Alan Longmuir,
Derek Longmuir, Eric Faulkner, Stuart "Woody" Wood
LATER MEMBERS OF NOTE: Ian Mitchell, Nobby Clark, John Devine,
Duncan Faure, Billy Lyall, Archie Marr, Eric Manclark,
Pat McGlynn, Dave Paton, Big Jim Sullivan
BEST KNOWN SONG: Saturday Night (#1, 1975)

Scotland's Bay City Rollers came closer to living up to the hype of "the next Beatles" than any of the other numerous bands so touted (Badfinger, Klaatu, Pilot, etc.) but still fell well short. Outfitted in tartan knickers, they became a worldwide sensation with teenage girls screaming at their every move on stage. Legal troubles stemming from the excesses of the rock and roll lifestyle derailed the group. Some of the members have been unable to escape the spotlight due to arrests, but not always convictions, for various illegal activities.

Before any of this trouble there was The Longmuir Brothers and later The Ambassadors. This then was changed to the name The Saxons. Their ambition was to be worldwide stars and it was decided The Saxons was not going to fly in America. The group decided to take a map of the United States and randomly stick a pin in it and take the name of the city or state where it landed. The last part of the name would be "Rollers" which they understood to mean "waves" to surfers.

Derek or Alan Longmuir (memories are hazy) was chosen for the appointed task. So the pin was placed and they became... The Arkansas Rollers. Everyone ok with that? According to Alan, "The Arkansas Rollers didn't sound quite right." So they tried again and this time hit Bay City, Michigan. It was agreed that they would henceforth be known as the Bay City Rollers.

Kamp, David, and Steve Daly. The Rock Snob*s Dictionary. New York: Broadway Books, 2005; Interview with Hannes A. Jonsson of the Derek Longmuir fan club.

The Beach Boys

GROUP FORMED IN: 1961
ORIGINAL MEMBERS: Brian Wilson, Carl Wilson,
Dennis Wilson, Mike Love, Al Jardine
LATER MEMBERS OF NOTE: David Marks,
Glen Campbell, Bruce Johnston
BEST KNOWN SONG: Good Vibrations (#1, 1966)

The creation of this family-related group (three Wilson brothers, cousin Mike Love, and friend Al Jardine) from Hawthorne, California, was driven by Brian Wilson. Formed while the boys were in high school, the names of various early combinations of the group members included Kenny & The Cadets, Carl & the Passions, and the Pendletones (an homage to the Pendleton shirts favored by surfers).

The decision to choose a name related to the surfing craze of the early '60s was bolstered by Dennis Wilson, the only member of the group who ever took up the hobby. While trying to impress Hite and Dorinda Morgan, song publishers associated with the local Candix label, Dennis described how popular surfing was becoming and how kids were listening to the surf report in the morning to plan their days accordingly. In fact, Brian had already written a song dedicated to the sport entitled "Surfin'" that they said they would be happy to audition for the label.

The Morgans were duly impressed with the group but suggested the more commercial name of The Beach Boys. The initial reluctance to accept another name change was soon forgotten as "Surfin'" became the group's first single, leading to such other surf-related hits as "Surfin' Safari," "Surfin' USA," and "Surfer Girl."

In more recent years much legal action has ensued over the rights to use the Beach Boys name. Love and Jardine, two of the three surviving members, have waged court battles in trying to maintain control of the well-known moniker.

Carlin, Peter Ames. Catch a Wave: The Rise, Fall & Redemption of the Beach Boys' Brian Wilson. *Emmaus, PA: Rodale, 2006.*

The Beatles

GROUP FORMED IN: 1960
ORIGINAL MEMBERS: Paul McCartney, John Lennon,
George Harrison, Stuart Sutcliffe, Pete Best
LATER MEMBERS OF NOTE: Ringo Starr (born Richard Starkey)
BEST KNOWN SONG: Hey Jude (#1, 1968)

The road leading to The Beatles is a well-worn path of pop music history. Paul McCartney joined John Lennon in the Quarry Men in July 1957. George Harrison joined seven months later. By August 1959 the Quarry Men consisted of those three plus guitarist and vocalist Ken Brown. The remaining trio changed their name to Johnny & the Moondogs when Brown quit over a dispute involving the division of gig money.

After Lennon's art school friend Stuart Sutcliffe joined to play bass, he convinced the others to rename the group the Beatals, in homage to Buddy Holly's Crickets. This was also a veiled reference to a gang in Marlon Brando's movie *The Wild One*. Lennon, always the punster, liked to think of the name as "beats all."

It was at this time the group began a Spinal Tap-esque period with a rotating series of drummers and band names. After adding 36-year-old drummer Tommy Moore, the band's name was changed to the Silver Beetles in May 1960. Moore left after two months and the group's name was tweaked to the Silver Beatles before adding drummer Norman Chapman for one month. Chapman was called to national service one month later and replaced by Pete Best.

It was at this point the group finally settled on the more simple moniker of The Beatles. The name was set but the lineup was not. Sutcliffe left in June 1961 (and subsequently died of a brain hemorrhage on April 10, 1962). The Liverpool lads added Ringo Starr to replace Best in August 1962, and the rest, as they say, is history.

Sandford, Christopher. McCartney. *New York: Carroll & Graf, 2006; Goldman, Albert.* The Lives of John Lennon. *New York: William Morrow, 1988; Frame, Pete.* The Beatles and Some Other Guys. *London: Omnibus Press, 1997.*

The Bee Gees

GROUP FORMED IN: 1959
ORIGINAL MEMBERS: Barry Gibb, Maurice Gibb, Robin Gibb

LATER MEMBERS OF NOTE: None
BEST KNOWN SONG: Stayin' Alive (#1, 1978)

Little is unknown about The Bee Gees. Their massive popularity between 1975 and 1979, when they had eight #1 hits topping the American charts for a combined 23 weeks, solidified their place in pop music history and propelled them into the Rock and Roll Hall of Fame.

One thing that is often misunderstood about the group is the origin of their name. While it is true that in later years the "Brothers Gibb" would not deny that the name of the group stood for the initials of this elongated nickname, the origin was certainly much different.

When Barry was twelve and the twins Robin and Maurice were not quite ten, the Gibb family moved from England to Brisbane, Australia. The family lived near a motor speedway and Barry would sell soft drinks to the patrons. In an effort to increase sales and reduce boredom, Barry and his brothers would set up a little stall under the grandstand during the lengthy between-race gaps and sing to grab the attention of the crowd.

The owner of the speedway was named Bill Goode (initials B.G.). He heard the boys and moved their venue to the public address system. In turn, a local radio disc jockey and race car driver named Bill Gates (initials B.G.) was racing one night and heard the Gibbs. He offered to play their songs on the radio and suggested the boys call themselves the B.G.s, after the initials of the two men who helped them get their start. Of course, Barry also had the same initials, so the name was accepted by everyone. Later when Maurice and Robin grew older and Goode and Gates became a fading memory, the group recast the name to mean Brothers Gibb.

Bilyeu, Melinda, Hector Cook, and Andrew Mon Hughes, with assistance from Joseph Brennan and Mark Crohan. The Ultimate Biography of the Bee Gees. London: Omnibus Press, 2000.

Berlin

GROUP FORMED IN: 1979
ORIGINAL MEMBERS: John Crawford, Terri Nunn,
Rick Olsen, Matt Reid, David Diamond, Rob Brill
LATER MEMBERS OF NOTE: Rod Learned, Mitchell Sigman,
Chris Olivas, Linda Dalziel, Dallan Baumgarten, Carlton Bost
BEST KNOWN SONG: Take My Breath Away (#1, 1986)

Berlin was the creation of John Crawford, who was raised in southern

California and developed a rebellious attitude toward his parents' comfortable lifestyle. "My parents were putting me into that little world where everything had to be the same. Everybody drives the same kind of car, wears the same suit to work, and the kids go to the same school and wear the same jeans from the Gap," said Crawford.

When he named his band Berlin, it was "a reaction against what was going on in L.A. at the time. It was the early days of the Knack, the Pop, The this, The that — all those twangy guitars and smiley boys and happy love songs, and it was driving me nuts." The name was selected to reflect an international flavor and, according to Crawford, "conjured up all sorts of decadent, kinky visions that may or may not have been rooted in reality but ... were nice and dark and different from the rest of the L.A. bands."

Crawford went through multiple personnel before settling on the lineup that recorded the EP *Pleasure Victim* for just $3,000 (artwork included). The lead singer was Terri Nunn who exuded the sexuality written into Berlin's lyrics. The synth-pop early style gave way to a straight-ahead rock sound by the 1986 LP *Count Three and Pray*, which included guitar work by Ted Nugent. This reflected Nunn's love of heavy metal.

Many critics dismissed Berlin as a raunchy synth-pop outfit. Their entire body of work suggests otherwise. Nunn is one of the great female voices in rock history. Crawford was a master song-crafter and Berlin should be reconsidered by anyone who knows nothing more of the group than "Take My Breath Away."

www.berlinpage.com; www.levity.com.

Big Brother & the Holding Company

GROUP FORMED IN: 1965
ORIGINAL MEMBERS: Peter Albin, James Gurley,
Sam Andrew, David Getz
LATER MEMBERS OF NOTE: Janis Joplin
BEST KNOWN SONG: Piece of My Heart (#12, 1968)

Known to most as Janis Joplin's band, Big Brother was actually a band in its own right before Joplin joined for her two-year tour of duty. However, it is fair to surmise the band would have been consigned to a Haight-Ashbury footnote were it not for the addition of Ms. Joplin's intense wail and persona.

The band became synonymous with the San Francisco psychedelic scene after its appearance at the 1967 Monterey Pop Festival, which helped push the group's first album with Joplin, the 1968 release entitled *Cheap Thrills*, to number one. This album also produced the group's only top-40 hit, "Piece of My Heart."

As was often the case with bands of the era, the name was particularly inventive and was created during a hazy drug-induced rap session. Peter Albin recalled, "We started out with the name Blue Yard Hill. We sat down and wrote a bunch of names on a piece of paper. One of theme was Big Brother and down at the bottom of the list was The Holding Company. We just joined the two names together and thought it was kind of funny. It had that kind of drug reference of The Holding Company [possessing drugs], and the 'Big Brother is watching you' political reference, but we were never really a drug band or a political band. It was an odd name for us, but it sounded right."

Many considered the name, although somewhat cumbersome, the coolest, most cutting-edge name of the early San Francisco bands. Local journalist Charles Perry remembers people wondering, "Oh wow, could you get busted for having a name like that?"

Echols, Alice. Scars of Sweet Paradise. The Life and Times of Janis Joplin. New York: Metropolitan Books, 1999; www.janisjoplin.net.

The Black Crowes

GROUP FORMED IN: 1984
ORIGINAL MEMBERS: Chris Robinson, Rich Robinson,
Johnny Colt (fka Charles Brandt), Steve Gorman, Jeff Cease
LATER MEMBERS OF NOTE: Eddie Hawrysch, Marc Ford, Sven Pipien
BEST KNOWN SONG: Hard to Handle (#26, 1991)

The earliest incarnation of the band formed by brothers Chris and Rich Robinson was called Greasy Little Toes. The group, formed in Atlanta, was a new member of an old breed, the southern roots, blues-based rock and roll band. They were most closely compared to the Rolling Stones (in attitude) and the Faces and Lynyrd Skynyrd (in music style).

The Crowes made fans in short order with their straight-ahead style, which in the late 1980s was conspicuously absent from the American music scene, except for Guns n' Roses. Despite the ability to sell albums and concert tickets, they never made much of a dent in the top-40. When the music tastes became grungier, the Crowes stuck to their guns and lost much of their momentum.

After the Greasy Little Toes, the Robinsons changed to Mr. Crowe's Garden. When they signed with Def American label, their record producer, Rick Rubin, tried to get the band to change to The Kobb Kounty Krows. Faced with the potential initials of KKK, this southern band could anticipate problems. The members were in no mood to answer the obvious questions from the public.

George Drakoulias, on staff at Def American, suggested a list of potential new names, including Confederate Crowes and The Stone Mountain Crowes. "Everyone just called us the Crowes when we hung out," explained Chris Robinson. "And we came up with Black Crowes-blackbirds. That was it." Once the name was decided, with Drakoulias's help, The Black Crowes extreme makeover resulted in a successful overhaul of their look, sound, and income stream with their 1990 debut album, the triple platinum *Shake Your Money Maker*.

Fricke, David. Good Old Rock & Roll Returns to the Top of the Charts. Rolling Stone *605 (May 30, 1991)*; Request *Magazine, June 1992 — Interview submitted by Chris Henne.*

Black Sabbath

GROUP FORMED IN: 1968
ORIGINAL MEMBERS: Ozzy Osbourne, Tony Iommi,
Terry "Geezer" Butler, William Ward
LATER MEMBERS OF NOTE: Dave Walker, Ronnie James Dio,
Ian Gillan, Tony Martin, Cozy Powell, David Donato,
Bev Bevan, Geoff Nicholls, Vinny Apice, Glenn Hughes,
Dave Spitz, Eric Singer, Ray Gillen, Bob Daisley, Jo Burt,
Terry Chimes, Laurence Cottle, Neil Murray, et al.
BEST KNOWN SONG: Iron Man (#52, 1972)

Have you been a member of Black Sabbath? If you answered no then you're in the minority. A very fluid lineup over the span of almost 30 years came full circle when the original lineup reunited in 1997 and toured as a unit for the next eight years. It may well be the only noteworthy band formed in the '60s with all its original members alive, much less still playing together. This is amazing considering the speed with which they lived their lives.

The band's influence on the heavy metal music scene is immense. Most would rank Sabbath just behind Led Zeppelin in the heavy metal hierarchy for bands of the era. However, where others have detoured from the pure faith, Sabbath has never been anything but a heavy metal band.

Originally called Polka Tulk Blues Band (later just Polka Tulk) and then Earth, the band decided on the final name change when they were booked at Henry's, a local club, under the mistaken belief that they were another band of the same name. They played to a house full of bow-ties expecting dance music, who instead got a dose of heavy metal blues. According to Tony Iommi, the band "died a death" that night. In order to avoid confusion the band adopted Black Sabbath as their new name.

Even members of the group themselves have several versions of the band name origin. Some say it was taken from a 1935 Boris Karloff movie of the same name. The most widely accepted explanation is that Geezer Butler was fascinated with author Dennis Wheatley and his supernatural tales, including his most well known, *The Devil Rides Out*, which resulted in a Butler-penned song entitled "Black Sabbath," from which the group name derived.

Rosen, Steven. Black Sabbath. *Cornwall, England: MPG Books, 1996; Sharpe-Young, Garry.* Black Sabbath. Never Say Die! *London: Cherry Red Records, 2003.*

Blind Melon

GROUP FORMED IN: 1989
ORIGINAL MEMBERS: Shannon Hoon, Rogers Stevens,
Christopher Thorn, Brad Smith, Glen Graham
LATER MEMBERS OF NOTE: Travis Warren
BEST KNOWN SONG: No Rain (#20, 1993)

Blind Melon might have become the truest descendants of the Grateful Dead had they not lost their leader, Shannon Hoon, to a drug overdose just as they were hitting their stride. Known as the group with the "bee girl" of the video from their breakthrough song "No Rain," Blind Melon was a band formed during the early 1990s that drew its inspiration from the Dead, Lynyrd Skynyrd, and Led Zeppelin, as opposed to many of its harder-edged alternative music contemporaries.

The band came together in Los Angeles from various parts of the United States. Hoon was familiar with Axl Rose from his earlier years growing up in Indiana. The group tried out several possible names such as Gristie, Frog, Mud Bird, Naked Pilgrims, Brown Cow, and Head Train. None of these struck a responsive chord.

Guitarist Brad Smith was born and raised in Mississippi. On his block, there lived about ten people whom his family considered hippies. They were poor but friendly. Brad's father would greet them by yelling, "What's happening, Blind Melons?" When Brad used this phrase on his new bandmates they adopted the name as their own. The band could relate to the original recipients of the greeting, considering themselves to be poor, friendly hippies as well.

Where Brad's father came up with the phrase is subject to speculation. He may have borrowed it from Cheech and Chong's fictional bluesman, "Blind Melon Chitlin," which itself was probably taken from real bluesman Blind Lemon Jefferson (melon is an anagram of lemon).

www.blindmelon.org; ; www.tv.com

blink-182

GROUP FORMED IN: 1992
ORIGINAL MEMBERS: Mark Hoppus, Tom DeLonge, Scott Raynor
LATER MEMBERS OF NOTE: Travis Barker
BEST KNOWN SONG: All the Small Things (#6, 2000)

This group is precisely called blink-182, without capitalization. They are a pop/punk band formed in southern California where the three original members grew up. Their style includes catchy melodies with lyrics often containing satire and occasionally laced with profanity, but played with more harmony than many of the contemporary alternative rock bands.

The group was originally called simply Blink and recorded its first demo from a recording made in Scott Raynor's bedroom. Early the following year they released their first full-length album, *Cheshire Cat*. In the wake of this release they received notice that legal action would be commenced by an Irish band also named Blink if the name was not changed. This resulted in an alteration to blink-182.

Rumors have abounded regarding the choice of the number. It has been reported to be the number of times Al Pacino utters the word "fuck" in *Scarface*. There was also a film starring Timothy Hutton entitled *Turk 182!* which may have influenced the band. A more ambitious suggestion is that it is the numerical positions in the alphabet of the letters "r" and "b," referring to the northern San Diego suburb of Rancho Bernardo. Another rumor has it that it is Matt Hoppus's ideal weight.

The band members claim the numbers were simply chosen at random. However, in an interview, Barker said the significance of the numbers derives from the U.S. radio code for "homicide," although the correct number is actually 187. The number 182 is the number corresponding to conspiracy. It sounds like a conspiracy of confusion when it comes to deciphering the meaning of this band's name.

Blondie

GROUP FORMED IN: 1974
ORIGINAL MEMBERS: Deborah Harry, Chris Stein, Clem
Burke, Billy O'Connor, Fred Smith, Julie, Jackie
LATER MEMBERS OF NOTE: Ivan Kral, Tish Bellomo, Snookie
Bellomo, Gary Valentine, Jimmy Destri, Frank Infante,
Nigel Harrison, Leigh Foxx, Paul Carbonara
BEST KNOWN SONG: Call Me (#1, 1980)

Blondie broke the punk mold just as they were becoming commercially successful by jumping from the CBGBs scene to record the discofied "Heart of Glass."
In so doing, they were considered sellouts by punk purists, but the rest of the
record-buying public fully embraced them throughout their various incarnations,
be it punk ("One Way or Another"), pop ("Call Me"), reggae ("The Tide Is High"),
or rap ("Rapture"), the latter three going to number one as did "Heart of Glass."

Deborah Harry was singing in a three-woman group called The Stilettos
when she met Chris Stein. They formed a band called Angel & the Snakes, which
included career Blondie member Clem Burke on drums. Soon two female backing vocalists by the names of Julie and Jackie were added and the name was changed
to Blondie. Some have reported that the reason for the name was the cat calls
Harry received from passing truckers on the streets of New York that started with
the intelligent phrase "Hey blondie...." While that may well have happened, the
truth was, as Deborah explained, "Julie, Jackie and I were all blonde, so it was an
apt name ... then, right before our first gig, Jackie dyed her hair dark brown."

Soon Julie and Jackie were replaced by the Bellomo sisters, Tish and
Snookie. The group changed its name to Blondie & the Banzai Babies. After
the backing vocalists were dropped the group name returned to Blondie. This
crew, with the later addition of Nigel Harrison, would serve as the band's personnel through its commercially productive years.

www.rip-her-to-shreds.com; www.mobile.mystrands.com; www.pgw.com; www.answers.com.

Blood, Sweat & Tears

GROUP FORMED IN: 1967

ORIGINAL MEMBERS: Al Kooper, Jim Fielder,
Fred Lipsius, Randy Brecker, Jerry Weiss,
Dick Halligan, Steve Katz, Bobby Colomby
LATER MEMBERS OF NOTE: David Clayton-Thomas,
Chuck Winfield, Lew Soloff, Jerry Hyman,
Dave Bargeron, Bobby Doyle, Jerry Fisher,
Joe Henderson, Lou Marini, Larry Willis, and others
BEST KNOWN SONG: Spinning Wheel (#2, 1969)

Blood, Sweat & Tears approached pop music from a new angle. Exuding the blues and fitted out with an influx of horns, it created a sound that promised to push the group to the top of the music scene. But infighting and defections left the group struggling to determine its leader and stay the steady course. The first three singles all reached #2, but the next peaked at 14, then 29, then 32, and then out of the top-40 altogether, never to return.

The original lineup contained two of the most prominent members, Al Kooper and Bobby Colomby. Though Kooper was a member for only one album, it was his vision and influence brought over from his former band, The Blues Project, that led the band down the path to eventual stardom. Colomby was also instrumental in organizing the band and reuniting Kooper and Steve Katz, who had been in The Blues Project but parted on bad terms.

In the years since Kooper left, Colomby has taken verbal shots at him. Their contradictory statements have muddied the waters on the origin of the band. In interviews, Colomby maintained the name was coined by Kooper while talking on the phone with a promoter and looking at the cover of the 1963 Johnny Cash album entitled *Blood, Sweat and Tears*.

Kooper agrees the name was his idea, but he refutes Colomby's facts, saying, "Bobby Colomby makes up stories about the name origin." The true source of the name was an after-hours jam at the Café au Go Go in New York City's Greenwich Village, where Kooper played with a cut on his hand that left his organ keyboard covered in blood. Says Kooper, "Blood, sweat and tears is what it took to put that band together."

Interview with Al Kooper; www.vh1.com; www.classicbands.com; www.rdrop.com.

Blue Öyster Cult

GROUP FORMED IN: 1967
ORIGINAL MEMBERS: Eric Bloom, Donald "Buck Dharma"
Roeser, Allan Lanier, Joe Bouchard, Albert Bouchard

LATER MEMBERS OF NOTE: Chuck Burgi, Richie Castellano, Jules
Rodino, Rick Downey, Thommy Price, Jimmy Wilcox,
Tommy Zvonchek, Ron Riddle, Jon Rogers, John Miceli,
Greg Smith, John O'Reilly, Danny Miranda, Bobby
Rondinelli, Kasim Sulton, Al Pitrelli
BEST KNOWN SONG: (Don't Fear) The Reaper (#12, 1976)

With its earliest roots in the psychedelic music scene, Blue Öyster Cult
(or commonly now "BOC") morphed into one of the more listenable and cere-
bral heavy metal bands in the 1970s. Formed with the assistance of rock journalist and later band manager Sandy Pearlman, the group originated and
released one album under the name *Soft White Underbelly*, which was a reference made by Winston Churchill to Italy during World War II.

The name was changed to "Oaxaca," which is a province in Mexico,
and a second album was released under that name. In 1968 the name changed
yet again, this time to the "Stalk-Forrest Group" with one single released,
and over an album's worth of other songs recorded. The name change per
album trend finally ended when the group settled on "Blue Öyster Cult" in
1970.

The origin of the current name derives from a poem written by Pearlman.
It was part of his *Imaginos* poetry written in the 1960s, which was later mined
more completely in the group's 1988 album called *Imaginos*. In the relevant
poem, the Blue Oyster Cult was a collection of aliens who had aggregated to
secretly guide Earth's history.

The band added an umlaut over the "O" in the name, leading to a trend
among later heavy metal bands such as Motörhead, Mötley Crüe, Queensrÿche,
and Spïnal Tap, which made fun of the trend by placing the umlaut over the "n."

Blues Traveler

GROUP FORMED IN: 1983
ORIGINAL MEMBERS: John Popper, Chan Kinchla,
Brendan Hill, Bobby Sheehan
LATER MEMBERS OF NOTE: Tad Kinchla, Ben Wilson
BEST KNOWN SONG: Run-Around (#8, 1995)

If any latter-day group has the right to sing blues music, it is Blues Traveler. The lengthy time spent by the group paying its dues was not uncommon
to many other groups. Added to that, however, was the serious car accident
involving leader John Popper, which left him wheelchair-bound for a while,

his later angioplasty procedure, and the drug overdose death of original bassist Bobby Sheehan. Blues Traveler certainly has blues cred.

Granted, the blues played by this band displayed little resemblance to Robert Johnson, Muddy Waters, or B.B. King. Popper's harmonica (harp) playing reflects more of Sonny Boy Williamson's imprint on the genre.

The band has always tried to reflect a no-nonsense approach to the blues, initially using the simple name Blues Band. What this moniker displayed in honesty it lacked in commerciality. The next name considered was Blues Entity, arising out of the notion that when the group jammed, a fifth member, or entity, was created. This name was also quickly dispatched for its lack of originality.

The name of Blues Traveler is the result of much more creative thought. The second half of the name was suggested by Popper following his viewing of the movie *Ghostbusters*. A villainous ghost featured in the movie is called "Gozer The Traveler," who was announced in one scene with the phrase "The Traveler has come." Popper suggested the new name without complete conviction, but the group members warmed to the name and soon it stuck. Once the song "Run-Around" became one of the biggest songs of 1995, everyone knew of Blues Traveler and, truly, the traveler had finally come.

www.bluestraveler.com.

Blur

GROUP FORMED IN: 1989
ORIGINAL MEMBERS: Damon Albarn, Graham Coxon,
Alex James, Dave Rowntree
LATER MEMBERS OF NOTE: None
BEST KNOWN SONG: Girls & Boys (#59, 1994)

Blur was not the original Britpop band (a.k.a. the 1990s British invasion that never quite made it across the pond). The Stone Roses beat them to it. But, modeled in the Roses's image, Blur briefly became England's most popular guitar-pop band of the 1990s until Oasis hit the scene.

While Blur's style and those of its British counterparts (the Roses, Happy Mondays, Elastica, Radiohead, etc.) were well received in their homeland, American music tastes had changed to the prevalent morose mood of grunge, essentially requiring those bands to change or stay out. This represented a 180 degree turn on the late 1970s when British tastes tended more toward angry punk while America was still bathing in the glow of the mirror ball.

Blur began as Seymour when it was being courted by Food Records, who liked everything about the band except the name. Andy Ross of the label told the band he thought the name was a "gay indie anorak name," before apologizing profusely, in case any members *were* gay.

The label prepared a list of names for consideration. They included Sensitize and Whirlpool. These were rejected as being too closely tied to the LSD-propelled Acid House scene. Other names considered were The Shining Path as well as The Government (talk about a full-circle from the punk days!). The one name everyone liked was Blur, which was adopted just before they signed with Food Records in March 1990.

Harris, John. Britpop. Cool Britannia and the Spectacular Demise of English Rock. *New York: Da Capo Press, 2004.*

Jon Bon Jovi / Bon Jovi

BORN: John Francis Bongiovi on March 2, 1962, in Perth Amboy, New Jersey
GROUP FORMED IN: 1983
ORIGINAL MEMBERS: Jon Bon Jovi, Richie Sambora, David Bryan, Tico Torres, Alec John Such
LATER MEMBERS OF NOTE: Hugh McDonald
BEST KNOWN SONG: Livin' on a Prayer (#1, 1987)

Everyone knows that the group Bon Jovi is named after lead singer Jon Bon Jovi. Following the lead of their charismatic heartthrob singer, the group Bon Jovi became the premiere American pop-metal band of the '80s and early '90s. The story here is how John Francis Bongiovi became Jon Bon Jovi and how the group came into existence.

Born John Bongiovi in New Jersey, Jon had designs on becoming a star in the music industry from an early age. At 13 he founded his first band, Raze. At 16 he created a 12-piece cover band called Atlantic City Expressway and later headed John Bongiovi and the Wild Ones. He learned guitar and harmonica and honed his vocal skills, leading him to take a job at Power Station recording studio, owned by his cousin Tony Bongiovi.

While at the record studio Jon met Billy Squier who agreed to produce several demos. One of the songs, "Runaway," was included on a compilation album of local talent in the New York metropolitan area. When A&R execs heard the song on the album (many of whom had passed on it previously), they finally came calling and Jon had a record deal. The problem was he had no band since he had used studio musicians on the demos.

Jon and the record company felt "Bongiovi" was in need of a makeover. Jon told Larry King, "When I got a record deal I was a solo artist and I put the band together around my record deal so we thought phonetics, get rid of the 'G-I,' change it to 'J' and there's your band name."

www.transcripts.cnn.com.

The Boomtown Rats

GROUP FORMED IN: 1975
ORIGINAL MEMBERS: Bob Geldof, Johnny Fingers,
Garry Roberts, Gerry Cott, Pete Briquette, Simon Crowe
LATER MEMBERS OF NOTE: none
BEST KNOWN SONG: I Don't Like Mondays (#73, 1980)

Hardly known in the United States before organizing Band Aid and Live Aid for famine relief in Ethiopia, Bob Geldof was well known in England and his native Ireland as the lead singer of the punk rock band called The Boomtown Rats. Before any of this, Geldof was working as a magazine journalist. He offered to help some friends launch a band, and before he knew it he was the lead singer. Geldof explained the naming process: "We'd thought of this name, the 'Nightlife Thugs,' because I thought you needed a name that suggested something before you've even heard the band."

The name Nightlife Thugs was to be used only once. Their first gig was in a school classroom for Halloween. During a break a girl brazenly propositioned Geldof. Bob had "been reading Woody Guthrie's book *Bound For Glory* and I'd come upon a bit when he was eight and he was in a gang called the Boomtown Rats," so, emboldened, "I turned around and walked over to this classroom blackboard, and I rubbed out the name Nightlife Thugs, which we were for a day, and I wrote the Boomtown Rats up there, because there was something more important than getting shagged, and that was to change the name of the band."

Bound for Glory, written in 1943, is a semi-autobiographical account of the plight of dust bowl refugees who migrated to California from Oklahoma during the depression of the 1930s. Guthrie had himself taken that path and met with much hostility and resentment. The book was also made into a movie in 1976 starring David Carradine.

Guthrie, Woody. Bound for Glory. *New York: Plume, 1943; www.bobgeldof.info; www.geocities. com; www.abc.net.au; www.arts.enotes.com; www.woodyguthrie.org.*

David Bowie

BORN: David Robert Jones on
January 8, 1947, in London, England
BEST KNOWN SONG: Fame (#1, 1975)

Is David Bowie rock's ultimate chameleon? A good case could be made but whereas the lizard responds and reacts to its surroundings, many of Bowie's changes have anticipated fashion and musical trends, not adapted to them. It is this quality that has kept Bowie relevant since the mid–1960s and placed him in the Rock and Roll Hall of Fame.

Born David Jones, he had his sights set on stardom from an early age, but fame did not shine its spotlight on him for a while. The early years found him in groups such as the King Bees, the Lower Third, and the Nazz. All along he had an appreciation for the unusual. He was different in appearance due to a paralyzed left pupil from a childhood fight that resulted in different colored eyes. But he would eventually be into something much more off-base that would make him stand out — his androgynous alter ego Ziggy Stardust, which stretched the bounds of glam rock.

Prior to Ziggy (which was really just a character, not a stage name), Bowie had been approached in 1965 by Ralph Horton, his manager at the time, and advised to change his name since there were already several Davids or Davy Joneses trying to find a foothold in the market, including the member of the Monkees.

The first thought was Dave Jay. No, this didn't convey the image he wanted. David looked up to Mick Jagger and, as legend would have it, Mick claimed "jagger" meant "knife" in Old English. David had a schoolboy fascination with the American Wild West and decided to use the name "Bowie," which was the name of a popular hunting knife used by Jim Bowie, hero of the Alamo. The name change effected a personality change as well. Ever after, when asked about his name change, Bowie would respond, "I was someone else before that."

Edwards, Henry, and Tony Zanetta. Stardust: The David Bowie Story. *New York: McGraw-Hill, 1986; Paytress, Mark.* Bowie Style. *London: Omnibus Press, 2000.*

The Box Tops

GROUP FORMED IN: 1966

Original Members: Alex Chilton, Gary Talley,
John Evans, Bill Cunningham, Danny Smythe
Later Members of Note: Rick Allen, Tom Boggs,
Harold Cloud, Swain Schaefer, Bobby Guidotti
Best Known Song: The Letter (#1, 1967)

The Box Tops began their existence in Memphis in 1963 as The Rockers but later became known as Ronnie & the Devilles with lead singer Ron Jordan. It was Jordan, not Alex Chilton, who was originally slated to sing lead on "The Letter," the song that would propel The Box Tops to stardom and the number one chart position in 1967.

"The first singer they brought me had too much attitude," remembered Dan Penn, producer of the group's first three albums. Jordan was replaced by 16-year-young Chilton, whose tough, swaggering voice belied his age. "He was a great little rock & roll singer," continued Penn. "After we cut the basic tracks for 'The Letter,' I overdubbed strings, horns, and the airplane on the fade. Then I mixed her down. I thought we had a pretty good little record, but I didn't know it was that good."

With Jordan no longer a band member, and following a discovery of another band recording at the time with the name of The Devilles, the group changed their name to The Box Tops. The group is considered one of the foremost purveyors of the blue-eyed soul sound. It has been said that no American band outside of the Righteous Brothers has looked whiter and sung blacker than the Box Tops.

The Box Tops went on to record four albums and had ten top-100 singles, although their only other significant hit was the #2 smash from 1968, "Cry Like a Baby." They broke up in 1970 when Chilton and Talley left to pursue other avenues, but they re-formed in 1996 to record together again.

www.orlandoweekly.com.

Bread

Group Formed In: 1968
Original Members: David Gates, James Griffin, Robb Royer
Later members of Note: Mike Botts, Larry Knechtel
Best Known Song: If (#4, 1971)

David Gates was the driving force behind Bread, the soft rock group who perfectly defined the genre in the early 1970s. The group's lilting melodies and heartfelt lyrics were displayed by Gates's beautiful voice and the group's stunning harmonies. Bread found its niche and never tried to be anything other than what it was, and was therefore rarely criticized for failing to create edgier music.

Gates left Oklahoma in 1960 and traveled to Los Angeles with a wife, two infants, and $200 in his pocket. Although he had a nightclub job waiting with some friends when he arrived, they were fired on the third night. Eventually he landed another gig and was able to put food on the table again. He hung out at the Crossbow Club and met other aspiring musicians such as Glen Campbell and Leon Russell (who, like Gates, was also from Tulsa). Gates began having success as a writer and producer, including assisting a group called The Pleasure Faire (or sometimes "Fair" without the "e"), which included Robb Royer, who subsequently introduced Gates to James Griffin. The trio decided to form a group.

It seems ironic that so many bands that contain prolific writers have such a hard time naming their groups; however, such was the case with Bread. According to Gates, "A bread truck came along right at the time we were trying to think of a name. We had been saying, 'How about bush, telephone pole? Ah, bread truck, bread.' It began with a 'B,' like the Beatles and the Bee Gees. Bread also had a kind of universal appeal. It could be taken a number of ways. Of course, for the entire first year people called us 'The Breads.'"

Smith, Joe. Off the Record: An Oral History of Popular Music. *New York: Warner Books, 1988; www.superseventies.com; www.jlindquist.net*

Buffalo Springfield

GROUP FORMED IN: 1966
ORIGINAL MEMBERS: Stephen Stills, Neil Young,
Richie Furay, Dewey Martin, Bruce Palmer
LATER MEMBERS OF NOTE: Jim Messina
BEST KNOWN SONG: For What It's Worth (#7, 1967)

An early American supergroup, Buffalo Springfield was second only to their progenitor The Byrds in stature in the realm of country/folk rock. In their short 25-month, three-album life, Buffalo Springfield left a tremendously influential body of work.

Record producer Barry Friedman (who later changed his name to Frazier Mohawk), played a large part in the history of the band. He suggested to housemate Stephen Stills that he could help a new band get started at the famed Troubador in Hollywood backing the Byrds if Stills could round up qualified musicians.

First, Richie Furay was enlisted. Next, Stills found Neil Young driving down Sunset Boulevard after having met him in Canada a year earlier. With Young came Bruce Palmer. Finally Dewey Martin was called upon to play the drums.

Friedman told the story about the group's name, "As far as the eventual name for the group, Buffalo Springfield, we pulled up in front of the house one day when they were repaving Fountain [Street]. There was a steam roller there and on the back it said 'Buffalo Springfield.' I said, 'Hey, that's a name!' I pried the sign off, took it into the house and nailed it on the wall."

The Buffalo-Springfield Roller Company resulted from the merger of the Buffalo Steam Roller Company and the Kelly-Springfield Road Roller Company. These companies were offshoots of other companies that were formed as early as 1890.

www.pucksfarm.com; www.steamtraction.com.

Bush

GROUP FORMED IN: 1992
ORIGINAL MEMBERS: Gavin Rossdale, Nigel Pulsford,
Dave Parsons, Robin Goodridge
Later MEMBERS OF NOTE: Sacha Putnam, Chris Traynor
BEST KNOWN SONG: Glycerine (#28, 1996)

Led by Gavin Rossdale, the British post-grunge band Bush has always had a bigger following in the United States than in their homeland. This is owing in large part to their sound, which channels Nirvana and other Seattle-based early '90s bands. Rossdale's 2002 marriage to American pop princess Gwen Stefani certainly enhanced his profile in the States.

Rossdale has given clues in various interviews as to the origin of the band's name. The most obvious and well-known reason was a reference to the London district where the band members lived called Shepherd's Bush. The references don't end there. "Bush can mean a number of things," says Rossdale. In addition to Shepherd's Bush, "of course there's the sexual connotation." He clarified his meaning here was gender neutral. A third reference is marijuana. When asked if he has any vices, Rossdale said, "Bush. That's pot in England." He added, "I also like the 'shhh' at the end of the word."

While the group was in Canada they went by the name of BushX because the Canadian rights to Bush were taken. Ultimately the Canadian band called Bush allowed the Rossdale's band to use the name Bush in Canada after the latter made two $20,000 donations to two Canadian charities.

One unintended meaning is the similarity of the name with that of U.S. president George H.W. Bush, who was just exiting the White House when the musical group was formed. The group has disavowed any connection between their name and the former U.S. head of state. It's perfectly plausible — four reasons are enough. Did they really need another?

www.westnet.com; www.gavin-rossdale.net.

The Byrds

GROUP FORMED IN: 1964
ORIGINAL MEMBERS: David Crosby, Gene Clark, Chris Hillman, Mike Clarke, James (later Roger) McGuinn
LATER MEMBERS OF NOTE: Kevin Kelly, Gram Parsons, Clarence White, John York, Gene Parsons, Hugh Masekela
BEST KNOWN SONG: Turn! Turn! Turn! (#1, 1965)

The Byrds were a launching pad for many music genres (folk rock, psychedelic, country rock, etc.) as well as offshoot groups (Crosby, Stills & Nash, Flying Burrito Brothers, McGuinn, Clark & Hillman, etc.). But before the band split and re-formed in many different incarnations, the Byrds created their own style of folk rock that resonated with the fans of Dylan and the Beatles alike. While they were influenced by those pop icons (find me someone from the '60s who wasn't), they are among the few who can rightly claim to have in turn influenced the Beatles and Dylan as well. With their trademark ethereal harmonies and McGuinn's jangly 12-string Rickenbacker, the Byrds left an imprint on the pop music scene and justifiably were inducted into the Rock and Roll Hall of Fame in 1991.

The band in its most formative stage was called "The Jet Set." As they developed a sound by working out of the Dylan catalogue, they decided to consider a different moniker. Gene Clark recounted, "It was actually over Thanksgiving dinner. We got the idea just from the turkey. It was sitting on the table and we were trying to think of a name and I said, 'How about the Birdses?' because Dino Valenti had written a song called *Birdses* and it was actually a very clever song, very cute."

Roger responded, "No, how about just 'Birds'?" After some discussion the idea came about to spell the name "Byrds" in the same vein as the Beatles had changed the spelling of their band from Beetles. Gene seconded the suggestion. The group voted on the new name and it was unanimously accepted.

Einerson, John. Mr. Tambourine Man: The Life and Legacy of the Byrd's Gene Clark. *New York: Backbeat Books, 2005.*

The Cars

GROUP FORMED IN: 1976
ORIGINAL MEMBERS: Ric Ocasek (born Richard Otcasek),
Benjamin Orr (born Benjamin Orzechowski), Greg
Hawkes, Elliot Easton, David Robinson
LATER MEMBERS OF NOTE: Todd Rundgren ("The New Cars")
BEST KNOWN SONG: Just What I Needed (#27, 1978)

The Cars became the most commercially successful American band spawned by the new wave movement. Led by charismatic and enigmatic leader Ric Ocasek, The Cars took full advantage of their new wave image on MTV, and Ocasek's marriage to supermodel Paulina Porizkova didn't hurt either.

In the early '70s Ocasek met Benjamin Orr (who was nicknamed "Benny Eleven Letters" for his lengthy original last name of Orzechowski), in Ohio, then relocated to Boston where they met Greg Hawkes and formed the folk band called Milkwood. When their lone album, *How's the Weather,* failed to chart, the group split up. Later Ocasek and Orr formed another group called Richard & the Rabbits, a name suggested by Jonathan Richman of rival new wave band Modern Lovers (which also contained future Cars drummer David Robinson — more on him later).

The next Ocasek/Orr endeavor became Captain (or Cap'n) Swing, which saw Elliot Easton join and Hawkes return to the fold. As their musicianship and songwriting evolved, the group began to receive local airplay. The final member of The Cars original lineup was Robinson, who came over from Modern Lovers in 1976, bringing with him the artistic style that the group had been lacking.

Robinson's contributions dovetailed perfectly into the new wave music scene and they were evident in the group's album artwork. It was Robinson who suggested that the group change its name to The Cars. Ocasek was quoted as saying, "It's so easy to spell; it doesn't have a 'z' on the end; it's real authentic. It's pop art, in a sense."

www.thecarszone.com; www.ticketmaster.com.

Cheap Trick

GROUP FORMED IN: 1974

ORIGINAL MEMBERS: Rick Nielsen, Bun E. Carlos
(born Brad Carlos), Tom Petersson, Robin Zander
LATER MEMBERS OF NOTE: Pete Comita, Jon Brant
BEST KNOWN SONG: I Want You to Want Me (#7, 1979)

Aside from bassist Tom Petersson's hiatus from 1981 to 1987, Cheap Trick sports one of the most consistent lineups for any band that has been together for over 35 years. The four original and current members converged from various bands in the Illinois/Wisconsin area in the early 1970s. When Rick Nielsen and Petersson got together they formed Fuse, which was later to be called Sick Man of Europe.

Eventually Bun E. Carlos replaced the drummer and, with lead singer Robert Antoni, toured the local circuit. The group name was very fluid at this point. Carlos said, "We changed our name every weekend. We were Ozzie & Harriet, Wham Bam Thank You M'am, and The Bun Birds one gig."

The band's classic lineup finally took shape with the arrival of Robin Zander, who joined Nielsen, Petersson, and Carlos in 1974. The group's name (which was back to Sick Man of Europe) was also in for an extreme makeover. When the band members attended a concert by Slade, Petersson commented that the group was "doing every cheap trick in the book on stage." The others felt this was a clever phrase (which could be interpreted several ways) and decided they should be called Cheap Trick.

They signed a record deal at Epic after being seen in a bowling alley gig by producer Jack Douglas. Their first three albums garnered a lukewarm response in the United States but were huge sellers in Japan. This set the stage for their breakthrough album recorded live in Japan at the Nippon Budokan Hall. The group's energy was captured and displayed with the accompaniment of rapturous screams from their female Japanese fans, serving as a springboard for the group's popularity at home and in Europe.

www.billionbrads.home.att.net.

Chubby Checker

BORN: Ernest Evans on October 3, 1941,
in Andrews, South Carolina
BEST KNOWN SONG: The Twist (#1, 1960 and 1962)

Chubby Checker is the undeniable king of the dance craze song. Everyone knows him for "The Twist," but he also had less memorable songs such as "The Hucklebuck," "The Pony," "The Fly," "She Wants to Swim," and "Let's Do the Freddie." He also milked the "twist cow" for "Let's Twist Again," "Twistin' U.S.A," "Slow Twistin,'" and "Twist It Up," in addition to his famous two stints at #1 for the original version.

Ernest Evans was born in South Carolina but raised in Philadelphia. As a teenager he worked in a poultry market. When his boss heard that Dick Clark needed someone to do singing impressions, he immediately thought of Ernest, since the lad was always singing while he worked.

Ernest remembers, "I showed up doing my Fats Domino and this lady walks in the room and she said, 'You're Chubby. Chubby Checker, like Fats Domino.' She said that and then walked out of the room and that was the end of it. That lady was Mrs. Dick Clark, and that was the start of my record career. My boss had been calling me Chubby ever since I started working for him. I said, 'I don't like that.' He said, 'You're working for me, I am the boss, and your name is Chubby. That is it.' I've often said that the public gave me everything, even the name."

When Chubby recorded "The Twist," he wondered how to get the point of the dance across to the public. As it was explained to him, "It's like putting out a cigarette with both feet, and wiping your bottom with a towel, to the beat of the music. That little formula literally changed this planet." Zsa Zsa Gabor jump-started the dance craze when she did it at the Peppermint Lounge in New York. Columnist Earl Wilson reported what he saw and soon everyone was doing the Twist.

Smith, Joe. Off the Record: An Oral History of Popular Music. New York: Broadway Books, 2005.

Chic

GROUP FORMED IN: 1976
ORIGINAL MEMBERS: Nile Rodgers, Bernard Edwards,
Tony Thompson, Alfa Anderson, Norma Jean Wright
LATER MEMBERS OF NOTE: Luci Martin, Fonzi Thornton,
Robert Sabino, Raymond Jones, Andy Schwartz,
Sammy Figueroa, Michelle Cobbs, Karen Milne, Cheryl
Hong, Valerie Haywood, Sylver Logan Sharp, Jessica Wagner,
Richard Hilton, Jerry Barnes, Omar Hakim, Bill Holloman
BEST KNOWN SONG: Good Times (#1, 1979)

The writing, producing, and recording team of Nile Rodgers and Bernard

Edwards are best know for the funkified disco created by their most successful endeavor, Chic. Many are also aware of their dance-pop fingerprints on
such other projects as David Bowie's "Let's Dance," Madonna's "Like A Virgin," and Diana Ross's "Upside Down." Based on this knowledge, most people
would be shocked to know that Rodgers and Edwards initially tried to be anything *but* disco artists.

The first band started by Rodgers and Edwards was a rock band called The
Boys and later The Big Apple Band. "When I first started, all I played was super
heavy-duty rock and roll," said Rodgers. "To be a guitarist in a heavy glitter
band was the whole thing. To be Hendrix or Jimmy Page was success to me."
Despite their musicianship, Rodgers and Edwards could not attract a record
deal because blacks (Jimi Hendrix excluded) were not taken seriously in rock
music.

A hit by Walter Murphy & the Big Apple Band (remember "A Fifth of
Beethoven?") led to another name and style change. About this time disco was
on the rise and, with the addition of female vocalists, they put their indelible
stamp on the genre when they formed Chic. The group name was intended to
reflect a high-brow concept. "We knew that we didn't look chic, and we didn't
act chic, but as musicians and producers we knew how to do our jobs. That's
what set us apart from other bands," recalled Rogers.

www.fullsail.com; www.chictribute.com; www.discomuseum.com.

Cinderella

GROUP FORMED IN: 1984
ORIGINAL MEMBERS: Tom Keifer, Eric Brittingham,
Michael Smerick, Tony Destra
LATER MEMBERS OF NOTE: Jeff LaBar, Jim
Drnec, Fred Coury
BEST KNOWN SONG: Don't Know What
You Got (#12, 1988)

Cinderella is a hair-metal band of little particular distinction from the era
of heavy hairspray. Brought to the attention of Mercury Records by Bon Jovi
while toiling in local club hell, the band had to make a favorable impression
on the strength of its live shows because their demos, as lead singer Tom Keifer
put it, "were terrible. We were very green in the studio, so the demos weren't
a good representation."

The band enjoyed a fair amount of success, releasing eight top-100 hits over a four plus year career but never cracking the top 10. By the time of their third album, the band was moving to more of a bluesy sound, which drew more from the Rolling Stones than from Bon Jovi. While the band may have been hitting its stride, the taste of the public was moving away from the pop-metal sound and more toward grunge. After a four-year hiatus, Cinderella released its final album to mostly deaf ears.

The most interesting aspect of the band is its name. Keifer explains, "We were actually sitting around watching TV one night, flipping through an HBO guide. We had been kicking around different names, and we saw the name Cinderella for the movie in the guide. It wasn't the Disney version though, it was the porno version. But that really didn't have anything to do with us selecting the name. We just thought it was cool.

"In the early '80s, most band names were very obvious to the sound of their music. If it was a heavy band, it was a very heavy name. So we were a hard rock band with a name that really didn't sound like what we sounded like. I always thought that was cool with bands like Queen, Kiss, or Sweet. A light name describing something heavy. And it just kind of caught on."

www.wisconsin-music.com.

The Clash

GROUP FORMED IN: 1976
ORIGINAL MEMBERS: John Mellor
("Joe Strummer"), Mick Jones, Paul Simonon,
Nicky "Topper" Headon, Keith Levene
LATER MEMBERS OF NOTE: Peter Howard,
Terry Chimes, Vince White, Nick Sheppard
BEST KNOWN SONG: Rock the Casbah (#8, 1982)

In the grand rock music scheme of things, the Clash was to the Sex Pistols what the Rolling Stones had been to the Beatles—ever in the shadow of their predecessors with a chip on their collective shoulder, trying to dethrone the king. But as the Sex Pistols were more about nihilism than melody, the Clash was a little less of the former and much more of the latter. The stronger musicianship and song-writing of the Clash were the reasons for their ultimate breakthrough in the United States, a market the Sex Pistols never cracked. However, their thinly veiled desire to make it big worldwide and their signing with big label CBS left many punk purists wondering whether the Clash were truly one of their own.

Shortly after the band was formed they mulled over several names, including the Phones, the Mirrors, the Outsiders, the Psychotic Negatives, and the

Weak Heart Drops (or just the Heartdrops). None of these captured the essence of the band.

Then one day, while reading London's *Evening Standard* newspaper, Paul Simonon was struck by the word "clash" and how often it appeared in titles and subtitles as shorthand not only for violent confrontation but also for disagreement and friction of any kind. This was the kind of impression the group desired to make, especially during their live performances. All except Keith Levene were in favor of the name, but he was outvoted four to one and the name was official.

Gray, Marcus. Last Gang in Town: The Story and Myth of the Clash. *New York: Henry Holt, 1995.*

Coldplay

GROUP FORMED IN: 1998
ORIGIANL MEMBERS: Chris Martin, Jonny Buckland,
Will Champion, Guy Berryman
LATER MEMBERS OF NOTE: none
BEST KNOWN SONG: Clocks (#29, 2003)

Coldplay is the brainchild of Chris Martin and Jon Buckland. They met at University College London in September 1996. For a time Martin considered forming a boy band much like *NSYNC. Shortly thereafter Guy Berryman joined, as did Will Champion, who was proficient at piano and bass, but who accepted the challenge of learning to play drums from scratch.

Once the four members of the band had been assembled they first performed under the name Pectoralz. Later the group changed its name to Starfish for a gig at Camden Laurel Tree. The idea for the name Coldplay was not original to the band. Tim Rice-Oxley, a mutual friend of the group, was using the name for his band. Martin and his gang decided to appropriate the name (with Rice-Oxley's blessing) when the other band decided the name was too depressing and opted to call itself Keane.

The name Coldplay itself comes from a collection of poems by Philip Horky entitled *Child's Reflections, Cold Play*. The group chose to combine the words that were separate in the title of the poetry book.

Coldplay's sound has a freshness to it, with melodic harmonies and simplistic acoustic arrangements, often building to dramatic orchestrations. They have become the darlings of the British music scene, and Martin's marriage to Gwyneth Paltrow has raised the band's profile dramatically in the United States. Coldplay quickly became one of the most popular bands in the world in the early twenty-first century.

Collective Soul

GROUP FORMED IN: 1992
ORIGINAL MEMBERS: Ed Roland, Dean Roland,
Ross Childress, Will Turpin, Shane Evans,
LATER MEMBERS OF NOTE: Ryan Hoyle, Joel Kosche
BEST KNOWN SONG: Shine (#11, 1994)

Collective Soul was formed by a group of friends from Stockbridge, Georgia. The band is a post-grunge alternative rock unit equally proficient at hard-driving rock (*Shine, Gel, Heavy*) as melodic and introspective pop (*December, Listen, Run*). The founders of Collective Soul, brothers Ed and Dean Roland, were raised under the roof of a Baptist minister. Although they do not consider themselves a Christian band, they acknowledge a certain spirituality in their lyrics.

Ed's first band was called Marching Two Step, which included future Collective Soul drummer Shane Evans. This band met with virtually no success and eventually broke up. Ed and Dean then formed Collective Soul, which included Evans, Will Turpin, and Ross Childress. They managed to sign with Atlantic Records and their first release, "Shine," became an instant hit. The group's visibility increased dramatically at Woodstock '94 and as a supporting act for Aerosmith on an extended concert tour.

Collective Soul was chosen as the group's name from the 1943 Ayn Rand novel called *The Fountainhead*. In the book, Gail Wynand, the owner of the newspaper called the *New York Banner*, laments gaining power and making money by reporting the news and views of *others* instead of expressing his own independent beliefs. Resigned to his choices, Wynand says, "I knew what I was doing. I wanted power over a collective soul and I got it. A collective soul. It's a messy kind of concept, but if anyone wants to visualize it concretely let him pick up a copy of the *New York Banner*."

Rand, Ayn. The Fountainhead. *New York: Signet, 1943; www.geocities.com.*

Commodores

GROUP FORMED IN: 1968
ORIGINAL MEMBERS: Lionel Richie, Thomas McClary,
Ronald LaPread, William "Wak" King, Jr., Milan
Williams, Walter "Clyde" Orange

LATER MEMBERS OF NOTE: James Dean "J. D." Nicholas
BEST KNOWN SONG: Brick House (#5, 1977)

The Commodores formed while five of the six original members were in college at the Tuskegee Institute in Alabama. The members had all belonged to other bands before uniting — Lionel Richie, Thomas McClary, and William King were in The Mystics; Milan Williams was in The Jays; Ronald LaPread was in The Corvettes; Clyde Orange was in the J-Notes.

Of course, most people are familiar with Richie, who was lead singer for the group before departing on a highly successful solo career, but most are not aware that he was not the lead singer when the group formed. His involvement was as a sax player and he reluctantly began singing only on the songs he wrote. Eventually he was the band's front man for their big later hits, including the ballads for which the group became best known.

Since everyone came from different bands, they needed a new identity. They struggled over the decision of what to call their tight unit. Finally, in a moment of despair, they decided to blindfold King and have him open the dictionary and point to a word. This was how the "Commodores" name was chosen.

It is quite likely the Commodores were inspired to use this naming method by the 1960s doo-wop group The Earls, who had used the same technique to choose their name. There are risks implicit in relying on random choice. In a later interview with Earls group member Larry Chance, he quipped, "We're lucky we didn't put it up an eighth of an inch more ... we'd be called The Ears. But you know, that's how [they] did it with The Commodores. I always said if [King] put his finger up just a little bit more, it would've been The Commodes!"

www.thecommodores.homestead.com; www.classicbands.com

Alice Cooper

BORN: Vincent Damon Furnier on
February 4, 1948, in Detroit, Michigan
BEST KNOWN SONG: School's Out (#7, 1972)

The man who would become Alice Cooper was born in Detroit but grew up in Phoenix, Arizona. In high school young Vincent Furnier and a friend named Dennis Dunaway ran for the cross country team. They later decided to form a band with a few of their classmates. The band cut its teeth playing the

Cortez High School Letterman's Club Variety Show performing a lip-synched Beatles parody, together with wigs and the obligatory screaming girls at the foot of the stage (a setup by the band). This band performed under the name the Earwigs.

They soon changed the name of the group to the Spiders and replaced their lead guitarist. At this point they were primarily a cover band, although they did record two original singles, which received some airplay on local radio stations. The group members then moved to Los Angeles and changed the name to The Nazz after a Yardbirds song entitled "The Nazz Are Blue." Name number four was necessitated by the discovery that Todd Rundgren had been operating his band as The Nazz. The band held a meeting to settle the issue once and for all. One name considered was Husky Baby Sandwich, which received no support. Vincent had the inspiration to go with a spooky name, which reflected their theatrical stage show, and he suggested Alice Cooper, a name and identity that Vincent assumed personally as well.

Cooper claims he chose the name because it "conjured up an image of a little girl with a lollipop in one hand and a butcher knife in the other. Lizzie Borden. Alice Cooper. They had a similar ring."

He has also been quoted as saying, "Alice Cooper is such an all–American name. I loved the idea that when we first started, people used to think that Alice Cooper was a blonde folk singer. The name started simply as a spit in the face of society. With a name like Alice Cooper, we could really make 'em suffer." With the name, the Alice Cooper persona was born, and the godfather of shock rock had arrived.

Cooper, Alice, with Keith Zimmerman and Kent Zimmerman. Alice Cooper: Golf Monster. *New York: Crown, 2007; www.alicecooper.com.*

Elvis Costello

BORN: Declan Patrick MacManus on August
25, 1955, in Liverpool, England
BEST KNOWN SONG: Everyday I Write
the Book (#36, 1983)

Elvis Costello is treated in rock snob circles as a virtual god, for his knowledge of musical pop culture as much as for his musical output. This is not to diminish his contribution to rock music since many view him as heir-apparent to Bob Dylan as the next great rock and roll poet.

In the early years, while still going by his given name of Declan

MacManus, Costello was honing his skills with the band Flip City. Encumbered by the weight of this less-than-worthy band, he sent a demo tape to Jake Riviera at fledgling British label Stiff Records. Intrigued by the strength of Costello's songwriting, Stiff signed him and put him to work on his solo career.

By this time he was going by the name of D.P. Costello, taking the maiden name of his great-grandmother as his surname. However, the name was considered too prosaic for Stiff Records. Bear in mind, Stiff was also trying to "make a name" for itself and had developed a reputation for interesting advertisement slogans such as "You can lead a horse to water but you can't make it float" and "Contains no hit singles whatsoever." So Riviera decided that changing "D.P." to "Elvis" would get people to notice.

Notice they did. The timing couldn't have been worse (or better, in Stiff's opinion), when later that year Elvis Presley died. His legion of fans were none too happy with this Buddy Holly look-alike using the King's name. Costello was even quoted as saying, "It wasn't meant as an insult to Elvis Presley. It's unfortunate if anyone thinks we're having a go at him in any way." Eventually Elvis Costello did win over most of his detractors with his intellectual songs and eclectic style.

Thomson, Greame. Complicated Shadows: The Life and Music of Elvis Costello. *Edinburgh: Canongate, 2004; Clayton-Lea, Tony.* Elvis Costello: A Biography. *New York: Fromm International, 1998. Kamp, David, and Steven Daly.* The Rock Snob*s Dictionary. *New York: Broadway Books, 2005.*

Counting Crows

GROUP FORMED IN: 1991
ORIGINAL MEMBERS: Adam Duritz, David Bryson,
Matt Malley, Charlie Gillingham, Steve Bowman
LATER MEMBERS OF NOTE: Ben Mize, Dan Vickrey,
Jim Bogios, David Immergluck
BEST KNOWN SONG: Mr. Jones (#5 airplay chart, 1994)

Adam Duritz and David Bryson began playing together in a San Francisco band called The Himalayans. In 1989 they broke off from that group and formed a duo, calling themselves Sordid Humor, playing local coffeehouses and small clubs. Later the other members of what would be the Counting Crows were added, the name was changed, and by 1994 the group was a huge national sensation.

Many compare Duritz favorably with Bob Dylan because of his poetic turn of phrase and expressive vocals. Counting Crows music has the flavor of American trade rock and folk sensibilities, recalling Van Morrison. The dearth of groups in the mid 1990s playing this style of throwback music allowed the Crows to monopolize a corner of the market not tapped for over 20 years.

The source of the group's name is an old English rhyme to which reference was made in the movie *Signs of Life*. Duritz was watching the film while compiling a list of names for the band. In one scene, two guys are standing on a hillside trying to decide what to do with their lives. A flock of crows flies by and one of the guys says, "What was that line that your grandmother used to tell us about counting crows?"

In the old English rhyme the crows were actually magpies. The rhyme's author is attempting to divine the future by counting birds: "One for sorrow, two for joy, three for girls, four for boys, five for silver, six for gold, seven for a secret never to be told...." This part of the rhyme was also used in the Counting Crows's song "A Murder of One."

www.Anna-begins.com; www.rockonthenet.com; www.amiright.com.

The Cranberries

GROUP FORMED IN: 1990
ORIGINAL MEMBERS: Noel Hogan, Mike Hogan,
Fergal Lawler, Dolores O'Riordan
LATER MEMBERS OF NOTE: none
BEST KNOWN SONG: Linger (#8, 1994)

The origin of The Cranberries actually began before Dolores O'Riordan was a member. In the beginning there were Noel and Mike Hogan, Fergal Lawler and Niall Quinn, a friend who was also a member of The Hitchers. Quinn was asked to be the lead singer for the band they were putting together and he accepted with the proviso that he be allowed to continue with The Hitchers as well.

Quinn actually originated the name The Cranberries but feared it sounded like a band fronted by a girl, so he also suggested several variations. According to Quinn, "These included The Cranberry Saw Us, The Cranberry Doodles, The Crandoodles, and several more I can't remember. Without actually voting on it we discussed them and eventually settled on The Cranberry Saw Us." The name was a play on the term "cranberry sauce."

The band practiced regularly and were eager to cut its first demo. All, that is, except for Quinn, who preferred his drumming roll in The Hitchers to his lead singing roll in The Cranberry Saw Us. To soften the blow of leaving, he brought O'Riordan to the attention of the group. She had been singing in the school choir but was influenced by Sinéad O'Connor and was anxious to break away from school and sing professionally.

As soon as O'Riordan started singing the rest of the band knew they had found their new lead singer. They gave her a demo of a melody they had recorded and asked her to complete the lyrics. She returned with the lyrics completed and the band's biggest hit, "Linger," had been born. Soon the new foursome decided to shorten the name to "The Cranberries" because the name was now appropriate for this female-led band.

www.zombieguide.com; www.doloresoriordan.net.

Cream

GROUP FORMED IN: 1966
ORIGINAL MEMBERS: Eric Clapton,
Ginger Baker, Jack Bruce
LATER MEMBERS OF NOTE: None
BEST KNOWN SONG: Sunshine of Your Love (#5, 1968)

Eric Clapton's innovative guitar playing is legendary. Not to be overlooked, however, his involvement in the "super group" and "power trio" trends proved groundbreaking. Cream was among the first of both.

After playing in numerous blues-based bands in England in the mid–1960s (notably Bluesbreakers and Graham Bond's Organisation), the three members of Cream were seasoned veterans by the time Ginger Baker approached Clapton backstage after a Bluesbreakers gig in Oxford in June 1966 and asked him if he would like to start a band. Clapton was ready to leave the Bluesbreakers but insisted that Jack Bruce join the new band.

Baker and Bruce had become virtual enemies in Graham Bond's band, one time fighting on stage after Baker threw his drumsticks at Bruce only to have Bruce's double bass airmailed right back at him. Despite these differences, the prospects of the three virtuoso musicians breaking new ground was the deciding factor in getting together.

Naming the band was the next formality. Clapton suggested Sweet and Sour Rock 'n' Roll but, sensing a lack of enthusiasm for the suggestion he uttered, "We're the *cream*," when correctly referring to the respective talents of the group members. The reference ultimately became the genesis of the group's name.

Bruce explained, "He (Clapton) always said it was meant to be descriptive of the sound. I thought it was a good name, [though] we had to call it something [and] we were quite arrogant and full of ourselves in those days!" Bruce did confide, however, that Clapton may have had another reason for naming the band Cream, but he did not elaborate.

Schumacher, Michael. Crossroads: The Life and Music of Eric Clapton. *New York: Citadel Press, 2003; Thompson, Dave.* Cream: The World's First Supergroup. *London: Virgin Books, 2005.*

Creed

GROUP FORMED IN: 1995
ORIGINAL MEMBERS: Scott Stapp, Mark Tremonti,
Scott Phillips, Brian Marshall
LATER MEMBERS OF NOTE: Brett Hestla
BEST KNOWN SONG: With Arms Wide Open (#1, 1999)

Creed was one of the most successful and least understood post-grunge rock bands during their ten-year stint, with their first six singles hitting #1 on the *Billboard Magazine* mainstream rock charts (and seven total). The segment of the media that wished to label Creed couldn't determine whether they were a grunge, hard rock, or Christian band.

Since the band's acrimonious breakup in 2004, former lead singer Scott Stapp has confirmed he is a Christian but denies the band ever set out to have a Christian agenda in its music. As for their sound, many compared Creed's sound to Pearl Jam and Stapp to Eddie Vedder. While they may sound similar, their songwriting is quite different, as both have noted.

Stapp and Mark Tremonti began writing songs together in 1995 and they soon added Brian Marshall and Scott Phillips to the fold. Stapp and Tremonti had been calling themselves Naked Toddler, taken from the headlines of a newspaper article. Marshall, who had come from bands called Mattox Creed and Baby Fish Mouth, suggested they consider giving Naked Toddler a different name.

The band toyed with different variations using Creed with each person's name, such as Stapp's Creed, Phillips' Creed, and so on, but nothing seemed to work. Stapp finally made the suggestion to simplify the name to just Creed, because in his words, "I don't think they were really in tune with my lyrics yet and the word is a belief or a following or something you believe in, and that's what I was in search for and the name was perfect for me."

www.creed.com; www.passionbreedsfollowers.com; www.brianmarshallonline.com; www.mark-tremonti.com.

Creedence Clearwater Revival

GROUP FORMED IN: 1964
ORIGINAL MEMBERS: John Fogerty, Tom Fogerty,
Stuart Cook, Douglas "Cosmo" Clifford
LATER MEMBERS OF NOTE: None
BEST KNOWN SONG: Bad Moon Rising (#2, 1969)

CCR was truly an American band. Though brought up in California, John Fogerty created a sound with its roots in the American South, which brought forth images of Americana at a time when patriotism was in short supply and British pop was controlling the radio.

The Golliwogs, as they were first known, were badly in need of a new name. Not only was the name utterly silly, but it also came across as a blatant and tardy attempt to cash in on the British Invasion, which was precisely *not* what CCR would be about. The name conspired to hold them back because the dynamic of the San Francisco music scene was moving away from the type of sound coming out of England.

The group struggled with new names such as Deep Bottle Blue, Muddy Rabbit, and Gossamer Wump. Tom Fogerty mentioned that he knew someone with the unusual name of Credence Nuball. The group members liked the sound of his first name but suggested adding another "e" to form Creedence, like a creed, something in which to believe.

The Clearwater part also had dual meaning. It came initially from an Olympia Beer ad, which reportedly came from cool, clear water. This also appealed to the band's environmental sensibilities.

Finally, "Revival" meant many things to the band, from the imagery of a revival show to a feeling of a resurgence for the band and finally to a revival of musical values to bring back the simplicity of rock and roll in the face of the prevailing acid rock scene. When the three names were put together the group knew it had its name. Stu Cook called it "a name weirder than Buffalo Springfield or Jefferson Airplane."

Bordowitz, Hank. Bad Moon Rising: The Unofficial History of Creedence Clearwater Revival. *Woodbridge, CT: Schirmer Books, 1998.*

Culture Club

GROUP FORMED IN: 1981
ORIGINAL MEMBERS: George "Boy George" O'Dowd,
Roy Hay, Michael Craig, Jon Moss
LATER MEMBERS OF NOTE: None
BEST KNOWN SONG: Karma Chameleon (#1, 1984)

Culture Club symbolized much of what was good and bad about the New Romantic era in pop music. The androgynous look of lead singer Boy George and his quick wit kept the group constantly in the spotlight and in heavy rotation in the early MTV era (way back when the original station actually played music videos). Ultimately group tensions exacerbated by romantic issues and George's heroin addiction took the band out of the spotlight as quickly as it appeared.

Boy George was born George O'Dowd. He was very coy and enjoyed being the focus of attention. George enjoyed his sexual ambiguity and felt a connection with the reggae scene. He admired some of the names disc jockeys used, including King Tubby, Prince Jammy, and Jah Whoosh since George himself had been a DJ. So with his dreadlocks, white smock, and campy persona, George O'Dowd felt the nickname "Boy George" would suit him to a tee.

Originally called Sex Gang Children, the group decided to opt for a more radio-friendly name. Considerations included Caravan Club and Can't Wait Club. Something clicked when Jon Moss observed, "Look at us. An Irish transvestite, a Jew, a black man, and Anglo-Saxon." The clash of cultures that brought the members together was the genesis of Culture Club, the descriptive and apt name ultimately chosen for the band.

George, Boy, with Spencer Bright. Take It Like a Man: The Autobiography of Boy George. *New York: HarperCollins, 1995.*

The Cure

GROUP FORMED IN: 1977
ORIGINAL MEMBERS: Robert Smith, Laurence
"Lol" Tolhurst, Michael "Mick" Dempsey
LATER MEMBERS OF NOTE: Porl Thompson, Simon Gallup,

Andy Anderson, Boris Williams, Roger O'Donnell,
Perry Bamonte, Jason Cooper
BEST KNOWN SONG: Love Song (#2, 1989)

The Cure was formed by schoolmates at the Notre Dame Middle School in Crawley, Sussex, England. The earliest version containing Robert Smith, Lol Tolhurst, and Mick Dempsey was called The Obelisk. Smith later played in a band called "the group" as well as his older brother's band, The Crawley Goat Band.

Smith later got back together with Dempsey and two others to form Malice and play a heavy rock sound. This band became increasingly influenced by the emergence of punk rock. A year later the band changed its name to Easy Cure, drawing the name from a song of the same name written by Tolhurst. Under the new name the band entered and won a talent contest advertised as "Wanna Be a Rock Star?" which led to a recording contract with Ariola-Hansa.

This relationship was short-lived, however, when Ariola-Hansa refused to support the band's direction and Easy Cure never actually released any material. At this point Smith assumed leadership as well as lead vocal responsibilities and convinced the group to shorten the name to The Cure, since, in his opinion, Easy Cure sounded too "hippyish and American west coast." He also preferred a name starting with "The." The Cure began as one of the seminal goth bands, but in later years it achieved mainstream success and stands out as one of the most enduring and popular bands to emerge from the punk rock scene.

www.amiright.com.

Bobby Darin

BORN: Walden Robert Cassotto on May 14, 1936,
in the Bronx, New York
DIED: December 20, 1973, in Los Angeles, California
BEST KNOWN SONG: Mack the Knife (#1, 1959)

Bobby Darin was a musical jack-of-all-trades. He did his best to stay one step ahead of anyone who wanted to categorize him in any particular genre. Was he a Rat Pack wannabe or was he a rock and roll singer? Was he a folk rocker or Vegas lounge singer? He was, in fact, a man who lived a life that many other men envied. Married to Sandra Dee. Huge hit single which won him a

Grammy in the Best New Artist category in 1959. Movie actor worthy of Oscar nomination. And, not least, a member of the Rock and Roll Hall of Fame in 1990.

Before any of this success could germinate, young Walden Robert Cassotto felt the need for a different moniker — something of a marquee-grabber. Not to mention that changing one's name was the first order of show business. So he experimented with different names such as Robert Walden, Walden Roberts, Bobby Walden, and Bobby Titan.

How he settled on Bobby Darin is subject to debate, as Bobby himself told several different versions of the story. One story is that he was walking past a Chinese restaurant advertising Mandarin cuisine with the first three letters of the neon sign missing. Another is that he used the name of Darren McGavin and tweaked the spelling.

A third, more plausible story, has Bobby picking "Darin" out of the phone book. This story was repeated by Darin in a later interview with David Frost. He recounted, "The letter 'D' has always attracted me, and I just went to the phone book and I just ran it down until I found one that was spelled slightly differently ... and I just changed it a little bit."

Starr, Michael Seth. Bobby Darin: A Life. *Lanham, MD: Taylor Trade Publishing, 2004.*

Deep Purple

GROUP FORMED IN: 1968
ORIGINAL MEMBERS: Ritchie Blackmore, Rod Evans,
Jon Lord, Ian Paice, Nicky Simper
LATER MEMBERS OF NOTE: Ian Gillan, Roger Glover,
David Coverdale, Glenn Hughes, Tommy Bolin,
Joe Lynn-Turner, Joe Satriani, Steve Morse
BEST KNOWN SONG: Smoke on the Water (#4, 1973)

This band, tabbed by the *Guinness Book of World Records* as the world's loudest, was appropriately named considering deep purple would be the color of your ears if you sat near a speaker during a concert. The group was driven by Ritchie Blackmore, who was the force behind the guitar-dominated heavy metal trademark sound.

The band started with the name Roundabout before all the members had been enlisted, but once the original lineup was in place there was a certain lack of enthusiasm for the moniker. Some of the other names considered and rejected were Concrete God, Fire, and Orpheus. Jon Lord said, "Bands used to name themselves what they were, like Fred Smith and the So and So's, but we were formed after that had gone out. But realize that once the band's accepted, you can use any name."

The one suggestion that met with some general approval was Deep Purple. Blackmore said it was the name of his grandmother's favorite song—a 1930s tune that had developed into one of the postwar period's most cherished musical numbers. He also liked the fact that it doubled as a nickname for a popular strain of acid.

Another corollary was the trend, whether intentional or not, of using the name of colors in band names, such as Black Sabbath, Frijid Pink, Redbone, and Greenslade. So in the spring of 1968, Jon Lord announced the new name of his group just before performing from the roof of a Danish television studio, perhaps giving the Beatles an idea or two.

Thompson, Dave. Smoke on the Water: The Deep Purple Story. Toronto: ECW Press, 2004.

Def Leppard

GROUP FORMED IN: 1977
ORIGINAL MEMBERS: Joe Elliott, Rick "Sav"
Savage, Pete Willis, Tony Kenning
LATER MEMBERS OF NOTE: Steve Clark, Frank Noon,
Rick Allen, Phil Collen, Vivian Campbell
BEST KNOWN SONG: Pour Some Sugar on Me (#2, 1988)

Def Leppard is the poster child band for perseverance. In the group's lifetime they have overcome the death of one member, the loss of an arm of the drummer, and a painfully long lack of acceptance in their homeland of England despite enormous success in America. Through it all they survived and flourished to become the quintessential hard rock band of the 1980s.

Just prior to its permutation into Def Leppard, the band germinated as Atomic Mass with Sav Savage, Pete Willis, Tony Kenning, and Nicholas Mackley. Fate intervened in 1977 when Joe Elliott missed his bus home from work and bumped into Willis who he knew from school. "I knew he played guitar," recalled Elliott, "and as I'd started playing too. I thought I could be Malcolm Young to his Angus [AC/DC]. When he said his band were looking for a singer I said, 'I'll do it.' I was in the band for six weeks before I had to sing a note for them. I remember getting a thumbs down from Sav initially."

Elliott had been dreaming of becoming a rock star for years. While in art class at school he was fond of designing posters for imaginary bands. One name he scribbled on a notebook was Deaf Leopard but didn't envision it as a serious band name at the time. Nevertheless he suggested it as a new name for Atomic Mass and it met with surprising acceptance.

Savage asked and answered, "Did I think it was a rubbish name? Strangely, no. From the start people likened it to Led Zeppelin, so it gave us the right image." It was Kenning who suggested the spelling change to Def Leppard in order to avoid comparison to punk bands.

www.deflepparduk.com.

Depeche Mode

GROUP FORMED IN: 1980
ORIGINAL MEMBERS: Andy Fletcher, Martin Gore,
Vince Clarke, David Gahan
LATER MEMBERS OF NOTE: Alan Wilder
BEST KNOWN SONG: Personal Jesus (#28, 1990)

The earliest music of Depeche Mode, before Andy Fletcher, Martin Gore, and Vince Clarke even worked under that name, involved guitars and synthesizers. Soon after David Gahan joined in 1980 they decided to fully embrace the synthesizer sound as their own. In so doing, Depeche Mode became the most admired synth-pop band to emerge from the 1980s.

Depeche Mode survived and flourished into the twenty-first century largely on the strength of the huge 1990 album *Violator*, which spawned three of the group's biggest hits in the United States and, with the help of MTV, introduced any yet unknowing Americans to the group that was already enormously popular in their homeland of England and throughout Europe.

In 1979 Gore and Clarke comprised half of a four-piece band they called "The French Look." While this band was still together, Gore and Clarke began another band in 1980 (with Fletcher) called "Composition of Sound." The two bands even played together at St. Nicholas School Youth Club. Gore, Clarke, and Fletcher decided to merge their talents and add Gahan to create a new group. According to Gore, "He (Gahan) was doing fashion design and window display and used the magazine *Depeche Mode* as a reference. It means hurried fashion or fashion dispatch. I like the sound of that."

Depeche Mode (the magazine) is a French fashion publication. It has been widely translated as hurried or fast fashion, possibly owing in part to Gore's comments. The French verb *se depecher* means to hurry. However, more technically the phrase means fashion update or fashion news dispatch.

www.eightyeightynine.com; www.tuug.org; www.lyricsfreak.com.

Derek and
the Dominos

GROUP FORMED IN: 1970
ORIGINAL MEMBERS: Eric Clapton, Bobby Whitlock,
Jim Gordon, Carl Radle, Dave Mason
LATER MEMBERS OF NOTE: George Harrison,
Duane Allman (both studio only)
BEST KNOWN SONG: Layla (#10, 1972)

Eric Clapton was a seasoned veteran of many of England's great bands of the 1960s, including the Yardbirds, Bluesbreakers, Cream, and Blind Faith. His reputation as one of the three greatest guitar players in the world was a double-edged sword. Clapton's ego was sufficiently stroked by the "Eric is God" graffiti slogan prominent throughout his home country, but he was not an extrovert by nature.

Derek and the Dominos was the result of Clapton's desire to be simply a part of a group, not the focal point. Bobby Whitlock first suggested the new group to Clapton and the other members were quickly recruited. The group's first public appearance was billed as a Clapton solo show but just before going on stage, Eric decided the band needed a name.

One suggestion was Del and the Dominos, Del being a nickname for Clapton. Del and Eric were combined as Derek and the band had its name. The ruse that Clapton was not the focal point of the band was transparent and somewhat comical. When sales faltered for the band's masterpiece, "Layla," the band's label, Polydor, distributed thousands of "Derek is Eric" buttons. But truthfully any inference the record-buying public didn't see through the veil was ludicrous since it was perhaps the worst-kept secret in rock.

Schumacher, Michael. Crossroads: The Life and Music of Eric Clapton. *New York: Citadel Press, 2003.*

Devo

GROUP FORMED IN: 1972
ORIGINAL MEMBERS: Mark Mothersbaugh,

Bob (Bob 1) Mothersbaugh, Gerald Casale,
Bob (Bob 2) Casale, Alan Myers
LATER MEMBERS OF NOTE: Jim Mothersbaugh,
David Kendrick, Josh Freese
BEST KNOWN SONG: Whip It (#14, 1980)

Devo is one of America's original and innovative new wave groups. Always campy and fun, Devo was born of much more serious stuff. To look at or listen to the group, one would not imagine that the event that led the group to coalesce was the infamous killing of four protesting students on the campus of Kent State University by National Guard troops on May 4, 1970. Prior to that day Gerald Casale had joked about his concept of human de-evolution. Post May 4, 1970, it was a joke to Casale no more.

Also on campus during that time were Bob Lewis and Mark Mothersbaugh. The three recruited Gerald's brother Bob, Rod Reisman, and Fred Weber and they formed the Sextet Devo, performing in 1973 at the Kent State Creative Arts Festival. The set list included such standards as "Sun Come Up Moon Go Down," "Subhuman Woman," and "Here Comes Peter Cottontail." Gerald said of the crowd in attendance, "They didn't know what to make of us.... Our sound then was like Chinese Computer Music."

After the first gig, the band simplified its name to Devo, which was defined by the group as the devolving of human life, or, according to Bob Casale, "Everything in the universe degenerating from its most complex to simple form. That's all that's going on. Devo is just based on the facts."

Mark Mothersbaugh described the early music as "very dissonant, slow and plodding. It was only later when we heard things like the Ramones that we decided that fast was the way to go. At the time we were playing at Ohio unemployment speed!" Such was the evolution of de-evolution.

www.freedomofchoice.com; www.simonreynolds.net; www.everything2.org; www.experts.about. com; www.huboon.com.

Dire Straits

GROUP FORMED IN: 1977
ORIGINAL MEMBERS: Mark Knopfler,
David Knopfler, John Illsley, Pick Withers
LATER MEMBERS OF NOTE: Hal Lindes, Alan Clark,
Terry Williams, Guy Fletcher, Jack Sonni, Omar Hakim
BEST KNOWN SONG: Money for Nothing (#1, 1985)

Dire Straits is led by one of the greatest and most underappreciated guitarists of all time, Mark Knopfler. Mark and his brother David are the sons of a Jewish Hungarian architect who fled his native land and moved to Glasgow, Scotland, where Mark was born.

After attending Leeds University and later moving to London, Mark joined his first band, Brewer's Droop. This group allowed him to hone his skills but was leading him nowhere professionally. He obtained a teaching position to pay the bills and formed a rockabilly/R&B group called the Café Racers about which he recalls, "We just played pubs in London. I didn't use any effects. It was just straight in, no messing about. The group was just guitar, bass, drums and a singer."

The Café Racers featured both Mark and his brother David, along with John Illsley and drummer Pick Withers. They were sharing a flat in South London when they played at a punk festival headlined by Squeeze. A friend of Pick's commented about the dire straits the band was in financially and suggested it would be an appropriate moniker. The band heeded his advice and became Dire Straits the very next gig.

The band's big break came after they recorded a demo and left it at the house of BBC Radio London DJ Charlie Gillett to solicit his opinion. Gillett so liked the tape he played it on his Honky Tonk show, which was heard by Phonogram A&R man John Stainze. Shortly thereafter the band had a record deal with the Vertigo label and, on the strength of its first single, "Sultans of Swing," the group would be in dire financial straits no longer.

www.superseventies.com; www.geocities.com.

Dr. Hook

GROUP FORMED IN: 1968
ORIGINAL MEMBERS: Ray Sawyer, Dennis Locorriere, Bill Francis, Jay David, George Cummings
LATER MEMBERS OF NOTE: Rik Elswit, Jance Garfat, John Wolters, Bob "Willard" Henke, Rod Smarr
BEST KNOWN SONG: The Cover of the "Rolling Stone" (#6, 1973)

When Dr. Hook finally did make the cover of *Rolling Stone* on March 29, 1973, they were depicted in caricature form. In fact, the group's name wasn't even mentioned. They were unceremoniously referred to as "What's-Their-Names." Following the top-10 hit, which echoed the secret fantasy of every fledgling rock group, *Rolling Stone* magazine felt compelled to celebrate the honor but did not treat the country-rock group with full respect. After all, "The Cover of the Rolling Stone" was only the group's second top-40 hit.

In retrospect, it was appropriate. After struggling to make a name for themselves, Dr. Hook began recording offbeat songs written by cartoonist, poet, and author Shel Silverstein. Not only were the band's songs unusual, so were its stage antics. In essence, the group really was a caricature of itself. After realizing a fair amount of fame, Dr. Hook began writing solid songs and became a regular resident of the top-40 chart between 1976 and 1982.

Contrary to popular belief, Ray Sawyer, the leather eye-patch-wearing lead singer, is not Dr. Hook. The group's name came courtesy of George Cummings. He recalls, "In 1968 Ray, Dennis [Locorriere] and I were working in 'The Bandbox,' a club in Union City, New Jersey. I had just formed the band and the owner asked me to come up with a name so he could put a sign up in front of the club. I borrowed a pencil from him and on a piece of paper wrote 'Doctor Hook & The Medicine Show, straight from the South, serving up soul music.' That's exactly how the name came about."

www.doctorhook.com.

The Doobie Brothers

GROUP FORMED IN: 1970
ORIGINAL MEMBERS: John Hartman, Dave Shogren,
Tom Johnston, Pat Simmons
LATER MEMBERS OF NOTE: Michael Hossack, Tiran Porter,
Keith Knudson, Bill Payne, Jeff "Skunk" Baxter,
Michael McDonald, Chet McCracken, John McFee,
Cornelius Bumpus, Bobby Lakind, Willie Weeks
BEST KNOWN SONG: China Grove (#15, 1973)

Most people either favor the Tom Johnston–led Doobie Brothers (the early material) or the Michael McDonald–led version. Which one was better? There's no right answer, because the group found tremendous success with both versions. The evolution of the group's sound from Johnston's rock and blues style to McDonald's blue-eyed soul style had much to do with its longevity — almost as if the music came from two different groups.

John Hartman, Dave Shogren, and Tom Johnston performed together in a band called Pud. They added Pat Simmons and soon thereafter Tiran Porter replaced Shogren. After legendary session player Skunk Baxter (1974) and McDonald (1975) joined, the group's best lineup was in place.

Now, about the name. Many times the obvious inference of the meaning of a group's name is the wrong inference. This is *not* one of those times! Sure enough, it means exactly what you thought it means. Did they worry about political correctness? Not hardly. This was the early 1970s. They all got a good laugh out of the suggestion made by friend of the band Keith "Dyno" Rosen to use the name The Doobie Brothers. One can almost imagine the scene amid the smoke-filled room strewn with munchies.

But as is always the case, the band makes the name. The Doobie Brothers were not promoting anything except their music. No cannabis poster-children were they. And throughout their numerous farewell and reunion tours, legions of fans have been thrilled to see them smoking on stage (figuratively speaking) for the better part of four decades.

www.modbee.com.

The Doors

GROUP FORMED IN: 1965
ORIGINAL MEMBERS: Jim Morrison, Ray Manzarek,
Robby Krieger, John Densmore
LATER MEMBERS OF NOTE: Doug Labahn, Leroy
Vinegar, Jerry Scheff, Lonnie Mack
BEST KNOWN SONG: Light My Fire (#1, 1967)

The Doors was a one of a kind band. An American group formed by Jim Morrison and Ray Manzarek, both students at the UCLA film school who found a common interest in music and drugs. After Robby Krieger and John Densmore were brought on board from The Psychedelic Rangers, the group developed their act with an emphasis on Manzarek's electric organ work and the highly poetic, literate, and politically tinged lyrics of Morrison, as well as his deep, sonorous voice. Morrison was at first a reluctant front man, but with success came a complete transformation to over-the-top extrovert, resulting in an arrest for indecent exposure at a Miami concert.

The band took its name from the title of a book by Aldous Huxley, *The Doors of Perception,* a 1954 novel detailing Huxley's experiences when taking the mind-altering drug mescaline. Morrison himself could quote Huxley at length. In turn, *The Doors of Perception* borrowed from a line of poetry by the eighteenth-century poet William Blake: "If the doors of perception were cleansed, every thing would appear to man as it is: infinite. For man has closed himself up, till he sees all things through narrow chinks of his cavern."

Morrison saw himself as the door separating the known from the unknown. He wanted people to go through him for knowledge and enlightenment. The Doors, the culture of the time, and the drugs that eventually took his life prematurely created the perfect vehicle for Morrison to be that metaphoric door.

Hopkins, Jerry, and Danny Sugerman. No One Here Gets Out Alive: The Biography of Jim Morrison. *New York: Warner Books, 1980; Huxley, Aldous.* The Doors of Perception. *New York: Harper, 1954.*

Duran Duran

GROUP FORMED IN: 1978
ORIGINAL MEMBERS: Stephen "Tin Tin" Duffy,
Simon Colley, Nick Rhodes (real name
Nicholas James Bates), John Taylor
LATER MEMBERS OF NOTE: Simon LeBon, Andy Taylor,
Roger Taylor, Warren Cuccurullo, Sterling Campbell
BEST KNOWN SONG: Hungry Like the Wolf (#3, 1983)

No group defined the 1980s New Romantic music (a/k/a the second British Invasion) like Duran Duran. Their looks and style, which captured the essence of the decade, were on display for all to see around the clock on MTV, where the Birmingham quintet received prime exposure.

The group referred to its music as the Sex Pistols meets Chic, but it owed much more to the latter than the former, considering ex-Chic founder Nile Rodgers produced for the boys but Johnny Rotten was never seen on the board. Therefore the music tends heavily toward the brittle funk style created by Chic with a slightly harder '80s edge.

The group was named technically before the inclusion of Simon LeBon, Andy Taylor, or Roger Taylor. While at a local pub called the Hole in the Wall, John Taylor asked Stephen Duffy (the first lead singer) if he had seen the movie *Barbarella* the night before. It was the ultra-camp 1960s sci-fi film starring Jane Fonda as a voluptuous space agent of that name, on a mission to locate an evil renegade scientist called Durand Durand (yes, that is the correct spelling), played by Milo O'Shea. As it so happened, Barbarella also happened to be the name of a punk hangout frequented by the boys.

According to Duffy, "Taylor and I stood in the stairwell outside the college kitchen, Victorian and untouched since the war. He said that we should call ourselves Duran Duran. It was an exciting moment. To hear the space-age name in such a dark old place, to hear the future christened in the past. For some time it was by far the best thing about the band."

Malins, Steve. Duran Duran. Notorious: The Unauthorized Biography. *London: Andre Deutsch, 2005.*

Bob Dylan

BORN: Robert Allen Zimmerman on
May 24, 1941, in Duluth, Michigan
BEST KNOWN SONG: Like a Rolling Stone (#2, 1965)

Bob Dylan, considered by many to be rock's consummate poet, did not take his stage name from the poet Dylan Thomas, contrary to popular belief. Born Robert Zimmerman and still nicknamed "Zimmy" by rock snobs, Dylan decided on a name change as early as his junior year in high school. He told one of his friends, "I know what I'm going to call myself. I've got this great name — Bob Dillon."

It was yet another year before he began using the new name regularly. He had his sights set on fame and Zimmerman was too cumbersome. Ethel Merman was already a star who had shed the same last name but simply shortened it by one syllable. Her famous quote was "Can you imagine the name Zimmerman in bright lights? It would burn you to death!"

Dylan has flatly denied borrowing the moniker from the famous poet. He acknowledged reading some of Thomas's poetry but he felt their styles were too different. Some have suggested that the name may have come from television character Matt Dillon from the show *Gunsmoke.*

Instead he has claimed to have taken it from an uncle with the last name of Dillion (with the extra "i"). He registered at the University of Minnesota as Robert Zimmerman but to his friends he was known as Dillon, with the slightly different spelling from his uncle's name. Later, after he had achieved some recognition in New York, the spelling begin appearing as Dylan.

Shelton, Robert. No Direction Home: The Life and Music of Bob Dylan. *New York: Ballantine Books, 1986.*

The Eagles

GROUP FORMED IN: 1971
ORIGINAL MEMBERS: Glenn Frey, Don Henley,
Randy Meisner, Bernie Leadon
LATER MEMBERS OF NOTE: Don Felder,
Joe Walsh, Timothy B. Schmidt
BEST KNOWN SONG: Hotel California (#1, 1977)

When the four original members of The Eagles converged on the Los Angeles Troubadour scene in the late 1960s (Glenn Frey from Michigan, Don Henley from Texas, Randy Meisner from Nebraska, and Bernie Leadon from Minnesota), they brought with them such divergent musical influences as the Everly Brothers, the Byrds, the O'Jays, the Beach Boys, and the Temptations. They first played together as a unit backing Linda Ronstadt at a July 1971 Disneyland gig and realized immediately the combination of their talents and influences created something special.

Shortly thereafter they had a record deal with David Geffen's Asylum label and they needed a name for the group. Leadon wanted a concise name with an image. Frey wanted a street-smart name that sounded as if it could double as a name for a Detroit gang. Henley was interested in a name with an Indian vibe and everyone wanted something tough and possibly with some mythological connotations.

Once The Eagles was suggested by Frey there was almost immediate agreement. It resonated an attitude (think "Jets" of West Side Story), it was a symbol of America, and it didn't hurt that it sounded like the Beatles. But pragmatic as the band was, they realized that a name is only what you make it. And for the past four decades, through several personnel changes and an extended hiatus, the members of The Eagles have made the group name synonymous with edgy, smart, and all-American rock and roll of the highest order.

Eliot, Marc. To the Limit: The Untold Story of the Eagles. *Boston: Little Brown, 1998.*

Earth, Wind & Fire

GROUP FORMED IN: 1969
MEMBERS THROUGHOUT GROUP'S HISTORY: Maurice
White, Verdine White, Fred White, Philip Bailey, Larry

Dunn, Andrew Wolfolk, Roland Bautista, Ralph Johnson, Ronnie Laws, Michael Beale, Wade Flemons, Jessica Cleaves, Sherry Scott, Alex Thomas, Chet Washington, Don Whitehead, Yackov Ben Israel, John Paris, David Whitworth, Myron McKinely, Greg Moore, Vadim Zilberstein, Gary Bias, Bobby Burns, Jr., Reggie Young, Krystal Bailey, Kimberly Johnson
BEST KNOWN SONG: Shining Star (#1, 1975)

Earth, Wind & Fire included the services of many but was the creation of one: Maurice White. White grew up in Chicago working with some of the great soul and jazz artists of the 1960s. He formed the "Salty Peppers" and had a modicum of local success before leaving the group and moving to Los Angeles.

White formed Earth, Wind & Fire in 1969 and so named the group because of his interest in astrology. "I came up with the name because my astrological chart had no water in it: Earth, Air & Fire didn't sound right so I used 'wind' instead, and I literally drew a picture of what I wanted the group to look like. I was reading Napoleon Hill's book, *The Laws of Success* and I put the drawing in the back of the book," said White.

His supernatural interests didn't end there. He has visited Stonehenge and the ruins of ancient Indian civilizations in an effort to discover the mysteries of the universe. He said, "If you're alive inside, you have to have some curiosity and enthusiasm about the universe. I've always been interested in mysterious things. Stonehenge, the Mayans, the Incas, the Pyramids and the Sphinx."

White's studies have translated to the artwork on the group's albums. White confessed, "On EWF's *All In All* album, I put a lot of symbols on there purposely to create some curiosity so that people would think and start to raise questions about what life is about, and think about all the symbols that they had been seeing all these years."

www.members.aol.com; www.soulwalking.co.uk.

Electric Light Orchestra (ELO)

GROUP FORMED IN: 1970
ORIGINAL MEMBERS: Jeff Lynne, Roy Wood, Bev Bevan
LATER MEMBERS OF NOTE: Richard Tandy, Michael d'Albuquerque, Steve Woolam, Mike Edwards, Colin Walker, Wilfred

Gibson, Mik Kaminski, Hugh McDowell, Louis Clark,
Kelly Groucutt, Melvyn Gale, Bill Hunt
BEST KNOWN SONG: Don't Bring Me Down (#4, 1979)

Electric Light Orchestra will always be considered a vehicle for Jeff Lynne, and for good reason. Lynne has been the consistent face and voice of the band throughout its entire history. But the true father of the band was Roy Wood, who recruited Lynne in 1970 to The Move from Lynne's band Idle Race. The Move had been very successful in England with Wood at the helm, whereas Idle Race seemed to be aptly named, getting apparently nowhere fast.

When Wood, Lynne, and Bev Bevan remained as the only members of The Move, they set out with a new direction and name — Electric Light Orchestra. The name was selected for multiple meanings. Electric light was certainly one source (such as a light bulb — a bright idea, for instance), as was evident by the light bulbs shown on the group's first two albums.

The other part of the name refers to light orchestras, which are small orchestras with just a few cellos and violins. ELO's modus operandi was to splice classical and rock music together, using a modified string section. Wood was inspired by Denny Laine's Electric String Band and he decided to create his own version with the electric guitars leading the strings, thus the "Electric Light Orchestra." Propelled by Wood's vision and Lynne's brilliant pop sensibilities, ELO would become one of the most unusual and successful groups of the '70s and early '80s.

www.superseventies.com.

Eurythmics

GROUP FORMED IN: 1980
ORIGINAL MEMBERS: Annie Lennox, David A. Stewart
LATER MEMBERS OF NOTE: none
BEST KNOWN SONG: Sweet Dreams (#1, 1983)

Following a four-year romantic relationship (and breakup) and a stint with the group The Tourists, Annie Lennox and Dave Stewart decided their professional relationship and chemistry were too strong to part company. As a result they formed one of the most successful duos of the 1980s, calling themselves Eurythmics.

Although a duo in terms of consistent personnel, a different set of backing musicians was employed for every record and tour. Lennox explains, "People start off in bands all equal due to their love of music and ultimately they end up hating each other because they've been on tour for so long. We didn't want that to happen to us, so we decided to change things every year or so. The only constant was our creative relationship."

Lennox drew the name from a dance technique she was taught as a child called eurythmy. Devised in 1905 by Emile Jacques-Dalcroze, professor of harmony at the Geneva Conservatory, the technique incorporates a system of rhythmical bodily movements to spoken word or with musical accompaniment for educational purposes. The premise was to interpret words or music with graceful choreography. This was taught to children in Canadian and European schools, including the British school Lennox attended.

The music Eurythmics produced was synth pop, usually with a danceable beat. The name was certainly appropriate for the group's style. Also the duo felt proud of their European heritage and the first three letters of the name hint of this connection. They have been quoted as saying, "We always felt more European than exclusively British."

www.millennialchild.com; www.musicrememdy.com; www.community.middlebury.edu.

Evanescence

GROUP FORMED IN: 1998
ORIGINAL MEMBERS: Amy Lee, Ben Moody
LATER MEMBERS OF NOTE: John LeCompt, Terry Balsamo,
Will Boyd, Rocky Gray, Tim McCord, David Hodges
BEST KNOWN SONG: Bring Me to Life (#5, 2003)

Although the founders of Evanescence claim their Christian faith is a big part of their lives and comes through in some of their music, they don't like being called a Christian band. Evanescence is an alternative rock band with Amy Lee singing lead, possessing the most powerful woman's voice in rock music since Ann Wilson. When the members became aware the band was being promoted as part of the Christian rock scene they made it clear they did not wish to be so categorized and their record company issued a press release asking that their albums be removed from Christian retail outlets.

When Lee and Moody began playing together they went through a series of names for their group, such as Childish Intentions and Stricken. It is highly likely that if the band had stayed with either of these names there would be no confusing them for a Christian band.

In the end they arrived at "Evanescence," which comes from the word *evanescent*, meaning disappearance, or the act of vanishing away. Lee likes the name because it is mysterious and puts a picture in the listener's mind. She said in an interview that the name "means to dissipate like a vapor. It puts an image in your head like a ghost or specter that isn't really there."

Following the huge success of their six-time platinum album entitled *Fallen*, which spawned five singles, Evanescence did not vanish from the music scene as their name might imply, even after Moody's departure in 2003. That is, unless you try to find them in your local Christian music outlet.

www.encyclopediaofarkansas.com; www.gurl.com.

Fastball

GROUP FORMED IN: 1996
ORIGINAL MEMBERS: Miles Zuniga,
Tony Scalzo, Joey Shuffield
LATER MEMBERS OF NOTE: none
BEST KNOWN SONG: The Way
(#5, airplay chart, 1998)

Fastball is best known for the hit LP *All the Pain Money Can Buy* with the single "The Way," one of the most infectious pop songs of the '90s. Like many latter-day bands, Fastball has followed the same formula—choose a group name that has several possible interpretations and then be coy when asked the meaning. But Fastball was not the band's first choice for a name. In fact, it was about their fifth name in two years. And to be precise, changing their name to Fastball really wasn't their choice as much as it was their record company's.

Among the first names for the group were Starchy and Star 69, which itself is a sexual innuendo. Tony Scalzo legitimized the inference by stating, "To me, rock 'n' roll is just one step up from being a porn star. I don't do it because it possesses any earth-shaking importance, I do it because it's fun and makes me feel good."

The band then opted to change the name to Magneto, but this was short-lived when another band claimed prior rights, so they amended it to Magneto U.S.A. Still, the record company demanded a different name. The group made a list of 12 to 14 names and Fastball was the one they picked. They deny the obvious baseball reference, but they allow the public to make their own conclusions regarding whether it refers to quickie sex. Another interpretation is that this is a straight-shooting band that comes right at the listener with their best stuff.

Zuniga later lamented throwing the pitch called by their label, "because I've learned that when a lot of people hate something (in this instance, Magneto U.S.A.), it's probably really good. At least you're getting a reaction." Zuniga later wished they had used Magnetic Heads but it was too late, and Fastball it remained.

www.soundclick.com; www.uk.music.yahoo.com; www.rollingstone.com.

The 5th Dimension

GROUP FORMED IN: 1965
ORIGINAL MEMBERS: Marilyn McCoo, Billy Davis, Jr.,
Florence LaRue, Lamont McLemore, Ron Townson
LATER MEMBERS OF NOTE: Lou Courtney, Joyce Wright,
Phyllis Battle, Greg Walker, Willie Williams, Van Jewel
BEST KNOWN SONG: Aquarius / Let the Sunshine In (#1, 1969)

Although Marilyn McCoo and Billy Davis, Jr., were eventually married and had four hits as a duo, The 5th Dimension was started by McCoo and Lamont McLemore, who had been in a group with two others called the Hi-Fi's. When the Hi-Fi's split, they recruited Florence LaRue (who, like McCoo, had previously been a beauty pageant winner), Lamont McLemore, and his cousin, Davis. The three additions all had extensive music backgrounds. The new group called itself The Versatiles.

This new quintet struggled to break through until they came to the attention of Johnny Rivers, who signed them to his fledgling label, Soul City Records. One condition to their signing was to update their image and change their name. McCoo recalled, "He said The Versatiles had sort of an old ring to it. So, we all went home and the next day came back with a list of names. Ronald came in with the name The 5th Dimension. We knew right away that was it. We all voted for The 5th Dimension. It said everything we wanted to say."

The story from McLemore gives a little more insight. He and his wife, Bobette, wanted to name the group The 3rd Dimension because 3D movies had just come out. But since the group was made up of five people, it was named The 5th Dimension.

The band was very productive from 1967 to 1973, placing 20 songs in the top-40. Various lineup changes took place after McCoo and Davis left, but the original quintet reunited in 1990. Any hopes for further reunions with the original five came to an end when Townson died in 2001.

www.classicbands.com; www.findarticles.com.

Firefall

GROUP FORMED IN: 1975
ORIGINAL MEMBERS: Rick Roberts, Larry Burnett,
Jock Bartley, Mark Andes, Mike Clarke
LATER MEMBERS OF NOTE: David Muse
BEST KNOWN SONG: You Are The Woman (#9, 1976)

Formed in the image of the Eagles, the Byrds, and Buffalo Springfield, Firefall continued the country-rock style of its ancestors through the latter half of the 1970s, losing steam in the early part of the 1980s as the group failed to change with the musical tastes of the record-buying public.

The group members represented a wealth of talent from various other bands, including the Flying Burrito Brothers, the Byrds, Spirit, and Jo Jo Gunne. Firefall was formed in Boulder, Colorado, and its members were very ecology-minded. The group's name refers to a spectacular event witnessed by Rick Roberts that took place nightly in Yosemite Park.

Each evening from 1880 until 1968 in the historic park, at Glacier Point, a huge campfire would be burning. At 9:00 p.m. a man would call out, "Let the *fire fall!*" while a crowd would wait silently for a response. A faint reply would follow from the top of the mountain, at which time the great bonfire of red fir bark would be pushed over the edge of the cliff, appearing to the onlookers below as a glowing waterfall of sparks and fire. The nightly tradition was finally ended in 1968 by a Park Service director due to the congestion caused in the park and the damage to the meadows from the trampling of onlookers.

The image of this spectacle was burned into Roberts's memory, so to speak. In 1973, as his new, unnamed band was about to play their first gig, he suggested Firefall. The name seem to have fit these country-tinged soft-rockers as they followed the well-lit path burned by those torchbearers that had come before.

www.firefall.com; www.firefall.info.

Five For Fighting

GROUP FORMED IN: 1997
ORIGINAL MEMBERS: John Ondrasik, Michael
Chaves, Solomon Snyder, Randy Cooke
LATER MEMBERS OF NOTE: none
BEST KNOWN SONG: Superman (It's Not Easy) (#14, 2001)

Five For Fighting is more like a solo performer (John Ondrasik) and his backing band. He (they) burst onto the scene in 2001 with their smash "Superman" which was already a hit prior to the events in New York City on September 11, but became a theme song for many associated with the rescue efforts, thrusting Ondrasik and crew into the pop culture mainstream.

By now, even those who are not hockey fans know that the group's name is a reference to a five-minute penalty assessed against a player for fighting with an opponent. "I've always been a huge sports fan and have spent my share of time in the penalty box that is the music biz," said Ondrasik, speaking metaphorically.

Ondrasik gives the inspirational credit for the name to National Hockey League defenseman Marty McSorley, who is one of the most penalized players in league history. "In the mid '90s I was making my first record and I had come from a hockey game to the studio and the record company was there. They were like, you gotta have a band name. That night McSorley and [highly penalized forward Bob] Probert had gotten into one of their famous 'discussions' and I threw out, 'How about Five For Fighting.' They seemed to like that and being a big hockey fan I was like, 'Let's go with it.'"

In retrospect Ondrasik's patience has worn thin from the questions about the name. "It is annoying to do the Five For Fighting story. Sometimes I wish I had just called it 'A', but frankly, it's all about the songs, not the name of the band, and not really me."

www.insidehockey.com; www.dreamsawake.com; www.associatedcontent.com; www.myspace. com/fiveforfighting.

The Flaming Lips

GROUP FORMED IN: 1983

ORIGIANL MEMBERS: Wayne & Mark Coyne,
Michael Ivins, Dave Kostka
LATER MEMBERS OF NOTE: Richard English, Nathan Roberts,
Johnathan Donahue, Ronald Jones, Steven Drozd
BEST KNOWN SONG: She Don't Use Jelly (#55, 1995)

Do you know The Flaming Lips? Most casual music fans do not. But to rock snobs and recording artists they are revered. Formed by brothers Wayne and Mark Coyne in Oklahoma City, the Lips are the best respected unknown band around. Their music has been described as everything from scuzz-rock, dream pop, noise pop, neo-psychedelic, experimental rock, American underground, alternative pop/rock, to acid-bubblegum. Their influences include Pink Floyd, Led Zeppelin, The Stooges, The Jesus & Mary Chain, Black Flag, and Dead Kennedys. So now you know — The Flaming Lips are like every band and no band you've ever heard before.

Although hit single success has largely eluded the group, the Lips have lasted a quarter of a century and their legend continues to grow. Quasi-concept albums *The Soft Bulletin* (1999) and *Yoshimi Battles the Pink Robots* (2002) have help make Wayne the "Justin Timberlake of the Volvo-owning set" according to admitted rock snobs David Kamp and Steven Daly.

On at least one occasion the band called itself the Chrome Leeches, but on the eve of the Lips's first serious gig, they had not settled on a name. The first offered by Wayne was Tijuana Toads, but the band made him come up with another. Flaming Lips was his second suggestion. And so it was.

The band has encouraged a number of myths about the meaning of the name. One is that it was the title of a porn flick. Another was a reference to burning your mouth when smoking a roach. How about the story that it came to Wayne as a vision from the Virgin Mary? None of these is true. The name simply appealed to Wayne as a bit of psychedelic surrealism. Michael Ivins has said keeping the name was the hardest thing they ever did. "We were supposed to change it after the first night, 'cause nobody liked us, but it was just too much trouble to come up with another one," he remembers.

DeRogatis, Jim. Flaming Lips. Staring at Sound. *New York: Broadway,* 2005. Kamp, David, and Steven Daly. The Rock Snob*s Dictionary. *New York: Broadway,* 2005.

Fleetwood Mac

GROUP FORMED IN: 1967

ORIGINAL MEMBERS: Peter Green, Mick Fleetwood,
Bob Brunning, Jeremy Spencer.
LATER MEMBERS OF NOTE: John McVie, Christine Perfect
(nee McVie), Bob Welch, Lindsey Buckingham,
Stevie Nicks, Billy Burnette, Rick Vito
BEST KNOWN SONG: Don't Stop (#3, 1977)

Most are aware that Fleetwood Mac is the combination of the last names of Mick Fleetwood and John McVie, but many would be surprised to know that the group was so named before McVie was even a member! Peter Green, Fleetwood, and McVie had played together for a short time in 1967 with John Mayall in the Bluesbreakers. While still members of the Bluesbreakers, Green, Fleetwood, and McVie recorded a few tracks in the Decca Studios using studio time bought by Mayall for Green as a birthday present. One track recorded at that session, "a three-minute twelve-bar R&B shuffle with a fast tempo tapped on the high hat cymbal," according to Fleetwood, was entitled "Fleetwood Mac." It was so named by Green in honor of his favorite rhythm section.

When Fleetwood and Green left the Bluesbreakers, they decided to form a new band. They enlisted the services of guitarist and vocalist Jeremy Spencer and prodded McVie to be the fourth member. When McVie proved initially reluctant to leave the Bluesbreakers, Green hired Bob Brunning, who came on board realizing his time would be short.

Green still liked the sound of the name Fleetwood Mac and decided to use it for the band's name, whether or not McVie would join. The name provided Green (who had tired of the star-guitar-as-God hype) some anonymity and was further evidence of the confidence he had in persuading McVie to capitulate, which he did within a month.

Fleetwood, Mick, with Stephen Davis. Fleetwood: My Life and Adventures in Fleetwood Mac. *New York: William Morrow, 1990; Frame, Pete.* Rock Family Trees. *London: Omnibus Press, 1980.*

Foghat

GROUP FORMED IN: 1970
ORIGINAL MEMBERS: "Lonesome" Dave Peverett,
Rod Price, Tony Stevens, Roger Earl
LATER MEMBERS OF NOTE: Nick Jameson,
Craig MacGregor, Eric Cartwright
BEST KNOWN SONG: Slow Ride (#20, 1976)

When Foghat got rolling with its brand of boogie-blues hard rock, it was difficult to get out of the way. That suited the fans just fine, since the group knew how to rock a sold-out house with the best of them in the mid–1970s. Forays by the band into the lighter side of the rock spectrum (power ballads) felt less sincere than, say, Kiss. Better to keep the train rockin' and rollin' down the tracks.

Early efforts to name the band met with little more than snickers from the band members. Concrete Parachute and Titanium Turtle were among the earliest entrants to reach the dumpster. According to Roger Earl, they were trying to work names like "So And So's Retroactive Show or The Solid Senders, Brandy this and Wine that."

"Dave (Peverett) liked to have monikers for everybody," Earl continued. "So he was Lonesome Dave and he was also Jaxman. And he had this character he would draw called Luther Foghat. He also tried to talk Chris Youlden, who was our singer in Savoy Brown, into calling himself Luther. But Chris couldn't see the wisdom in that. And I was Skins Willie Johnson for some reason. So Dave said, 'How about Luther Foghat?' And we said, 'All right, how about just Foghat?'"

"What does it mean?" asked Earl.

"It means us, doesn't it?" replied Peverett.

That said it exactly. Most bands believe the name doesn't make the band, the band makes the name. No question Foghat certainly *has* made its name in rock music.

www.classicrockrevisited.com; www.foghat.com.

Foo Fighters

GROUP FORMED IN: 1994
ORIGINAL MEMBERS: Dave Grohl, Pat Smear,
Nate Mendel, William Goldsmith
LATER MEMBERS OF NOTE: Taylor Hawkins,
Franz Stahl, Chris Shiflett
BEST KNOWN SONG: Best of You (#18, 2005)

From the ashes of Nirvana grew a band whose seed had actually germinated before Kurt Cobain's untimely demise. The group's drummer, Dave Grohl, had actually learned the guitar first and had been writing songs since his early teens. However, he resisted the temptation to force them on his group, fearing the songs might negatively affect Nirvana's chemistry. He recorded numerous original tunes in the privacy of his home and wrote "Foo Fighters" on the tape boxes.

Grohl's opportunity to perform the songs came all too soon. After gathering his wits about him following the news of Cobain's suicide, Grohl set out to form his own group, which he also called Foo Fighters. The name was taken from mysterious balls of orange and red light encountered by the U.S. Army in the skies over Germany just after World War II. The unidentified flying objects were named foo fighters and their true nature has never been determined. The army took the name from comic strip character Smokey Stover, whose favorite expression was "Where there's foo, there's fire."

Much has been made of Grohl's interest in UFOs. He even named his record label Roswell Records, and he gave an exclusive performance at the U.S. Air Force base in Roswell, New Mexico, which is the site where a UFO allegedly crashed in 1947. But one gets the impression Grohl feels it is a little overplayed. He skirts the issue and says, "People suppose I'm obsessed with outer space, which I'm just not. I love reading about it, I love science fiction movies, but I don't pray to the alien God in my pyramid temple. It just doesn't happen."

www.foofighters.com; www.realnetworks.com; www.fusionanomaly.net; www.answers.com; www.fooarchiv.com.

Foreigner

GROUP FORMED IN: 1976
ORIGINAL MEMBERS: Mick Jones, Lou Gramm
(born Louis Grammatico), Ian McDonald,
Dennis Elliott, Al Greenwood, Ed Gagliardi
LATER MEMBERS OF NOTE: Rick Wills, Johnny Edwards,
Jeff Jacobs, Bruce Turgon, Andrew "Ravens Claw" Peters,
Mark Schulman, Thom Gimbel, Ron Wikso, Brian Tichy,
Denny Carmassi, Jason Bonham, Jeff Pilson, Kelly Hansen
BEST KNOWN SONG: Cold As Ice (#6, 1977)

Foreigner, formed by Mick Jones and Ian McDonald, rocketed to stardom so fast with their eponymous debut album that they were unable to perform encores at their early concerts because they had played all ten songs they knew. When their second album, *Double Vision*, was an equally big hit, Foreigner had established itself at the pinnacle of the arena rock scene, where they stayed throughout the 1980s.

The band has been criticized for being formulaic. However, Foreigner is to be credited with creating its own successful style of memorable hard rock guitar licks and catchy melodies. Foreigner even brought in Junior Walker to play sax on *Urgent* and the vocals of Jennifer Holliday and the New Jersey Mass Choir on *I Want to Know What Love Is*.

The band name origin would seem obvious since the group was originally comprised of members from both sides of the Atlantic. While it was a good fit, the selection process was not quite so simple. Per Lou Gramm, "We went from Nothing to being called Trigger. For a while we were being called The Romeos. I'd tell everybody, 'I can't live with that.' We were going through encyclopedias, porno magazines, paperback novels. We just would come up with lists of 50 names and before we'd start rehearsal we'd exchange lists and see if anything appealed to us as far as a name goes. Mick came in with Foreigner right out of a dictionary or something. It didn't blow any of us away, the name, but it was comfortable. It had positive connotations."

www.foreignerfiles.com.

Frankie Goes
to Hollywood

GROUP FORMED IN: 1980
ORIGINAL MEMBERS: Holly Johnson, Paul Rutherford,
Brian Nash, Mark O'Toole, Peter "Ped" Gill
LATER MEMBERS OF NOTE: none
BEST KNOWN SONG: Relax (#10, 1985)

This is another example of a group that merits mention in this book not for its prodigious output but for its highly unusual name. There is little argument that in 1984 and 1985 Frankie Goes To Hollywood (FGTH to those in the know) had the attention of most people. Whether it was their video for "Relax," to the shocking lyrics of the song itself, to their ban of the song from the British radio airwaves, to the striking black and white t-shirts worn by every New Romantic artist (FRANKIE says...), FGTH was momentarily at the top of the mountain.

This begs the question, however, of which was faster — getting to the top or plummeting back into the valley of oblivion again? The follow-up song to "Relax" was "Two Tribes," a commentary on cold-war politics. In the video, look-alikes of U.S. president Ronald Reagan and Russian leader Konstantin

Chernenko battle in a mud wrestling match. The metaphor was lost on most of the record-buying public who would rather have FGTH make them dance than make them think. This was the beginning of the group's demise, which became official when they broke up in early 1987.

The group was performing under the name of Hollycaust for a while (a play on Holly Johnson's name). The change of name was discussed in interview format on the B-side of the 7-inch version of "Relax," called "One September Monday." In the interview by Paul Morley of their record label Zang Tuum Tumb (ZTT), Holly Johnson reveals that the new name was derived from a magazine headline entitled "Frankie Goes To Hollywood" above a story about Frank Sinatra's move from Las Vegas to Tinseltown. Once again, "Holly" was a part of the name.

www.knittingcircle.org.uk.

Frankie Valli & the 4 Seasons

GROUP FORMED IN: 1961
ORIGINAL MEMBERS: Frankie Valli (born Francis Stephen Castellucio), Tommy DeVito, Bob Gaudio, Nick Massi (born Nicholas Macioci)
LATER MEMBERS OF NOTE: Charlie Calello, Joe Long
BEST KNOWN SONG: December, 1963
(Oh, What a Night) (#1, 1976)

This is much more than the story of how the 4 Season became the 4 Seasons. Consider the path Frankie Valli took to arrive at his long-lasting stage name. He was born Francis Stephen Castelluico in Newark, New Jersey. He first recorded in 1953 as Frankie Valley. He chose this name in honor of his favorite female singer, Texas Jean Valley. When he first hooked up with Tommy DeVito (and two others) they formed the Variatones and later changed the name to the Four Lovers. To accommodate this group name, Frankie Valley became Frankie Love, as it was customary for the group leader's name to be listed in front of the group.

After being dropped by their record label, Frankie recorded a solo record as Frankie Tyler. He later rejoined the Four Lovers but the group then used a variety of names including Frankie Valle & the Romans. Thus Frankie had returned to the first stage name, without the "y" on the end. He was not through by a long shot.

You still with me? Try to keep up. After hooking up with producer and songwriter Bob Crewe, the group was in for another name change. Valli recalls, "We were auditioning at a nightclub in a bowling alley in Union (N.J). I looked up at the sign and said, 'What a great name for a group — the Four Seasons.'" The group has actually gone by The 4 Seasons, using the numeral "4" instead of the spelled out word. It was also at this time Frankie began spelling his last name "Valli," so as to "re–Italianize" himself.

Think we're done? Not so fast. Most of the 47 top-100 songs released by this group over the next 34 years were credited to Frankie Valli & the 4 Seasons. However, three of their releases (one each in 1965, 1966, and 1967) were credited to "The Wonder Who?" Why? Who knows.

Talevski, Nick. The Unofficial Encyclopedia of the Rock & Roll Hall of Fame. Westport, CT: Greenwood Press, 1998; www.nj.com.

Garbage

GROUP FORMED IN: 1994
ORIGINAL MEMBERS: Shirley Manson, Bryan "Butch" Vig, Steve Marker, Doug "Duke" Erickson
LATER MEMBERS OF NOTE: none
BEST KNOWN SONG: Stupid Girl (#24, 1996)

Garbage is simply one of the best rock bands of its time. The ingredients were all present — a true superstar female rock vocalist and her backing band that is capable of turning their excellent musicianship into gold with production wizardry. The finished product allowed fans of alternative music the opportunity to actually *enjoy* their music again, instead of just commiserate with it.

Butch Vig was born Bryan Vig. The origin of his nickname came from the butch haircuts his father gave him as a child. Vig's reputation in the music biz came from producing some of the biggest acts of the grunge and alternative era, including the Smashing Pumpkins, Sonic Youth, Soul Asylum, and Nirvana (yes, Butch was at the helm of the most influential album of the 1990s, *Nevermind*). With free studio time, Vig, Steve Marker, and Duke Erickson would record their own material, then experiment with it as if they were producing their own band — a notion they entertained for a while.

Finally the talk of starting a band turned to action. Tired of listening to their own voices, the guys sought out a female vocalist. They spotted Scottish singer Shirley Manson on MTV performing with her group Angelfish. Two auditions later she was hired and the group was formed.

The name had already been chosen. One day when Vig was remixing noise samples for Nine Inch Nails, his friend and fellow percussionist Pauli Ryan commented, "this [stuff] sounds like garbage to me," to which Vig replied, "Yeah, but at some point I'm going to turn this garbage into a song." What the master producer actually did was turn Garbage into a group, making one man's trash an industry's treasure.

www.garbage.suite.dk.

Genesis

GROUP FORMED IN: 1967
ORIGINAL MEMBERS: Peter Gabriel, Anthony Phillips,
Tony Banks, Mike Rutherford, Chris Stewart
LATER MEMBERS OF NOTE: John Silver, John Mayhew,
Steve Hackett, Phil Collins, Bill Bruford, Chester
Thompson (tour), Daryl Stuermer (tour), Ray Wilson
BEST KNOWN SONG: Invisible Touch (#1, 1986)

The Genesis of Peter Gabriel was prog rock, quirky, complex, and theatrical. The Genesis of Phil Collins was successful. Does this mean Collins's style was better? Not necessarily. Only more radio friendly. But it certainly serves as an interesting dichotomy of a group that lasted the better part of 40 years.

Formed in 1967 from members of Charterhouse School, the group had no intention of ever playing live. Rather, the quintet considered itself a songwriting cooperative that would demo songs they hoped other artists would want to record. When their reputation grew as the best band in the school, they cut a cassette in the hopes of obtaining a record deal.

A Charterhouse alum named Jonathan King took them under his wing. He had become a novelty hit-maker and was interested in a career as a music producer. After listening to and liking the tape (especially Gabriel's vocals), King contacted Gabriel to suggest they meet to discuss the group's future. King told the boys their name would be Genesis, which really had nothing to do with the group but was in reality King's allusion to the genesis of his career as a music producer, although he was later quoted as suggesting the name signified the "beginning of a new sound and feeling."

No sooner had he christened the band than his record company pointed out there was already a group in the United States of the same name and suggested a change. King considered and dismissed the handful of new ideas that had been passed along to him such as Gabriel's Angels and Champagne Meadow, returning instead to his original choice.

Thompson, Dave. Turn It on Again: Peter Gabriel, Phil Collins & Genesis. *Faversham, Kent, England: Backbeat Books, 2005.*

Gin Blossoms

GROUP FORMED IN: 1987
ORIGINAL MEMBERS: Bill Leen, Doug Hopkins,
Jesse Valenzuela, Richard Taylor, Chris McCann
LATER MEMBERS OF NOTE: Robin Wilson, Dan Henzerling,
Scott Johnson, Phillip Rhodes
BEST KNOWN SONG: Til I Hear It from You (#11, 1996)

Bill Leen and Doug Hopkins first played together a few years after graduating from high school in Tempe, Arizona. They spawned an impressive number of bands. Their first band was called Moral Majority, so called when a friend used Doug's name to join Jerry Falwell's organization.

From there Leen and Hopkins changed the personnel and band name to the Psalms. Internal conflicts caused the group to disband and Algebra Ranch was formed. Similar circumstances led to the dissolution of this incarnation as well.

Leen and Hopkins moved to Portland and played in a band called Ten O'Clock Scholars, before returning to Tempe and recruiting Jesse Valenzuela (guitar and lead vocals), Richard Taylor (rhythm guitar), and Chris McCann (drums). This band bore the name of the Gin Blossoms. The term gin blossom refers to the damaged capillaries in the nose of someone suffering from vascular rosacea. This condition can be aggravated by excessive alcohol consumption. The band was inspired to use the name from a famous picture of comedian W. C. Fields that appeared in Kenneth Anger's book *Hollywood Babylon II*, along with the caption describing Fields's "terminal case of gin blossoms."

The band members were reputed to live up to their group's name, although not to the same extent as the drinking reputation attributed to W. C. Fields. They were known for some disreputable antics after rounds of power drinking. One of the widely reported misdeeds involved poking holes in the low ceiling above the stage when performing at Long Wong's, one of the local clubs.

Anger, Kenneth. *Hollywood Babylon II*. *New York: Plume, 1984; www.ginblossoms.info; www.users.on.net.*

Go-Go's

GROUP FORMED IN: 1978
ORIGINAL MEMBERS: Belinda Carlisle (born Belinda
Jo Kurczeski), Jane Wiedlin, Margot Oliverra, Elissa Bello
LATER MEMBERS OF NOTE: Gina Schock,
Kathy Valentine, Charlotte Caffey
BEST KNOWN SONG: Our Lips Are Sealed (#20, 1981)

The Go-Go's were born out of the punk influences of the late 1970s. Former high school cheerleader Belinda Carlisle went by the stage name of Dottie Danger as the drummer in a punk band called The Germs. After practicing with them a few times she contracted pneumonia and left the band.

Jane Wiedlin was not the cheerleader type. Her life was changed after attending a Sex Pistols performance in 1978. Calling herself Jane Drano, she was playing guitar in punk bands in the Los Angeles area. After Wiedlin met Carlisle they decided to form a band with Margot Oliverra and Elissa Bello, which they called The Misfits. When deciding who would play what, Carlisle opted for singing since, according to her, "I am much too lazy to play drums."

The Misfits' first gig was in a place called The Masque, which was in the basement of a porno theater. Just prior to the gig the band members were in Denny's Restaurant on Sunset Strip when Wiedlin suggested the group change its name to the Go-Go's. The name may owe in part to the world famous Whiskey a Go Go, where they made some of their earliest appearances.

Within a short time Bello and Oliverra left, replaced by Gina Schock, Charlotte Caffey, and Kathy Valentine, which has remained the Go-Go's lineup ever since. The Go-Go's ultimately became the most popular all-female band to emerge from the punk and new wave era.

www.members.fortunecity.com; www.geocities.com; www.beautifulatrocities.com.

Goo Goo Dolls

GROUP FORMED IN: 1986

ORIGINAL MEMBERS: Johnny Rzeznik,
Robby Takac, George Tutuska
LATER MEMBERS OF NOTE: Mike Malinin,
Brad Fernquist, Korel Turnador
BEST KNOWN SONG: Iris (#1, 1999)

The Goo Goo Dolls are a post-grunge alternative rock band formed in Buffalo, New York. Although they fancy their early work as heavy metal in the vein of The Replacements, the band has rounded into a melodic rock band that has produced a lengthy string of hit songs and legions of fans.

The band was originally called the Sex Maggots at a time when they would play with other nondescript bands in a local club and were paid in beer. Once the group was good enough to have an actual booking under their own name, a promoter strongly advised them to change the name. The group's sound was still pretty rough and closer to heavy metal than radio-friendly rock. In fact, their first recording contract was with heavy metal label Metal Blade. But Robby Takac confessed in a later interview they now realize that those early recordings aren't nearly as hard as they once thought. "At the time it seemed really heavy and so we thought it would be ironic to have a name like a bunch of little girls," he said.

The new name was chosen from an ad in a *True Detective* magazine. "Buffalo is not exactly a metropolis and it (Sex Maggots) was considered offensive, so we changed it to 'Goo Goo Dolls,'" said Johnny Rzeznik.

The band had come to regret the silliness of the name. "If I had five more minutes, I definitely would have picked a better name," said Rzeznik. They "toyed with the notion of calling the band Goo or calling the band GGD," says Takac, but by that time they had a wide following and the name recognition was far more important.

www.fanclubs.org; www.annecarlini.com; www.insidecx.com.

Grand Funk Railroad

GROUP FORMED IN: 1968
ORIGINAL MEMBERS: Mark Farner, Don Brewer, Mel Schacher
LATER MEMBERS OF NOTE: Craig Frost, Dennis Bellinger,
Bruce Kulick, Max Carl, Tim Cashion
BEST KNOWN SONG: We're an American Band (#1, 1973)

Grand Funk Railroad is one of the best liked (by fans) and least liked (by critics) rock bands of the 1970s. Formed as a boogie blues band, they built a devoted fan base with constant touring, a loud, simple take on the blues-rock power trio sound, and strong working-class appeal. They expanded their style to include a number one cover of Little Eva's "Locomotion" and they left their legacy with the autobiographical hard rock hit "We're an American Band."

The band history was recounted by Don Brewer as follows, "We were originally a garage band, the Jazzmasters, which I started in the basement of my house in Swartz Creek, Michigan, near Flint, in 1963. Then the group was called The Pack until Terry Knight, a local DJ with a big ego, joined us and we were called Terry Knight and the Pack. When he left, we became The Pack again, then The Fabulous Pack. We were clearly in search of a name."

Brewer and Mark Farner left The Fabulous Pack and recruited Mel Schacher from ? And the Mysterians. Terry Knight left the performance side of the music business and became the group's manager. They renamed themselves Grand Funk Railroad, borrowing from the western subsidiary of a railroad line that was headquartered in Montreal, Canada, called Grand Trunk Western Railway, but more commonly known as the Grand Trunk Railroad. According to Brewer, "That railroad gave us an idea. With funk music coming up in rock in the late '60s, we thought it would be a great play on words: 'trunk,' 'funk.'"

www.classicbands.com; www.irvineworldnews.com

Grateful Dead

GROUP FORMED IN: 1965
ORIGINAL MEMBERS: Jerry Garcia, Bob Weir, Ron
"Pigpen" McKernan, Phil Lesh, Bill Kreutzmann
LATER MEMBERS OF NOTE: Mickey Hart, Tom Constanten,
Keith Godchaux, Donna Godchaux, Brent Mydland,
Bruce Hornsby (tour only), Vince Welnick
BEST KNOWN SONG: Touch of Grey (#9, 1987)

The Grateful Dead were the great ambassadors of music's psychedelic era, lasting long after other acts had died, broken up, or compromised their musical roots. For that reason along with their fervent following, the Dead ranks among rock's greatest bands of all time. A mystical quality carried the Dead on the wave of an ever-growing throng of "Deadhead" fans willing to tour *with* the band throughout the country. Not until founder Jerry Garcia's death in 1995 did the band decide to call an end to the seemingly endless road show.

The first incarnation of the band was known as the Warlocks. Looking to begin anew, the band considered names such as The Hobbits, Vanilla Plumbego

(Weir's choice), and Mythical Ethical Icicle Tricycle (Garcia's choice). One day the band members were smoking DMT and decided to try Valentinian chance — fortune telling using a randomly selected passage from a book, in this case, Funk and Wagnalls's dictionary. "Grateful dead" was a folkloristic term for earth-tethered spirits freed from their earthly ties through human intervention. Seems to have hit the mark!

Garcia said, "It was one of those moments, like everything else on the page went blank, diffuse, just sorta *oozed* away, and there was *grateful dead. Big* black letters *edged* all around in gold, man, blasting out at me, such a stunning combination." Originally the rest of the band didn't take to the name but eventually their friends and fans convinced them how perfect it was and the band members succumbed to the inevitable.

Jackson, Blair. Garcia: An American Life. *New York: Viking, 1999; Brightman, Carol.* Sweet Chaos: The Grateful Dead's American Adventure. *New York: Clarkson Potter, 1998.*

Green Day

GROUP PERFORMED IN: 1989
ORIGINAL MEMBERS: Billie Joe Armstrong, Mike
Dirnt, John Kiffmeyer (a/k/a Al Sobrante)
LATER MEMBERS OF NOTE: Frank "Tre Cool" Wright
BEST KNOWN SONG: Good Riddance
(Time of Your Life) (#11-airplay charts, 1998)

Born in the mold of the great punk rock bands, Green Day plays with an energy and enthusiasm not heard in America since the days of the Ramones. They are the new standard for the post-grunge punk revival, influencing an entirely new generation of neo punk bands, including Sum 41 and Good Charlotte, to name a few.

The band was originally named Sweet Children, a name that couldn't have been further from the image the group wanted to portray. A new record deal with Lookout Records prompted the band to devise a new name. The label executives suggested the band choose a name they could easily visualize on the cover of a CD.

The band selected the name Green Day as an inside joke. The group first heard the words uttered by the muppet Ernie on *Sesame Street* and then started using "green day" to refer to smoking pot (picture a green haze of smoke filling the room). Armstrong even wrote a song entitled "Green Day," which was recorded on the album *1039/Smoothed out Slappy Hour.* In addition, the group's first drummer, Al Sobrante, wrote "Green Day" on the back of his jacket.

Even after deciding on the name, the group admits being somewhat embarrassed by it. When Hoobastank hit it big, Mike Dirnt was quoted as saying, "At last a band with a worse name than us." But as opposed to Sweet Children, the name Green Day signaled a new and maturing band, no longer the innocent youngsters their former name implied, whether or not they ever *were* sweet or innocent in the first place.

Spitz, Marc. Nobody Likes You: Inside the Turbulent Life, Tunes and Music of Green Day. New York: Hyperion, 2006; www.greendayauthority.com.

The Guess Who

GROUP FORMED IN: 1963
ORIGINAL MEMBERS: Chad Allan (born Allan Kobel),
Randy Bachman, Bob Ashley, Jim Kale, Garry Peterson
LATER MEMBERS OF NOTE: Burton Cummings,
Kurt Winter, Greg Leskiw, Don McDougall,
Bill Wallace, Dominic Troiano
BEST KNOWN SONG: American Woman (#1, 1970)

The Guess Who devised (accidentally) truly one of the most unusual methods of obtaining a name in rock history. The group began in Winnipeg, Canada, as Chad Allan and the Reflections (later changed to Chad Allan and the Expressions), with Allan Kobel changing his stage name to Chad Allan. The group's beginnings coincided with the Beatles and the British Invasion. The Expressions were in tune with the times which were a-changin', and they tried to market themselves as if they themselves were Brits.

The early returns were met with limited success. Then in 1965 they recorded a cover version of British rocker Johnny Kidd's "Shakin' All Over," which they believed could be their breakthrough hit. In a weak marketing ploy, the song was released with the words "Guess Who?" under the title, with the hope people would wonder if this was a new band from England. Farther down in smaller print was the group name. To look at the cover, the "Guess Who?" part looks more like a B-side song than a realistic question as to artist.

Be that as it may, the song was their first hit in the United States, climbing to #22 in 1965. Early the next year, Chad Allen left the group to concentrate on his studies. He was replaced by 17-year-old Burton Cummings, who would be the voice of the group from then on. At that point the group's label, Quality Records, decided the group should permanently change its name to

"Guess Who?" since many disc jockeys had been erroneously announcing the band by that name when playing "Shakin' All Over," and was finally changed to The Guess Who in 1968.

www.tsimon.com.

Guns n' Roses

GROUP FORMED IN: 1985
ORIGINAL MEMBERS: Axl Rose (born William Bailey),
Izzy Stradlin (born Jeffrey Isbell), Tracii Guns,
Rob Gardner, Ole Beich
LATER MEMBERS OF NOTE: Slash (born Saul Hudson),
Steven Adler, Michael "Duff" McKagan, Matt Sorum,
Dizzy Reed, Gilby Clarke, Robin Finck, Tommy Stinson,
Chris Pitman, Richard Fortus, Ron "Bumblefoot" Thal,
Frank Ferrer, Bryan "Brain" Mantia, Josh Freese,
Paul Tobias, Buckethead
BEST KNOWN SONG: Sweet Child O' Mine (#1, 1988)

Slapping the music world up the side of the head, Guns N' Roses was a phenomenon of the late 1980s that made hair bands look wimpy and drove the last vestige of the New Romantic era completely out of town. The band's debut album, *Appetite for Destruction,* represented a new dawn for hard rock, changing rock music from just a good time to something dirtier, more raw and more dangerous. The band's appetite for *self*-destruction led to its premature demise after just four years as kings of heavy metal.

Rose was raised under the name William Bailey, which was his step-father's last name. At the age of 17, he learned his biological father was William Rose, so he changed his name to W. Rose. He formed a local band called Axl and later adopted the group name as his own first name.

Rose left Indiana for LA and met up with fellow Hoosier Izzy Stradlin. Together they played in the band Hollywood Rose. Ole Beich and Rob Gardner played with Tracii Guns in L.A. Guns. Guns N' Roses was formed by a marriage of the talents and names of Tracii Guns and Axl Rose together with the aforementioned bandmates. Soon afterward Guns and Gardner were replaced with Slash and Duff McKagan. As a group, Guns n' Roses were unrepentant both on and off stage and, using their own brand of heavy metal, built the bridge over which many would walk into the '90s music scene.

www.mobile.mystrands.com; www.tags.lyricsfreak.com.

Heart

GROUP FORMED IN: 1970
ORIGINAL MEMBERS: Roger Fisher, Steve Fossen, Michael
Derosier, Howard Leese, Ann Wilson, Nancy Wilson
LATER MEMBERS OF NOTE: Mark Andes, Denny Carmassi,
Fernando Saunders, Denny Fongheiser, Ben Smith,
Mike Inez, Craig Bartok, Debbie Shair, Rick Markmann
BEST KNOWN SONG: Magic Man (#9, 1976)

Led since 1970 by Ann Wilson, the greatest female rock vocalist of all time, Heart has confounded critics by surviving and flourishing for more than four decades. The confluence of bands that flowed into what became the group's base lineup is like a complicated genealogy chart and came from three distinct directions.

First, the men of Heart. Brothers Roger and Mike Fisher joined with Steve Fossen to form The Army in 1963. The name is ironic since Mike later became a conscientious objector to the Vietnam War, precipitating his move to Canada (he apparently felt he had already served his time in The Army). The Army later changed personnel and its name to White Heart, Carl Wilson & Heart (no relation to the Beach Boys or Ann/Nancy), and then Heart.

In 1970 Ann Wilson answered an ad placed by Roger and Steve for a female vocalist. She had been a member of several bands herself, including Ann Wilson & the Daybreaks and A Boy and His Dog (a group name she surely was glad to ditch). When Ann joined Heart, the group stopped being Heart and became Hocus Pocus.

The third piece to the puzzle was Ann's sister Nancy Wilson, who had been playing acoustic guitar in clubs while attending college in Oregon. After being assured by Ann that the group would have an acoustic side and wouldn't be all straight-ahead "rock and roll hoochie-koo," Nancy joined the band in Vancouver, Canada, where it had relocated. At this point the band returned to its previous name of Heart and the pieces were in place for the world to be rocked by Ann and rolled by Nancy for years to come.

www.members.tripod.com; www.phoenixheart.org.

Herman's Hermits

GROUP FORMED IN: 1964

ORIGINAL MEMBERS: Peter Noone
(a/k/a Herman), Derek Leckenby, Keith
Hopwood, Karl Green, Barry Whitwam
LATER MEMBERS OF NOTE: none
BEST KNOWN SONG: I'm Henry VIII, I Am (#1, 1965)

As it is with any teenage idol (or band led by one), revisionist history is quick to downplay an individual's popularity and/or talent. While nobody will win an argument that Herman's Hermits could compete with the Rolling Stones in a talent show, Peter Noone and his band were most certainly a commercial force to be reckoned with in the mid–1960s, even outselling the Beatles worldwide in 1965 (by their estimate, anyway). Despite or perhaps because of their blatant Englishness, Herman's Hermits played a significant role in the British Invasion of America. From 1965 to 1966 the group had nine consecutive top-10 hits in the Untied States and 10 total.

The band started without Noone under the name The Heartbeats, playing clubs around Manchester, England. Noone was in attendance at one of these outings and jumped up on the stage to sing a few impromptu numbers. He had been performing on television for several years and so was well prepared to lead the group despite being only 15 years old.

The owner of the pub where the group rehearsed commented on how much Noone resembled Sherman, the cartoon character in *Peabody's Improbable History*, which was an offshoot series to the *Rocky and Bullwinkle* cartoon series. In the cartoon, Peabody, a professorial dog who wore glasses, and his young companion Sherman, travel back in time to interact with and sometimes alter historical events (which never turn out to go like the history books taught).

Amused by the similarity, the band intended to call Noone by his new nickname; however, they misunderstood the name and referred to him as Herman, not Sherman. Herman was, according to Noone, "a real nerdy character." The band was then renamed Herman and His Hermits, and later shortened to Herman's Hermits.

Smith, Joe. Off the Record: An Oral History of Popular Music. New York: Warner Books, 1988; www.hermanshermits.com.

The Hollies

GROUP FORMED IN: 1962
ORIGINAL MEMBERS: Alan Clarke, Graham Nash,
Vic Steele, Eric Haydock, Don Rathbone

LATER MEMBERS OF NOTE: Terry Sylvester, Bernie Calvert,
Mikael Rickfors, Carl Wayne, Tony Hicks, Bobby
Elliott, Ray Stiles, Steve Laurie, Ian Parker, Peter
Howarth, Alan Coates, Dennis Haines, Steve
Stroud, Jamie Moses, Dave Carey
BEST KNOWN SONG: Long Cool Woman (#2, 1972)

The Hollies were a Manchester, England, product of the 1960s, heavily influenced by the Everly Brothers in their approach to harmonies, although the Hollies used three (rather than two) part harmonies in most of their songs. Only the Mamas & the Papas and the Beach Boys were able to put forth a harmonic sound that exceeded the Hollies during the '60s. Borrowing from the example set by the above-mentioned American acts, the Hollies created their own highly successful style with nearly 20 top-20 hits in the United Kingdom and 12 top-40 hits in the United States over two decades.

A pervasive belief throughout the years was that the group took their name to pay homage to Buddy Holly. While the group did indeed respect Holly's work, the truth is that the name has nothing to do with him. They were going by the name of The Deltas in 1962 when, during the Christmas season, they convened at Graham Nash's house. Noticing the holly-decorated surroundings they decided (perhaps jokingly) to name their group The Hollies. The embarrassment surrounding the truth of the name origin may have led band members to encourage and perpetuate the Buddy Holly myth.

They intended to use the name only temporarily until something better came along. Nothing ever did. Soon enough they began hitting the charts and creating goodwill with the name, making the Hollies one of the most successful acts of the British Invasion. Merry Christmas.

www.hollies.co.uk.

The Honeydrippers

GROUP FORMED IN: 1984
ORIGINAL MEMBERS: Robert Plant, Jimmy Page, Jeff Beck,
Robbie Blunt, Andy Sylvester, Kevin J. O'Neil,
Ricky Cool, Jim Wickman, Keith Evans
OTHER CONTRIBUTORS: Paul Shaffer, Brian Setzer, Nile Rodgers
BEST KNOWN SONG: Sea of Love (#3, 1985)

In the wake of the death of Led Zeppelin drummer John Bonham in 1980, and the resulting demise of the band, Robert Plant sought to heal his wounds by pursuing a solo career. Plant's efforts resulted in four hits, including "Big Log" and "In the Mood" in 1983. These songs signaled a departure for the former lead singer of the most influential hard rock band of all time. For a change, Plant was showing his softer side and his interest in beautiful melodies with lyrics that came from deep inside his heart. Without the restraints of the group dynamic, Plant was able to sew his own musical oats, and these songs were the first and best evidence of the direction in which he was heading.

Once Plant decided to reenter the realm of group recording in 1984, he created a band called The Honeydrippers. This represented a completely different tangent for Plant but one closer to Zeppelin's blues roots. The group was formed with Jimmy Page, Jeff Beck, and studio musicians. The influences from which Plant drew are evident in the band name.

There were two sources for the name. First was Roosevelt "Honeydripper" Sykes, an American blues musician who influenced blues piano with a thundering boogie style. He died July 17, 1983, just before Plant created his band, and he served as the main source of inspiration. The other source was Joe Liggins, a jazz, blues, and R&B pianist whose instrumental called "The Honeydripper" was a hit in 1945, topping the R&B chart for a record 18 weeks.

www.allmusic.com; www.geocities.jp.

Hoobastank

GROUP FORMED IN: 1995
ORIGINAL MEMBERS: Douglas Robb, Dan Estrin,
Markku Lappalainen, Chris Hesse
LATER MEMBERS OF NOTE: Josh Moreau
BEST KNOWN SONG: The Reason (#2, 2004)

Hoobastank is a modern rock band formed in Agoura Hills, California (Los Angeles suburb), in 1995. Chris Hesse, Doug Robb, and Dan Estrin knew each other from high school, which happened to be the same school attended by Linkin Park's Mike Shinoda and Brad Delson. They were also friends with members of the band Incubus.

Among the things that set Hoobastank apart from other bands of their ilk are tight harmonies and strong hooks. Robb sings with feeling, giving life to the relevant lyrics.

Another thing setting the band apart is the name. Originally the group spelled its name Hoob*u*stank but found people had problems with the way the group wanted it pronounced. Robb said, "Actually people were calling us Hoo-boo-stank. It makes sense ... I mean if I didn't know the name of the band and I saw Hoobustank I would [pronounce it that way] too, so we changed it to the 'a' for the new record. It's still pronounced the same."

As of yet, nobody outside the inner circle of the band has cracked the code as to the meaning of the band name. The party line is that the name has no particular meaning, but reading between the lines hints of something more. Robb has been quoted as saying, "It doesn't mean anything. And it's really cool, it's one of those old high school inside-joke words that didn't really mean anything." The group refuses to divulge what *was* the inside joke. Considering the content of most high school jokes, maybe it's best left unknown by the general public.

www.in-your-ear.net; www.forums.fortminor.com.

The Hooters

GROUP FORMED IN: 1980
ORIGINAL MEMBERS: Eric Bazilian, Rob
Hyman, David Uosikkinen
LATER MEMBERS OF NOTE: Bobby Woods, John Kuzma, Rob Miller,
John Lilley, Andy King, Mindy Jostyn, Fran Smith, Jr.
BEST KNOWN SONG: And We Danced (#21, 1985)

A musical group formed by men calling themselves The Hooters. We all know the inspiration for that name, don't we? It's not what you might think.

Eric Bazilian and Rob Hyman began together in a group they called Baby Grand. Although they enjoyed liberal airplay in their hometown and support among the local club scene, their first album fell far short of platinum. "It went lead, and we're not talking Zeppelin," they quipped.

Bazilian and Hyman added David Uosikkinen and they played their first gig as a trio on July 4, 1980. Once the Hooters began to play it seemed they never stopped. Their popularity continued to grow until they achieved national recognition in 1985. Their music included several instruments not normally associated with rock bands, including accordion, mandolin, violin, and melodica.

What, you may ask, is a melodica? Therein lies the origin of the group's name. A melodica is a keyboard harmonica manufactured by such companies as Hohner and Samick. The instrument is also known as the melodion, melodia, pianica, clavietta, or hooter.

The first time the band was in the studio recording a demo tape, it borrowed a melodica from some friends. John Senior, the engineer at the session, kept yelling, "Give me more *hooter!*" When it was suggested that the group use the instrument's nickname for its new name, there was initial skepticism. But the term grew on the members, all except for Uosikkinen, who was ultimately outvoted, and the band became The Hooters.

www.geocities.com.

Hootie & the Blowfish

GROUP FORMED IN: 1989
ORIGINAL MEMBERS: Darius Rucker, Mark Bryan,
Dean Felber, Jim "Soni" Sonefeld
LATER MEMBERS OF NOTE: none
BEST KNOWN SONG: Hold My Hand (#10, 1995)

Hootie & the Blowfish are the classic example of the fickleness of rock music fans. Toiling in anonymity for five years after forming at the University of South Carolina, the group shot into the stratosphere with their album *Cracked Rear View,* which has sold over 16 million copies. The band's second album, *Fairweather Johnson,* debuted with the momentum of the former album, pushing it to #1 but it quickly lost steam as a large portion of the record-buying public felt it represented no musical growth by the band.

Hootie & the Blowfish were easy targets, since they were not controversial. The band simply liked playing its brand of light-hearted American blues-based pop/rock in the wake of the grunge era. Others saw Rucker as a sell-out, a black man singing "white music" and hosting charity golf events. This narrow-minded thinking caused a backlash, leaving only true fans to support the band.

A common misconception is that Hootie is Rucker and the Blowfish are the rest of the ensemble. Actually nobody in the band is a Hootie or a Blowfish. Rucker was in choir in college and knew other members of the choir on whom the nicknames were bestowed. Hootie was so nicknamed because of his owl-like appearance due to his round face and glasses. Blowfish likewise received his nickname due to his facial appearance, which included chubby cheeks. When the four members of the band were deciding on a name they reflected back on the two unusual choir members and put them together to form Hootie & the Blowfish.

The Human League

GROUP FORMED IN: 1977
ORIGINAL MEMBERS: Martyn Ware, Ian
Craig Marsh, Philip Oakey, Adrian Wright
LATER MEMBERS OF NOTE: Joanne Catherall, Susanne
Sulley, Ian Burden, Jo Callis, Russell Dennett, Neil Sutton
BEST KNOWN SONG: Don't You Want Me (#1, 1982)

The members of The Human League took their influences from David Bowie and Roxy Music, and, in turn, influenced an entire generation of synth-pop groups, arguably including the majority of the New Romantic era bands. Their trick was to use synthesizers in a warmer and more melodic way than had been done before, while also incorporating computer technology to produce lyrics.

The group began when Martyn Ware, Ian Craig Marsh, and Adi Wright formed The Future, so-named for their forward-looking philosophy and willingness to embrace new technology. In 1977 school chum Philip Oakey was added as vocalist because "he looked like a pop star." His first order of business was to get an odd hairstyle because when considering pop stars, "the only thing that I could think of that made them all different was a hairstyle," Oakey once said.

With the new lineup, the group decided to change their name. After considering ABCD, they opted for The Human League, which was taken from a sci-fi board game called *Star Force*. Per Ware, "There were all these scenarios in the back (of the game) for various wars in the future, and one of these, for a stage around about 2180, where there were two main empires—The Pansantient Hegemony and The Human League. The Human League centered around Earth and the scenario was called The Rise of the Human League. So we stole it." Probably a wise choice. "The Pansantient Hegemony" doesn't roll off the tongue quite as well.

www.dma.be; www.ex-rental.com.

Icehouse

GROUP FORMED IN: 1977
ORIGINAL MEMBERS: Iva Davies (born Ivor Arthur Davies),
Keith Welsh, Bob Kretschmer

LATER MEMBERS OF NOTE: Anthony Smith, John Lloyd
BEST KNOWN SONG: Electric Blue (#7, 1988)

Australia's Icehouse is huge ... down under. With over 30 hits in 20 years
in their native land, this synth-pop group is one of Australia's most successful
bands. Led by former oboe player Iva Davies, Icehouse has also achieved a modicum of international success, placing six songs in the top 100 in the United
States, including their biggest hit, "Electric Blue," in 1988.

The band was formed as Flowers in 1977, soon becoming well known
around Sydney as a note-perfect cover band. Flowers signed a record deal in
1980 with Regular Festival Records and released an album entitled *Icehouse* that
was led off by the title track, a haunting melody written by Davies when he lived
next door to a halfway house for convalescing psychiatric and drug-addicted
patients. The album title: *Icehouse* is Australian slang for insane asylum.

When Flowers looked to succeed abroad a problem arose because the name
was already being used by another group. The band's overseas label, Chrysalis
Records, ran a name suggestion competition among staff members. A prize was
given for the name considered the best alternative for Flowers. The name
selected: Industrial Chilli.

Obviously the band didn't feel as strongly about being called Industrial
Chilli as did Chrysalis Records. The success of the *Icehouse* album and song were
very meaningful for Davies and the rest of the band, especially since the album
helped the band win the award for best new talent at the Countdown Awards
in 1981. At the end of the tour to promote the new album it was announced
that henceforth the band would be called Icehouse. The band obviously had a
sense of humor about the name, considering that their second-biggest American hit was entitled "Crazy."

www.spellbound-icehouse.org.

Billy Idol

BORN: William Michael Albert Broad on
November 30, 1955, in Stanmore,
Middlesex, England
BEST KNOWN SONG: White Wedding
(#36, 1983)

For a young man, William Broad was an old-sounding name. For an adult,

Billy Idol is a very young-sounding name. But that's how it was for the Brit known for his punk-styled, bleached blond hair, curled lip sneer, and punctuating fist pumps. Billy represents a cross between punk rock and hard rock, a bridge he may never have crossed if he and his bandmates hadn't been so good looking.

Young William was smart but not highly motivated, except for being mischievous. He claims to have been kicked out of the Boy Scouts for "snogging" with a girl. In school, his inattentiveness frayed the nerves of his teachers. Billy recalls receiving a particularly poor test back from a high school teacher, "He wrote in massive letters on one of my reports, William is I-D-L-E — idle. First I thought, 'Billy Idle.' But then I thought, 'Well, there's Eric Idle. I can't — But it could be Billy I-D-O-L. Oh, you maniac! That's right.'"

After the Broad to Idol transformation and emboldened by the Sex Pistols, he joined the seminal punk group Siouxsie & the Banshees. Soon he quit to form his own outfit called Generation X, which had some success in England. *Record Mirror* called them "one of the most entertaining and vibrant bands to spring from the initial British new wave explosion."

The problem with Generation X was they were too attractive to be taken serious as punks. Good skin, good teeth, and, by their own guilty plea, they declared they didn't partake in alcohol or drugs. This clean-cut aesthetic kept them from being accepted as serious punk rockers, so the group broke up and Idol moved to New York to pursue the very successful solo career for which he is now known the world over.

www.transcripts.cnn.com; www.accessmag.com.

INXS

GROUP FORMED IN: 1979
ORIGINAL MEMBERS: Michael Hutchence, Andrew Farriss,
Jon Farriss, Tim Farriss, Kirk Pengilly, Garry Beers
LATER MEMBERS OF NOTE: Jon Stevens, J. D. Fortune
BEST KNOWN SONG: Need You Tonight (#1, 1987)

Formed in Sydney, Australia, and aptly, but unimaginatively, at first called the Farriss Brothers, this sextet cut its teeth in the local pub scene. Relying on a mixture of new wave, dance, and straight-ahead rock as well as the energy and stage presence of lead man Hutchence, INXS dominated the American charts with six consecutive top-10 hits during their heyday from 1987 to 1990.

The Farriss Brothers were playing hard and promoting itself equally hard. Tim Farriss was placing flyers under windshield wipers in their home town when he was approached by Gary Morris, manager of the immensely popular band Midnight Oil. The band was offered a gig supporting Midnight Oil, and Morris subsequently became the band's first manager.

According to Morris, the name had to be changed as a first order of business. For a short time the band became The Vegetables. Then a better idea came to Morris while watching television. He saw an ad for a brand of jam called IXL. The ad featured a spokesman saying "*I excel* in all I do." Morris was also fond of the name of the band XTC (as in "ecstasy"). As a result, he roughly combined the two and came up with INXS (pronounced "in excess").

This name suited the band well because of their reputation for excessive behavior on and off stage. The guys hosted legendary parties at their Newport Beach house. On stage, Hutchence had a Jagger-esque style that found him flinging himself around like nobody else, giving the audience the impression the band was still partying while they worked. "In excess" also described their stage outfits, since the band took pride in wearing clothes not normally seen in public.

INXS, and Anthony Bozza. Story to Story: The Official Biography. *New York: Atria Books, 2005;* Hutchence, Tina, and Patricia Glassop. Just a Man: The Real Michael Hutchence. *London: Sedgwick & Jackson, 2000.*

Jefferson Airplane

GROUP FORMED IN: 1965
ORIGINAL MEMBERS: Marty Balin, Paul Kantner,
Jorma Kaukonen, Jack Casady, Signe Anderson, Skip Spence
LATER MEMBERS OF NOTE: Grace Slick, Spencer Dryden, Joey Covington,
Papa John Creach, David Freiberg, Craig Chaquico, Pete Spears, John
Barbata, Mickey Thomas, Aynsley Dunbar, Don Baldwin, Kenny
Aronoff, Brett Bloomfield, Mark Morgan
BEST KNOWN SONG: We Built This City (#1, 1985)

Word association: San Francisco, psychedelic rock, Surrealistic Pillow, mid–'80s schmaltzy power-pop. The correct answer is Jefferson Airplane / Starship on all counts. While the Grateful Dead was the other lead conspirator in the Haight-Ashbury scene, it was the Airplane that made the first leap from local to national success. Throughout its lengthy tenure and numerous personnel changes, the Jefferson Airplane eventually became the Jefferson Starship (in 1973) and ultimately just Starship (1985). With the name and personnel changes came style changes to match the taste of the record-buying public. While these changes actually increased the band's commercial popularity, they stripped the band of any semblance of their musical roots.

Some incorrect tales of how Jefferson Airplane was named include a slang term for a roach clip or the name of someone's pet dog or cat. The name was, in fact, an inside joke that got carried away.

Legendary bluesman Blind Lemon Jefferson was the hero of lead guitarist Jorma Kaukonen. According to Kaukonen, "Steve Talbot had named me Blind Thomas Jefferson Airplane. Steve Mann was Little Sun Goldfarb and Tom Hobson, another guitar player friend of mine, was Blind Outrage. The band was coming up with all these really stupid names and I said, 'If you want something really silly, try Jefferson Airplane.'"

Tamarkin, Jeff. Got a Revolution! The Turbulent Flight of Jefferson Airplane. New York: Atria Books, 2003.

Jethro Tull

GROUP FORMED IN: 1968
ORIGINAL MEMBERS: Ian Anderson, Mick Abrahams,
Glenn Cornick, Clive Bunker
LATER MEMBERS OF NOTE: Don Airey, Martin Allcock, Martin Barre,
Paul Burgess, John Evans, Andrew Giddings, Jeffrey Hammond,
Barrie Barlow, David Palmer, John Glascock, Dave Pegg,
Eddie Jobson, Mark Craney, Peter-John Vettese, Gerry Conway,
Dave Mattacks, Jonathan Noyce, Doane Perry, Tony Williams
BEST KNOWN SONG: Bungle in the Jungle (#1, 1974)

What is well known about Jethro Tull? The crazy antics of front man Ian Anderson. Their lengthy tenure in the music scene dating back four decades. Their improbable Grammy award for Best Hard Rock/Heavy Metal Album in 1988 in the inaugural year for the category.

What is not known? Much. Many incorrectly assume that Jethro Tull is one person or the name of a member of the band (Anderson is commonly mistaken as Tull). Also not well known are the countless musical identities of the group, from blues to folk to prog to something near hard rock. Through it all Jethro Tull has kept its fans and critics off balance.

Another fairly well-kept secret is the origin of the group's name. As it was toiling to establish an identity and, more importantly, score a second booking anywhere they played, the group began a series of name changes hoping something would resonate with the public. Tried and discarded were Candy Coloured Rain, Ian Henderson's Bag o' Nails, Bag o' Blues, and Navy Blue.

Finally Jethro Tull was pitched by agent Dave Robson, who had studied

history at the university. Jethro Tull is the name of an eighteenth-century agri-
culturist and inventor of the seed drill. The band members liked the gritty and
earthy connotations of the name almost as much as they liked being asked back
to a second performance at London's famous Marquee Club under that name.
According to Anderson, the name is "not something you get tired of like the
Orange Bicycle or the Psychedelic Banana."

Nollen, Scott Allen. Jethro Tull: A History of the Band 1968–2001. *Jefferson, NC: McFarland, 2002.*

Jimmy Eat World

GROUP FORMED IN: 1993
ORIGINAL MEMBERS: Jim Adkins, Tom Linton,
Rick Burch, Zach Lind
LATER MEMBERS OF NOTE: none
BEST KNOWN SONG: The Middle (#5, 2002)

This four-member band from Arizona consists of lifelong friends. They
first collaborated in junior high school playing Metallica covers but their music
evolved into a genre known as emo. Emo is the opposite of punk, dealing
with introspective issues instead of anarchy, personal emotions rather than
social issues, and the heavy chords are used to punctuate songs, not drive them.
     Don't tell Jimmy Eat World that they're emo, though. Like most bands,
they hate categorization. "I tell people we're just a rock band," says Jim Adkins.
"I used to cringe when someone asked us how it feels to play music in the
'emo movement.' I still cringe. I used to care, but now, whatever. People need
labels."
     One label the group put on itself is its name. The highly unusual name came
from Ed Linton, the younger brother of guitarist Tom Linton. Tom explains,
"Actually, it's a picture that my little brother drew. My brother Jim [Jimmy] beat
up my younger brother, Ed, and Jim ran into his room and locked the door, and
Ed drew this picture that said 'Jimmy Eat World,' and it was a picture of him eat-
ing the world. My brother Jim is kind of a big guy. A stupid name."
     It is quite likely little Ed, who was eight years old at the time, was inspired
by an episode of the cartoon show *Tiny Toon Adventures*, which featured a short
"film" by Dizzy Devil entitled "Dizzy Eat World!" showing Dizzy chomping the
earth to his own off-key Looney Toons soundtrack.

*www.chrisblackburn.com; www.timmcmahan.com; www.jimmyeatworld.com; www.youtube.
com.*

Elton John

BORN: Reginald Kenneth Dwight on March 25, 1947,
in Pinner, Middlesex, England
BEST KNOWN SONG: Candle in the Wind (#1, 1998)

More precisely, this artist is now known as Elton Hercules John. Working under his given name, Reg Dwight, he started his performing career splitting time between solo gigs and working with a band called Bluesology, which supported such acts as The Isley Brothers, Patti LaBelle, and, in 1966, Long John Baldry.

Looking for another outlet for his talent, Elton John auditioned for King Crimson and Gentle Giant without success. He later answered an ad in the *New Musical Express* meant to pair talented songwriters and lyricists. This resulted in his legendary partnership with Bernie Taupin, with whom Elton John had his white-hot 1970s success. This laid the foundation for a career filled with over 250 million records sold, over 50 top 40 hits (including at least one top 40 hit for 30+ consecutive years), a knighting by the Queen of England, and induction in the Rock and Roll Hall of Fame. Other than that, Sir Elton Hercules John hasn't accomplished much.

By the time he began writing with Taupin, John had decided to leave both Bluesology and his birth name behind. Desiring a memorable, brief stage name, Reg pilfered "Elton" from Bluesology's new sax player, Elton Dean, and "John" from Long John Baldry, whom Reg considered a mentor. For him, being called Reg "was kind of like a nightmare when I was young." He was quoted as saying, "I couldn't wait to be somebody else."

The final part of his new name is his adopted middle name, "Hercules." Oddly enough, he selected "Hercules" after the name of a horse in the British sitcom *Steptoe and Son*. Although seldom used or seen in print, the full three names appear on a deed poll changing his name on January 7, 1972.

Rosenthal, Elizabeth J. His Song. The Musical Journey of Elton John. New York: Billboard Books, 2001.

Journey

GROUP FORMED IN: 1973

ORIGINAL MEMBERS: Neal Schon, Gregg Rolie,
Prairie Prince, George Tickner, Ross Valory
LATER MEMBERS OF NOTE: Steve Perry, Jonathan Cain,
Aynsley Dunbar, Robert Fleischman, Steve Smith, Steve Augeri,
Deen Castronovo, Randy Jackson, Jeff Scott Soto
BEST KNOWN SONG: Open Arms (#2, 1982)

Rule #1 when forming a band: Never choose your group's name through a contest on the radio. Journey found this out the hard way. The story begins in 1973 just after Neal Schon and Gregg Rolie left Santana (along with manager Herbie Herbert) to form their own band. Drummer Gregg Errico joined and they became the Golden Gate Rhythm Section.

Still several years before the arrival of Steve Perry or Jonathan Cain, Herbert brought in Ross Valory on bass, George Tickner on guitar (both from the band Frumious Bandersnatch — really, no joke), and Prairie Prince replaced Errico on drums. Finally Herbert had his first solid lineup in place.

Then came the contest run by San Francisco radio station KSAN. The entries were many and varied. Among the humorous but unusable suggestions were Hippie-potamus and Rumpled Foreskin. Realizing none of the names would do, Herbert decided on Journey. Herbert said in a much later interview that an associate of his named Jack Villanueva first suggested the name. To hide the scam, the group created a fictitious winner.

In a 2003 interview, Gregg Rolie explained it this way: "Toby Pratt named us. The names were so awful from this real contest that we ended up using a name one of our own guys who worked in the office came up with. We had this contest so we couldn't tell people we didn't choose one of their names so we made up the name Toby Pratt. It turns out there was a real guy out there named Toby Pratt and I think we ended up having to give him something. The whole thing kind of backfired." Lesson learned.

www.journey-zone.com; www.classicrockrevisited.com; www.steveperryfanclub.homestead. com.

Keane

GROUP FORMED IN: 1997
ORIGINAL MEMBERS: Tim Rice-Oxley, Tom Chaplin,
Richard Hughes, Dominic Scott
LATER MEMBERS OF NOTE: none
BEST KNOWN SONG: Somewhere Only
We Know (#50, 2005)

Three of the members of Keane met in primary school in Battle, England, before they reconnected years later in high school and built a kinship through their love of music. They enlisted the guitar playing services of Dominic Scott and began a band initially called the Lotus Eaters.

Not long afterward, the band members became aware that they were using a name that had already been taken. The other Lotus Eaters were a new wave band from Liverpool that had minor success in the mid 1980s. They reportedly considered the name Coldplay before deciding it was too depressing and they allowed college chum Chris Martin to use it.

The band then opted for the name Cherry Keane, who was a lady known to Chaplin in his younger days. The exact role Cherry Keane played is muddled to this day. By one account she was a lunch lady at grade school in Battle. Another says she was a retired neighbor of Chaplin's who had been supportive of his musical dream when few others had. Yet another is that she was Chaplin's nanny. However, in an interview for *Q Magazine*, Chaplin said, "She was a kind old lady who helped make tea for the kids at school. People are saying she was my nanny but that's not really accurate." (The interviewer suggests a certain lack of conviction in Chaplin's story due to Chaplin's laughing demeanor at this point in the interview).

The band ultimately dropped the "Cherry" part and settled on their current moniker. This decision was made due to a mildly sexual subtext in the name. Also, some people had misunderstood the name to be Cherokee.

www.amplifiermagazine.com; www.lawrence.com; www.keane.at; www.ireland.com.

Chaka Khan / Rufus

BORN: Yvette Marie Stevens on March 23,
1953, in Great Lakes, Illinois
GROUP FORMED IN: 1970
GROUP MEMBERS: Chaka Khan, Andre Fischer,
John "JR" Robinson, Tony Maiden, Kevin Murphy,
Ron Stockert, David Wilinski, Bobby Watson
BEST KNOWN SONG: Solo—I Feel for You (#3, 1984)
Group — Tell Me Something Good (#50, 2005)

This story is a name-dropper's smorgasbord. First let's start with Chaka

Khan. She was born Yvette Marie Stevens. She grew up on Chicago's south side with four younger siblings. She was performing from an early age and even then she was referred to as "Little Aretha."

A few years later she became more aware of her African roots and volunteered to work for the Black Panthers's breakfast program. An African shaman christened her Chaka Adunne Aduffe Yemoja Hodarhi Karifi. Chaka means "Woman of Fire." Shortly thereafter she entered into a short-lived marriage with a bass player named Hassan Khan. Chaka joked later that she only married him for her stage name.

Digressing to when little Yvette was still just 11 years old, she formed her first group with her sister Yvonne called the Crystalettes, performing strictly covers of The Crystals and Gladys Knight and the Pips. During high school she sang with a group called Shades of Black. It was during this time she took the lengthy African name.

High school was not Chaka's thing. After ninth grade she dropped out and sang for a short while with a group called Lyfe, followed by another singing stint with a Chicago-based band named The Babysitters. This was during the time she was married to Hassan.

Yet another band whose presence she graced was called Lock and Chain. While performing with this band, Chaka was noticed by producer Bob Monaco who introduced her to a band called Ask Rufus, which got its name from a column in *Popular Mechanics* magazine so titled. Eventually Chaka joined the group, the name was shortened to Rufus, and her career finally had the launching pad Chaka Khan needed to stardom.

www.seand85.tripod.com.

The Kinks

GROUP FORMED IN: 1963
ORIGINAL MEMBERS: Ray Davies, Dave Davies,
Peter Quaife, Mike Avory
LATER MEMBERS OF NOTE: Ian Gibbons, Jim Rodford, Bob Henrit
BEST KNOWN SONG: You Really Got Me (#7, 1964)

The Kinks was arguably the seminal heavy metal band *and* punk band in rock history. And while it wasn't as heavy or punk as the bands that later defined the genres, it certainly was heavier and more punk than any band of their time. Unlike other British bands of the mid '60s, The Kinks avoided the later pull toward psychedelic music, staying true to their roots in the process. Formed by brothers Ray and Dave Davies, the lineup saw many personnel changes but the Davies remained constants until the '90s when the brothers pursued solo careers.

Originally the group was called The Ramrods (after a 1958 Duane Eddy instrumental hit), then The Ravens (in part after the 1963 Boris Karloff horror movie of the same name), and later yet the Boll Weevils (after an Eddie Cochran B-side), a name that Ray felt was a bit on the quaint side.

One night in a pub the band members were having a drink and someone commented on their attire. According to Ray, they were "wearing kinky boots, similar to those worn by Honor Blackman in *The Avengers.*" The general look of the group was out of the ordinary to say the least, especially the new drummer who looked "a little like a police identikit version of a pervert." Arthur Howes, the group's booking agent, suggested that they call themselves The Kinks and appear on stage in leather gear with whips. He felt the name was provocative and relevant, with the phrase "kinky sex" regularly appearing in the tabloids.

Initially Ray hated the idea, claiming "people will think that we're all weird," but he acquiesced, putting faith in the manager. He figured they could change the name if their first record flopped, so he didn't really care. "I hated my own name even more," said Davies, "but I had been walking around with that all my life, so who was I to complain."

Davies, Dave. Kink: The Outrageous Story of My Wild Years as the Founder and Lead Guitarist of the Kinks. New York: Hyperion, 1996; Davies, Ray. The Unauthorized Biography. New York: Overlook Press, 1994.

Kiss

GROUP FORMED IN: 1973
ORIGINAL MEMBERS: Gene Simmons (born Chaim Witz),
Paul Stanley (born Stanley Harvey Eisen), Peter Criss
(born Peter Criscuola), Ace Frehley (born Paul Frehley)
LATER MEMBERS OF NOTE: Eric Carr, Vinnie Vincent,
Mark St. John, Bruce Kulick, Eric Singer
BEST KNOWN SONG: Rock and Roll All Nite (#12, 1976)

Kiss was an amalgam of different acts (New York Dolls, Alice Cooper, Slade, to name a few), but despite their early borrowing, their ledger was ultimately balanced when others took equally from Kiss, including their image

(Mötley Crüe), stage show (Twisted Sister), and heavy metal power ballad (sadly, too many to mention).

Kiss is the outgrowth of Wicked Lester, a band formed by Gene Simmons and Paul Stanley. In an effort to enhance their prospects, they hired Peter Criss from an ad Criss placed in *Rolling Stone* magazine. Ace Frehley was later added and the original lineup was in place by early 1973.

There has been some speculation over the years that the group name has a dark meaning, such as an acronym for "Knights in Satan's Service," a claim that the group has consistently denied. In fact the name was created on the spur of the moment by Stanley. According to Simmons, "Paul was driving his Mustang and I was in the back seat, and Peter was in front, 'cause I'm deathly afraid of cars. Ace wasn't there. We were trying to think of a name, and then Paul, joking, said, 'How about Crimson Harpoon?' We all started laughing, and then he said, 'How about KISS?' And nobody laughed. It just fit."

After hearing of the decision, Frehley designed a button with the logo that the band adopted (except he had a diamond dotting the "i"). This logo caused some consternation because the "SS" resembled the symbol used by the Nazi military force. Frehley responded, "I wasn't thinking of the [Nazi] SS when I designed it. I was thinking more of lightning bolts. In fact, my first boots had lightning bolts down the side."

Lee, David, and Ken Sharp. Kiss: Behind the Mask. *New York: Warner Books, 2003.*

Kool & the Gang

GROUP FORMED IN: 1964
ORIGINAL MEMBERS: Robert "Kool" Bell, Ronald
Bell (a/k/a Khalis Bayyan), Robert "Spike"
Mickens, Dennis Thomas, Claydes "Charles"
Smith, George "Funky" Brown, Rick Westfield
LATER MEMBERS OF NOTE: James "J.T." Taylor,
Clifford Adams, Earl Toon, Jr., Curtis "Fitz"
Williams, Gary Brown, Odeen Mays, Skip Martin
BEST KNOWN SONG: Celebration (#1, 1981)

The roots of Kool & the Gang go way back to 1964, although they would not become household names until 1979. Their fortunes turned slowly as their jazz beginnings were phased out for a more funk and R&B sound that resonated with the dance trends of the late '70s.

Robert Bell was Kool & the Gang's founder. His nickname is "Kool," which explains at least part of the group's name. His first school band in Greenwich Village was called The Five Sounds Jr., which quickly changed to The Jazz Birds and later The Jazziacs.

When the group got a gig as a Motown/Stax revue band they changed their name once again, this time to The Soul Town Band, which referred to Soul Town, an organization around Jersey City that was trying to be a smaller version of Motown. All of these name changes occurred in the first two years of the band's existence.

The names just kept on coming. As the band began to develop a following apart from the revue, they broke away and decided to create yet another entity called Kool & the Flames. They might have actually kept this name but for James Brown's backing band, which was called The Famous Flames. Since Brown was much more famous, Bell deferred the name to him and switched (finally) to Kool & the Gang, which, according to Bell, "had a sort of street sound to it."

www.koolandthegang.com; www.remembertheeighties.com.

Led Zeppelin

GROUP FORMED IN: 1968
ORIGINAL MEMBERS: Robert Plant, Jimmy Page,
John Paul Jones, John Bonham
LATER MEMBERS OF NOTE: None
BEST KNOWN SONG: Stairway to Heaven
(unreleased as single, on 1971 album)

Considered by many as the definitive heavy metal band, by most accounts they were also the greatest live band as well. Not to mention Led Zeppelin can take as much credit as any other act for the increase in album sales (vis-à-vis singles) and the growth of AOR radio stations in the early 1970s.

When Jimmy Page recruited John Paul Jones from the studio circuit and Robert Plant from his pub outfit Band of Joy (from which John Bonham soon followed), he still used the name of his former band, the Yardbirds. After receiving veiled threats of legal action for the continued use of the name, Page was eager to make a change and Plant was in full agreement, since the material they were playing was certainly a departure from that of the Yardbirds.

Page favored a name that reflected a paradoxical combination of heaviness and lightness, finesse and bombast, with a touch of wit (not unlike Iron

Butterfly). Several years earlier, when John Entwistle and Keith Moon were giving consideration to leaving The Who and forming a super group with Jeff Beck and Jimmy Page, the former two were said to have joked that, had it ever become a reality, it would have gone down like a lead balloon. Later the joke was changed to a lead zeppelin and the imagery was not lost on Page, who decided that the term, with a slight spelling modification, would be the perfect name for his new foursome.

Shadwick, Keith. Led Zeppelin: The Story of a Band and Their Music 1968–1980. Faversham, Kent: Backbeat Books, 2005.

Level 42

GROUP FORMED IN: 1980
ORIGINAL MEMBERS: Mark King, Mike Lindup,
Phil Gould, Roland "Boon" Gould
LATER MEMBERS OF NOTE: Alan Murphy, Gary
Husband, Jakko Jakszyk, Nathan King,
Lyndon Connah, Sean Freeman
BEST KNOWN SONG: Something About You (#7, 1986)

Level 42 began as a jazz-funk fusion band and transformed in the mid 1980s into a synth-pop outfit with great success in England and Europe and slightly less in the United States. The group's name has occasionally been the subject of random speculation. One suggested source is Tower 42 in London. Opened in 1980, the 42-story tower was the tallest building in London for ten years until being eclipsed by One Canada Square.

Another supposed source of the band's name was the sign in an elevator in a tall building in the United States. Alternatively some have speculated it refers to the top floor of the tallest parking garage in the world, which happens to be located in Japan.

The truth is that Mark King and Boon Gould decided to call the group by a number, and initially they chose "88," which was the number of a bus they caught to the recording studio. This idea was abandoned when the band learned of the American R&B group from the early 1950s called Rocket 88. Other rejected names included Powerline and Kick in the Head.

King and Gould then turned their attention to a book they were reading called *The Hitchhiker's Guide to the Galaxy*. The book claimed the answer to the questions of life can be found in the number 42. The group agreed to use the number for their name but they later chose to add the word "Level" to fill the name out. (Interestingly, Tower 42 in London appears in some scenes of the television version of *The Hitchhiker's Guide.*)

www.level42.com; www.myvillage.com.

Loverboy

Group Formed In: 1980
Original Members: Paul Dean, Mike Reno (born Michael Rynoski), Scott Smith, Doug Johnson, Matt Frenette
Later Members of Note: Spider Sinnaeve
Best Known Song: Working for the Weekend (#29, 1982)

As one of Canada's most successful rock acts of all time, Loverboy reset the bar high following in the footsteps of The Guess Who and BTO. Already a veteran of 14 bands, group founder Paul Dean began Loverboy after being dumped from Streetheart without explanation. Realizing he lacked the vocal ability to be the lead singer for his own band, he turned to a local booking agent who hooked him up with Michael Rynoski, aka Mike Reno, formerly of the band Moxy.

Classically trained keyboardist Doug Johnson and bass player Scott Smith were added to the lineup. Dean's former bandmate from Streetheart, Matt Frenette was lured out of semi-retirement to man the skins. The group would, along with Rush and, later, Bryan Adams, go on to rule the Canadian rock scene for the decade of the '80s.

Their fame in the United States was largely tied to their groundbreaking use of MTV. Consistently using the most beautiful women to grace their music videos, together with their own good looks, they took full advantage of the medium.

Dean is credited with naming the group. There was some early indecision on what the name should be, but when Dean suggested Loverboy he received immediate consent. The name was perhaps subconsciously pulled from his youth, as he explained, "My mom tells me now, after all this time, that she used to call me 'loverboy' a lot when I was a kid. She'd always go, 'Hey, loverboy, time for bed.' Sounds kind of kinky, doesn't it? Of course, she didn't mean it like that."

www.web.295.ca.

The Lovin' Spoonful

GROUP FORMED IN: 1965
ORIGINAL MEMBERS: John Sebastian, Zal
Yanovsky, Steve Boone, Joe Butler
LATER MEMBERS OF NOTE: Jerry Yester
BEST KNOWN SONG: Do You Believe
in Magic (#9, 1965)

Like so many other musicians whose careers began in the '60s, John Sebastian, Zal Yanovsky, and crew were heavily influenced by the blues greats (and not-so-greats) of the '20s, '30s and '40s. Ironically, the music of The Lovin' Spoonful was anything but blues. In fact, it was downright perky. Their unabashedly melodic good-time songs served them well, commercially speaking, until a drug bust in 1967 ultimately led to Yanovsky's temporary exodus from the band, and Sebastian's permanent departure a year later.

The band's name was suggested by Fritz Richmond who, though not a member of the band, knew Sebastian well and shared his love of the bluesmen. On Sebastian's web site, Richmond is labeled a "washtub virtuoso," if there is such a thing. According to Sebastian, "I told him our sound was kind of like Chuck Berry meets Mississippi John Hurt and he immediately chimed in, 'Why not call it the Lovin' Spoonful?' So, we were named after a John Hurt song."

Mississippian John Hurt was an influential blues singer and guitarist who died in 1966. His career had an abortive start in 1928 when his first recorded work failed to generate any interest and his record company went out of business. He gave up recording until 1963 when folk musicologist Tom Hoskins located him and persuaded Hurt to play and record again, which he did to wide acclaim for the final three years of his life.

In 1964 he recorded "Coffee Blues" at the Newport Folk Festival, which included a line that referred to Maxwell House Coffee. As Hurt reminds us, "it's good till the last drop."

www.johnsebastian.com; www.harptab.com.

Lynyrd Skynyrd

GROUP FORMED IN: 1965

ORIGINAL MEMBERS: Ronnie Van Zant, Bob Burns,
Gary Rossington, Allen Collins, Larry Junstrom
LATER MEMBERS OF NOTE: Leon Wilkeson, Rickey Medlocke,
Artimus Pyle, Greg Walker, Ed King, Billy Powell,
Steve Gaines, Cassie Gaines, Johnnie Van Zant
BEST KNOWN SONG: Sweet Home Alabama (#8, 1974)

This band, along with Steely Dan and Jethro Tull (to name a few), are often incorrectly thought to be one person. Far from it, when the expansive list of group members is noted. However, the group name is a backhanded homage to one person, a high school gym coach from Robert E. Lee High School in Jacksonville, Florida, named Leonard Skinner.

Coach Skinner repeatedly warned Ronnie Van Zant, Bob Burns, and Gary Rossington to cut their hair or face discipline. The boys tried to skirt the rules by greasing down their hair with Vaseline but inevitably the ploy backfired come shower time after gym class. After some 20 to 30 trips to the principal's office, Gary was suspended for two weeks. Instead of submitting to the punishment he quit school altogether. Van Zant had already left school and Allen Collins had similar problems with a teacher just like Skinner at a separate school.

As a joke one night while playing in their band, which was called The One Percent, Ronnie introduced his band as Leonard Skinner. The crowd roared their approval, knowing full well the local meaning. The band members felt naming the band after their nemesis appropriately represented their refusal to submit to authority. In order to avoid the otherwise inevitable lawsuit, the spelling was changed to Lynard Skynard but the pronunciation was not. Shortly thereafter the spelling was again changed to the name we know today.

Brant, Marley. Freebirds: The Lynyrd Skynyrd Story. *New York: Billboard Books, 2002.*

Madness

GROUP FORMED IN: 1978
ORIGINAL MEMBERS: Mike Barson (Monsieur Barson),
Chris Foreman (Chrissy Boy), Lee Thompson (Kix),
Graham McPherson (Suggs), Mark Bedford
(Bedders), Daniel Woodgate (Woody)
LATER MEMBERS OF NOTE: Carl Smyth (Chas Smash)
BEST KNOWN SONG: Our House (#7, 1983)

As one of the best loved bands in England, Madness carried the banner for the ska revival of the late 1970s. Their early trademark "nutty sound" later morphed into a more radio friendly sound, incorporating elements of Motown, soul, and British pop. While the style change enhanced their image, they never quite won over America, placing only two hits in the U.S. top-40. Three of their signature songs ("One Step Beyond," "House of Fun," and "Baggy Trousers") failed to crack the U.S. top-100. Conversely, the band's first 20 singles all made it into the U.K. top-20.

The earliest form of the group took shape in 1976 when Mike Barson, Chris Foreman, and Kix Thompson formed a group they called The North London Invaders. In 1978 they added Suggs, Mark Bedford, and Woody Woodgate to the fold, sometimes using the Invaders name and sometimes calling themselves Morris and the Minors.

The band was always in touch with its ska and reggae roots. As such, the members held in high esteem Cecil Bustamente Campbell, aka Prince Buster, a Jamaican ska and rock-steady artist who created an impressive body of work in the 1960s. One of his songs was called "Madness." Barson and crew wished to pay homage to Buster and decided to change the group's name to Madness. They also named their "first child" after him, calling their debut single "The Prince." If that wasn't enough, they used Prince Buster's "Madness" on the B-side of "The Prince" single. To top it off, their first top-10 hit in England was "One Step Beyond," a remake of a Prince Buster song. Now that's a tribute!

www.geocities.com.

The Mamas & The Papas

GROUP FORMED IN: 1964
ORIGINAL MEMBERS: John Phillips, Michelle Phillips, Denny Doherty, "Mama" Cass Elliot (born Ellen Naomi Cohen)
LATER MEMBERS OF NOTE: Jill Gibson
BEST KNOWN SONG: California Dreamin' (#4, 1966)

With apologies to the Beach Boys, The Mamas & the Papas must be considered the greatest vocal group in pop music history. Their versatility in the use of male *and* female voices breaks the tie. Both groups flourished at a time when harmonies were the centerpiece of the pop song, as opposed to the focal points of the music of the '70s (drums for disco), '80s (synths for New Romantic), '90s (guitars for grunge) and '00s (bass for hip hop).

John Phillips and his much younger wife Michelle called upon Denny Doherty to form a folk trio based in New York. Doherty knew Cass Elliot from their previous involvement in The Mugwumps. Elliot was interested in keeping in touch professionally and personally with Doherty and in the Virgin Islands she met up with the trio, who were there for a working holiday. While there, Elliot was hit on the head with a lead pipe and after she was released from the hospital her vocal range had risen by 1 1/2 octave, which finally allowed her to sing the part required of her by John Phillips.

But the group was nameless. "We're all just lying around vegging out watching TV and discussing names for the group," recalls Doherty. "John was pushing for 'The Magic Cyrcle.' Eech, but none of us could come up with anything better, then we switch the channel and it's the Hell's Angels on this talk show.... And the first thing we hear is: 'Now hold on there, Hoss. Some people call our women cheap, but we just call them our Mamas.' Cass jumped up: 'Yeah! I want to be a Mama.' And Michelle is going: 'We're the Mamas! We're the Mamas!' Ok. I look at John. He's looking at me going: 'The Papas?' Problem solved."

Rounds, Dwight. The Year the Music Died. *Austin, TX: Bridgeway Books, 2007. www.denny doherty.com*

Marilyn Manson

GROUP FORMED IN: 1989
(PERSON) BORN: Brian Hugh Warner on
January 5, 1969, in Canton, Ohio
ORIGINAL MEMBERS: Marilyn Manson, Daisy Berkowitz,
Madonna Wayne Gacy, Sara Lee Lucas, Twiggy Ramirez
LATER MEMBERS OF NOTE: Olivia Newton Bundy,
Gidget Gein, Zsa Zsa Speck, Ginger Fish,
Zim Zum, John 5, Tim Skold

Marilyn Manson is a person as well as a group. The person was born in Ohio but raised in Florida. The group took Manson's name and were originally called Marilyn Manson and the Spooky Kids before the name was shortened to just the lead singer's name. Following Manson's lead, most of the members created their own stage names by combining the first names of female stars of movies or music with the last names of serial killers.

Manson himself created his nickname in order to hide his identity when writing about his music. In his autobiography *The Long Hard Road Out of Hell,* he describes how he was looking for a name with a lilt to it, like hocus-pocus or abracadabra. "The words Marilyn Manson seemed like an apt symbol for modern-day America," says Manson, "and the minute I wrote it on the paper for the first time I knew that it was what I wanted to become."

Manson was intrigued with the thought that everybody has a light and dark side, and neither can exist without the other. He feels man by nature is drawn to his evil (sinful) side, which is why when people ask him about his name, they always focus on the Manson (as in Charles) part instead of the Marilyn (as in Monroe) part. "Although she is a symbol of beauty and glamour, Marilyn Monroe had a dark side just as Charles Manson had a good, intelligent side," he says. "The balance between good and evil, and the choices we make between them, are probably the single most important aspects of shaping our personalities in humanity."

Manson, Marilyn, with Neil Strauss. The Long Hard Road Out of Hell. New York: Regan Books, 1998.

Maroon 5

GROUP FORMED IN: 1997
ORIGIANL MEMBERS: Adam Levine, Jesse Carmichael,
Mickey Madden, Matt Flynn, Ryan Dusick
LATER MEMBERS OF NOTE: James Valentine
BEST KNOWN SONG: This Love (#1, 2004)

If you are a female who has crossed paths with Maroon 5's Adam Levine, there's a good chance he will name something after you. The precursor to Maroon 5 was called Kara's Flowers, so-named for a girl all the guys in the band were fawning over. Much later, the mega-hit album of Maroon 5 was entitled *Songs about Jane*, inspired by a tumultuous relationship Levine had with an ex-girlfriend.

The band members first played together as freshmen in high school under the name Edible Nuns (fortunately not believed to be any nun in particular known to Levine). Later the original drummer left and was replaced by Amy Wood so the name was changed to Mostly Men. Kara's Flowers was officially formed in 1995 and played their first gig at Whisky a Go Go. The band's style owed much to Pearl Jam's Eddie Vedder, of whom Levine was a fan.

When Kara's Flowers failed commercially, the guys decided to head off to their respective colleges. Levine and Carmichael attended the State University of New York, where they were exposed for the first time to gospel, hip-hop, and, most importantly, Stevie Wonder. Upon their return to Los Angeles, Levine and Carmichael reunited the band and took on a new R&B style that alienated some fans but ultimately found a broader audience. After adding James Valentine, the group changed its name to Maroon and later to Maroon 5 when a name conflict was discovered. The name change represented the group's makeover and evolution. The band has refused to divulge the meaning of the current name, leaving it to our collective imaginations. Maybe it just signaled a fresh start. Per Levine, "If you name a band when you're 15, by the time you're 23 you're probably not gonna like it very much."

www.maroon5.com; www.radcyberzine.com; www.mtv.com.

matchbox twenty

Group Formed In: 1996
Original Members: Rob Thomas, Kyle Cook,
Brian Yale, Paul Doucette, Adam Gaynor
Later Members of Note: none
Best Known Song: Bent (#1, 2000)

Matchbox twenty is a rock band from Orlando, Florida, who broke away from the pack of post-grunge guitar bands (Goo Goo Dolls, Third Eye Blind, and the like) to become the most successful by far. In the process, lead singer Rob Thomas is one of the best known and most sought after singers in the business.

Thomas, Brian Yale, and Paul Doucette played together in Tabitha's Secret, a band they all agree was not very good. After overpaying their dues at local bars and fraternity parties they left the band, recruited Kyle Cook and Adam Gaynor, and formed Matchbox 20. Their first three albums sold in excess of 40 million copies and spawned fourteen singles.

The name came courtesy of Doucette. In an interview, Thomas explained, "Paul was a waiter and he, boringly enough, just saw it on a shirt and liked it. It was a jersey with a '20' on it and he saw the patches, and one of the patches said 'Matchbox.'" Despite the regular questions and kidding about the name, Doucette stands proudly defiant, "Quite honestly, I can't knock it, because I thought of it. It's my one proud moment. I can knock Rob's songs, but I can't knock the name." In 2000, just before releasing their second album (*Mad Season*), the group amended the name to matchbox twenty, with no capital letters and "20" spelled out.

Asked if he would prefer another name for the band, Thomas jokes,

"'Larry' was one of my favorites. People would say, 'What's the name of your band?' and you could go: 'Larry.' 'Who you gonna go see?' 'Larry.' That just seemed like the coolest thing to me. 'Hey, Larry's playing!'"

www.raininboxex.com; www.music.yahoo.com; www.mattsmusicpage.com.

Meat Loaf

BORN: Marvin Lee Aday on September 27, 1951,
in Dallas, Texas
BEST KNOWN SONG: Paradise by the
Dashboard Lights (#39, 1978)

Meat Loaf is one of the most theatrical male rock singers in the history of the genre. A Las Vegas act waiting to happen, he developed his style by paying dues in Broadway musicals, most notably *Hair*. A watershed moment in his career came when he won the role of Eddie in the Broadway and movie productions of *The Rocky Horror Picture Show.*

Meat's pop music career exploded with the 1977 rock music opus *Bat Out of Hell,* with the assistance of classically trained pianist and composer Jim Steinman and producer Todd Rundgren. Meat Loaf and Steinman parted company after the album and the former had virtually no further success until the pair reunited in 1993 for a sequel album that sold another five million copies.

With one of the stranger stage names in rock music history, Meat Loaf would not be the type of name that one would choose in order to become a matinee idol. Especially when the name-bearer tips the scales at over 300 pounds. Perhaps he just wanted to be known as the *biggest* act in pop music!

It should come as no surprise that the name chose *him.* He claims to have given several different accounts of the origin of the name. One story is that his football coaches called him that. Another is how he made a bet with some kid in high school that he would let his head get run over by a Volkswagen and afterward the kid remarked that he was dumb as a hunk of meat loaf.

Although these things did happen, it was actually his father who first coined the nickname. According to Meat Loaf, his father was jealous of the affection that his mother focused on her child instead of on her husband, leading to the not-so-flattering nickname. "Leave it to my dad to do that. He called me Meat Loaf almost from the time my mother brought me home (from the hospital)."

Meat Loaf with David Dalton. Meat Loaf: To Hell and Back. *New York: Regan Books, 1999.*

Metallica

GROUP FORMED IN: 1981
ORIGINAL MEMBERS: Lars Ulrich, James Hetfield, Lloyd Grant
LATER MEMBERS OF NOTE: Dave Mustaine, Ron McGovney,
Cliff Burton, Kirk Hammett, Robert Trujillo,
Jason Newsted, Lloyd Grant, Bob Rock
BEST KNOWN SONG: Enter Sandman (#16, 1991)

Metallica is the reigning undisputed heavyweight champion in three categories: hard rock, heavy metal, and thrash metal. Not since Led Zeppelin has a rock band been held in such high esteem. They have done it by not just knocking out ear-splitting headbanger noise, but by showing their musicianship and the intricate structures of their ever-improving song writing. However, they have never strayed far from their hard rock roots, and with every album they continue to add legions of fans to the fold.

Before Lars Ulrich put the band together, he became friends with a metal fan named Ron Quintana. They discussed the possibilities of starting a band, opening a record store, or starting a magazine, but they never jointly acted on these discussions. About the time the yet unnamed Metallica was forming, Quintana was working on his idea of producing a magazine to promote U.S. and British metal bands. He asked Ulrich to help him name the zine and offered a list from which to choose. Ulrich had his own list of potential group names such as Red Veg and Blitzer. When Lars saw Metallica on Quintana's list he quickly suggested the magazine be named Metal Mania, one of the *other* names, so Ulrich could appropriate Metallica for his own band.

Some have suggested this resulted in "petty larceny," but Quintana does not begrudge the name heist. "He had some really *bad* names himself. I guess mine wasn't much better because I ended up with *Metal Mania*—which isn't very original, but it worked."

Crocker, Chris. Metallica: The Frayed Ends of Metal. *New York: St. Martin's Press, 1993.*

Milli Vanilli

GROUP FORMED IN: 1988
MEMBERS: Originally thought to be Rob Pilatus and

Fabrice Morvan. Later learned to be John Davis,
Brad Howell, and Charles Shaw
BEST KNOWN SONG: Girl You Know It's True (#2, 1989)

So much has been made of the disgrace of Rob Pilatus and Fabrice Morvan, the lip-synching front men for the Frank Farian creation called Milli Vanilli, that little is known or written about the meaning of their name. There was a time, however, that everything the act released turned to gold (even multi-platinum). And although many had their suspicions about the pretty boys who moved their lips and bumped their bellies on stage, the record buying public either didn't know or didn't care — the songs were infectious and wildly popular, regardless from whose lips the words came.

The first album spawned five hits, including three number ones, a number two, and a number four. The album sold over five million copies in the United States alone and resulted in a Grammy award for Best New Artist in 1990. As we all know, the house of cards came tumbling down beginning with a glitch in the audio track during a concert in Connecticut when "Girl you know it's" repeated over and over until the flustered Vanillians ran from the stage. The ruse was soon up. The public backlashed. The Grammy was forfeited. And Pilatus died of a drug overdose in 1998.

Then it should come as no surprise that the group's name was a fabrication also. It was commonly held that Milli Vanilli was Turkish for "positive energy." Read my lips — not true. Milli means "national" in Turkish. Vanilli is not a Turkish word, not even for a flavor of ice cream. Another claim is that the name was taken from a now defunct dance club in Berlin. This may be true but cannot be verified. Finally, Milli was also the first name of Farian's production coordinator Milli-Ingrid Segieth. This is the most likely source. But who really cares, right? Nobody anymore — but a lot of people used to!

www.geocities.com; www.reference.com; www.crapfromthepast.com.

Moby

BORN: Richard Melville Hall on September 11, 1965,
in Harlem, New York
BEST KNOWN SONG: Southside (#14, 2001)

Moby is truly a complex contradiction of terms. He is an American icon of techno/house music, that cold faceless genre that is the grandchild of disco.

On the other hand, he has become a celebrity for his prodigious output (especially in the United Kingdom), thus personalizing his music in a way others before him have not.

Another contradiction is in the music he produces. Most techno is synth driven, but Moby, who is skilled on guitar and keyboard, has helped bring the genre to the mainstream by creating a techno/alternative mix drawing from punk, pop, and dance.

Whereas the roots of techno are in the hedonistic world of house music, Moby embraces the music while eschewing its values. Moby makes his personal views public, including on issues such as environmentalism, animal rights, politics, and organized religion. While not a saint, Moby lives his life on higher moral ground than many in his profession.

Most importantly (for purposes of this book), his chosen stage name contradicts with others he has used. Throughout his career, Moby has used various stage names, including Barracuda, Voodoo Child, Brainstorm, Lopez, The Brotherhood, U.H.F., and Mindstorm. But the one name that has followed him since childhood is Moby.

As a small child who grew into a small adult, Moby was saddled with a big name, Richard Melville Hall, deriving from a big legacy: His great-great grand uncle was Herman Melville, author of the literary classic *Moby Dick*. According to the techno guru himself, "So my parents nicknamed me 'Moby.' Kinda like naming a Chihuahua 'Killer.'" The tongue-in-cheek name apparently worked — Moby has become and remains a giant in the musical sea.

www.usaweekend.com www.discogs.com.

The Moody Blues

GROUP FORMED IN: 1964
ORIGINAL MEMBERS: Denny Laine, Ray Thomas,
Mike Pinder, Clint Warwick, Graeme Edge
LATER MEMBERS OF NOTE: Justin Hayward, John Lodge, Patrick Moraz
BEST KNOWN SONG: Nights in White Satin (#2, 1972)

The Moody Blues known by most people is the version who created "Nights in White Satin" with its ethereal qualities and pretentious poetry, but they were a different band before and after this period in the band's history. Upon formation, the group was steeped in blues music, having backed Sonny Boy Williamson and other American blues artists. In the group's later life they shed their prog rock skin, or at least conformed it to a more commercial sound for the 1980s, and they made a solid comeback with hits such as "Gemini Dream," "The Voice," and "Your Wildest Dreams."

Mike Pinder was a founding member and, with Ray Thomas, named the group. As a youngster Mike was taken with Duke Ellington's song "Mood Indigo," as much for the title as for the song itself, serving as inspiration for the first word of the band's name.

When working on the name, they decided to use the initials M and B, since one of the largest British breweries that owned all of the Birmingham clubs was named Mitchells and Butlers. Their ploy was to coax money from the company by pointing out the vague connection between the brewery's name and the group's.

Pinder claims that "actually I came up with the 'Blues' part first, because at that time we were playing blues. It was very easy to come up with 'Blues' for that, and the 'Moody' with an M because of my interest in the mood affecting changes of music. It had magical qualities to do things like that. That's how the name Moody Blues kind of happened, tied in with the M and B beer." The ploy was for naught, since Mitchells and Butlers never subsidized the band, which managed to do very well without it.

www.classicbands.com.

The Mothers of Invention

GROUP FORMED IN: 1964
ORIGINAL MEMBERS: Frank Zappa, Ray Collins, Jimmy
Carl Black, Roy Estrada, Elliot Ingber, Davy Coronado
LATER MEMBERS OF NOTE: Ian Underwood, Bunk Gardner, Arthur
Tripp, Don Preston, Jim "Motorhead" Sherwood, Aynsley
Dunbar, George Duke, Howard Kaylan, Mark Volman
BEST KNOWN ALBUMS: Freak Out! (1966), We're
Only in It for the Money (1968), Uncle Meat
(1969), Burnt Weeny Sandwich (1970)

The Mothers of Invention are one of only three bands listed in this book that never had a charting single. So why mention this group? Obviously the interesting name origin is a prerequisite. But also because the group served as the launching pad for Frank Zappa, one of the most interesting, talented, brilliant, and influential musicians of the rock era.

In 1964 Zappa joined a bar band from Los Angeles called The Soul Giants and immediately became the leader of the group. They were renamed The Mothers on Mother's Day. Anyone who knew Zappa assumed it stood for mother-fuckers. In 1965 record producer Tom Wilson signed them to MGM for a paltry advance of $2,500.

Their first recording, *Freak Out!*, would be just the second rock-and-roll double album of all time, released two months after Bob Dylan's *Blonde on Blonde*, which was the first. Zappa recalled the album and the events that led the group to change its name again, "By the time *Freak Out!* was edited and shaped into an album, Wilson had spent twenty-five or thirty thousand dollars of MGM's money — a ridiculous sum in those days, even for a double LP. We were then informed that they couldn't release the record — MGM executives had convinced themselves that no d.j. would ever play a record on the air by a group called The Mothers (as if our name was going to be *The Big Problem*). They insisted that we change it, and so the stock line is: 'Out of necessity we became Mothers of Invention' which is a turn on the phrase, 'necessity is the mother of invention.'"

Zappa, Frank, with Peter Occiogrosso. The Real Frank Zappa Book. New York: Touchstone, 1999.

Mötley Crüe

GROUP FORMED IN: 1981
ORIGINAL MEMBERS: Frank "Nikki Sixx" Ferranno, "Tommy Lee"
Bass, Bob "Mick Mars" Deal, "Vince Neil" Wharton
LATER MEMBERS OF NOTE: John Corabi,
Randy Castillo, Samantha Maloney
BEST KNOWN SONG: Girls, Girls, Girls (#12, 1987)

Are they better known for their music, tattoos, bad boy image, or Playboy/Baywatch wives? Take your pick because they all apply. Mötley Crüe proved more influential than commercially successful. No accurate count on the number of tattoos exists but suffice it to say they rival the *New York Times* for ink used. They are widely reputed for having more "sex, drugs and rock & roll" than any other band in rock history. And has any other band been affiliated with more beautiful women than Pamela Anderson, Heather Locklear, Donna D'Ericco, and Heidi Mark?

Another thing about the group is its name. First, the intentional misspelling. Second, the pretentious, cliché and liberal use of umlauts. Finally, the meaning and origin of the name itself.

Tommy Lee and Nikki Sixx had contacted Mick Mars in response to an ad he had placed that read "Loud, rude, aggressive guitarist available." Shortly thereafter Vince Neil joined the others after leaving his band, Rock Candy. The group had strongly considered calling itself Christmas, but discussions continued to see if something else resonated.

While Marrs was in his former band, White Horse, one of the band members, walked in and called the group "a motley looking crew." The original spelling attributed to the name is either Mottly Kruu or Mottley Cru, depending on your source. The group decided the new name would attract fans by itself and modified the spelling to Mötley Crüe, umlauts and all.

www.epinions.com; www.onlineseats.com.

Mott The Hoople

GROUP FORMED IN: 1969
ORIGINAL MEMBERS: Mick Ralphs, Terry "Verden"
Allen, Pete "Overend" Watts, Dale "Buffin"
Griffin, Ian Hunter (born Ian Patterson)
LATER MEMBERS OF NOTE: Luther "Ariel Bender"
Grosvenor, Morgan Fisher, Mick Ronson,
Nigel Benjamin, Ray Majors
BEST KNOWN SONG: All the Young Dudes (#37, 1972)

Evolving from the group Silence, Mott The Hoople was a hard rock glam band with strong R&B roots. Signed to Island Records in 1969, the group replaced injured lead singer Stan Tippens with Ian Hunter and forged ahead under the watchful eye of producer Guy Stevens. Stevens himself has a colorful history in the British music scene. He was responsible for suggesting the name of the band Procol Harum (see later in this book), as well as several brilliant album titles, including the Rolling Stones's *Sticky Fingers*. He was also reputed to have a wealth of knowledge of American R&B and was the one that gave the Stones many of their cover versions before they started writing their own material.

Stevens also spent time in Wormwood Scrubs, a prison in London, for a drug-related offense. While in the joint he read a book by Willard Manus called *Mott the Hoople*, which is the story of a misfit named Norman Mott who ends up joining a circus freak show in order to avoid being drafted to fight in Vietnam. Stevens decided the name would be perfect for a rock band, later telling his wife that it would look great on a marquee with "lots of o's and t's," but he asked her to keep the name a secret until he could apply it to the perfect group.

Although Mott The Hoople never achieved the mainstream success they craved, their early mixture of heavy metal and glam, together with a hipster cynicism, provided the groundwork for many British punk bands, most notably the Clash.

Manus, Willard. Mott the Hoople. *New York: McGraw-Hill, 1966; www.losingtoday.com; www.amazon.com; www.procolharum.com; www.hunter-mott.com.*

Mungo Jerry

GROUP FORMED IN: 1970
ORIGINAL MEMBERS: Ray Dorset, Colin Earl,
Paul King, Mike Cole, Joe Rush
LATER MEMBERS OF NOTE: John Godfrey,
Bob Daisley, Dave Bidwell, Paul Hancox,
Boris Williams, Dick Middleton, Steve Jones
BEST KNOWN SONG: In the Summertime (#3, 1970)

A one-hit wonder if ever there was one, Mungo Jerry surprisingly has continued to record as a band (no, it's not one person), ever since its one and only hit, "In the Summertime," peaked at number three in the United States and number one in England for seven weeks. The song also hit the top spot in 20 other countries.

The one constant member is founder Ray Dorset, lead singer on the big hit. The group's name is also one of a kind. The band's first big break came when Barry Murray signed them to Pye Records. At the time the group was answering to the name of The Good Earth Rock'N Roll Band. They had formerly been known as (in reverse chronological order) Memphis Leather, Camino Real, The Sweet and Sour Band, The Tramps, The Conchords, and The Buccaneers.

Murray felt Good Earth needed yet another name change (you know, eighth time's a charm). A few names were written on scraps of paper and Mungo Jerry was pulled out of a hat. The losing entries included The Incredible Shark, which had been the name that was written on the original acetate of the group's test recording at Pye Studios. The band was relieved when "Shark" was not drawn.

The name Mungo Jerry came from a character named Mungojerrie in T.S. Eliot's book *Old Possum's Book of Practical Cats* and later from the musical *Cats*. Together with his cohort in crime, Rumpleteazer, they are a mischievous pair who specialize in petty theft and creating chaos.

Eliot, T. S. Old Possum's Book of Practical Cats. *London: Faber & Faber, 1939; www.mungojerry.com; www.mungomania.com.*

Naked Eyes

GROUP FORMED IN: 1981
ORIGINAL MEMBERS: Pete Byrne, Rob Fisher
LATER MEMBERS OF NOTE: none
BEST KNOWN SONG: Always Something
There to Remind Me (#8, 1983)

One day Pete Byrne was crossing the Pultney Bridge in Bath, England, and he saw a woman accosting a man. He intervened on behalf of the man, Rob Fisher, and the two became friends after discovering a mutual interest in music. Eventually they formed the duo called Naked Eyes.

In the interim, Byrne and Fisher would be part of the band Neon, which also included Curt Smith and Roland Orzabal, who would later form Tears For Fears. Neon was primarily a vehicle for Byrne and Fisher so the music recorded had a strong Naked Eyes sound to it.

After Neon split, Byrne and Fisher remained together and adopted a sound that featured more synthesizers and drum machines and less guitars. When asked about the origin of the name, Byrne has this to say: "I made it up. We were looking for a name that suggested 'two' and Naked Eyes just popped into my head. I thought it was a great name, but the record label thought otherwise."

"I remember one meeting with about ten people," recalls Byrne, "and they were asking everyone what they thought. Some of the ideas were truly awful. Rob and I had thought up this mythical country singer with the rhinestones, etcetera, and christened him Boulevard Credibility and I suggested, as a joke, we call ourselves Boulevard Credibility. One of the marketing people leapt to his feet in agreement and I knew, then and there, that if I listened to these people I'd end up wearing a spandex kilt and Robin Hood shoes."

www.pjbmusic.com; www.discog.info.

New Order

GROUP FORMED IN: 1980
ORIGINAL MEMBERS: Bernard Sumner, Peter Hook,
Stephen Morris, Gillian Gilbert

LATER MEMBERS OF NOTE: Phil Cunningham
BEST KNOWN SONG: True Faith (#32, 1987)

New Order is the electronic dance group that was created from Joy Division when the latter's lead vocalist, Ian Curtis, committed suicide in 1980. "We were devastated ... but, to be honest, we were angry too," said Bernard Sumner. "We were like, 'What are we supposed to do now, Ian?' It was all we knew. We'd given up our jobs." After the stunning development that transpired shortly before the group's second album was released, the remaining members chose to soldier on, but with a change of name to New Order.

Several years earlier and an ocean away, Ron Asheton, a former member of The Stooges, had formed a band he named The New Order (as a reference to Adolf Hitler's New Order of the Third Reich from *Mein Kampf*). Asheton even put Nazi paraphernalia on the group's album cover to emphasize the point.

The British New Order has publicly denied its name has anything to do with Nazi Germany. Their manager, Rob Gretton, came up with the name. Gretton was very private and rarely submitted to interviews before his death in 1999, so the precise origin of the name is uncertain. It is generally believed that he had spotted an article in the daily newspaper, *The Guardian*, entitled "The people's New Order of Kampuchea" and the phrase caught his eye.

Other names considered, if only fleetingly, were Stevie and the JDs, Sunshine Valley Dance Band, and The Eternal. Had the band chosen to be called the Sunshine Valley Dance Band, its chances of being confused with Hitler would probably have been greatly reduced.

www.neworderonline.com; www.writersclub.iafrica.com.

Nickelback

GROUP FORMED IN: 1995
ORIGINAL MEMBERS: Chad Kroeger, Mike Kroeger,
Ryan Vikedal, Brandon Kroeger
LATER MEMBERS OF NOTE: Ryan Peake, Daniel Adair
BEST KNOWN SONG: How You Remind Me (#1, 2002)

Nickelback is a hard rock band from Alberta, Canada. A commercially but not necessarily critically successful band, Nickelback has maintained a strong legion of avid fans, making them one of the most popular bands of the early twenty-first century.

The group was formed by brothers Chad and Mike Kroeger. A cousin, Brandon, was also an early member but left the band in 1997. Early on, the group benefited from the Canadian law known as Cancon (short for Canadian content), which requires radio and television broadcasters to air a certain percentage of content that is at least partly written, produced, presented, or otherwise contributed to by persons from Canada.

However, the group's second album, *The State*, propelled them into the mainstream and ensured Nickelback secured extensive airplay without the aid of government regulations. The third album, *Silver Side Up*, which included the huge breakthrough hit "How You Remind Me," pushed Nickelback well beyond the Canadian borders as international superstars.

Mike Kroeger claims the group couldn't decide what to call themselves, even after recording their first songs. The group's name came about as a result of Mike's experience as a cashier at a Starbucks in Vancouver. He suggested the name Nickelback since he found himself constantly receiving $2.00 for a $1.95 coffee and saying "Here's your *nickel back*." One wonders, if the price of coffee was $1.75, would the group be confused for football players? (Think about it.)

www.kidzworld.com; www.mmguide.musicmatch.com.

Night Ranger

GROUP FORMED IN: 1981
ORIGINAL MEMBERS: Jack Blades, Kelly Keagy,
Brad Gillis, Alan "Fitz" Fitzgerald, Jeff Watson
LATER MEMBERS OF NOTE: Gary Moon, Michael Lardie
BEST KNOWN SONG: Sister Christian (#5, 1984)

The group's roots can be traced to Rubicon, a horn-driven pop group from the '70s. When Rubicon broke up, Jack Blades, Kelly Keagy, and Brad Gillis stayed together and played as Stereo. Soon they recruited ex-Montrose keyboardist Alan Fitzgerald and guitarist Jeff Watson and changed the name to Ranger. This name came under fire from The Rangers, a country band that claimed legal rights to the name. This led to a final change to Night Ranger, and finally the band was ready to attack the pop music world.

Unfortunately the pop music world was not quite ready for Night Ranger. As they say, timing is everything. When Night Ranger began in 1981, their timing was not good. They had a hard rock sound in the heart of the new wave era. According to Jack Blades, "Nobody wanted to hear us at that time and every time we played a show in San Francisco everybody would yell out '1975' and put us down. If you think about what was going on at that time in the music industry, it was like Blondie and the Cars, A Flock of Seagulls, Haircut 100 and they thought we were dinosaurs. They wanted us to cut our hair and wear skinny ties."

The group persevered. As MTV was just getting started, Night Ranger's "Don't Tell Me You Love Me" was among the first few videos played, so heavy rotation was assured. "Because MTV was new, all these kids were watching MTV and suddenly there is this rock band with screaming guitars and stuff with two lead vocals," recounts Blades. "That kind of just propelled us and that is how it got started." Finally the timing was right for Night Ranger as they helped usher in the rejuvenation of hard rock, leading to hair bands, grunge, and alternative music.

www.classicrockrevisited.com.

Nine Inch Nails

GROUP FORMED IN: 1988
ORIGINAL MEMBERS: Trent Reznor
LATER MEMBERS OF NOTE: Adrian Belew,
Jeordie White, Josh Freese, Alessandro Cortini,
Aaron North, many others in studio and on tour
BEST KNOWN SONG: Closer (#41, 1994)

For all intents and purposes, Nine Inch Nails (NIN) is one person, Trent Reznor. He created the "group" and writes all the songs. Additional musicians are hired to help out in the studio and on tour, although Reznor is a classically trained pianist and able to play many of the instruments himself.

The music produced by NIN is most often described as industrial metal; however, purists of the genre demur at the classification, claiming Reznor's songs are too close to pop. It would be unwise to attempt to classify NIN under any one umbrella since the songs vary among industrial, heavy metal, rock, pop, alternative, and electronica.

The origin of the name Nine Inch Nails has been the subject of much speculation over the years. Theories abound that the following things, which reportedly are each nine inches long, were the source of the name: (1) the nails used to crucify Jesus; (2) nails used to seal coffins; (3) the Statue of Liberty's finger nails; or (4) Freddy Krueger's finger nails (*A Nightmare on Elm Street*).

According to Reznor, the meaning is not nearly that convoluted. "I don't know if you've ever tried to think of band names, but usually you think you have a great one and you look at it the next day and it's stupid. I had about 200 of those. Nine Inch Nails lasted the two week test, looked great in print, and could be abbreviated easily. It really doesn't have any literal meaning. It seemed kind of frightening. Tough and manly. It's a curse trying to come up with band names."

Huxley, Martin. Nine Inch Nails. New York: St. Martin's Griffin, 1997; Axcess Magazine.

Nirvana

GROUP FORMED IN: 1986
ORIGINAL MEMBERS: Kurt Cobian, Krist
"Chris" Novoselic, Chad Channing
LATER MEMBERS OF NOTE: Jason Everman,
Dan Peters, Dave Grohl, Pat Smear
BEST KNOWN SONG: Smells Like Teen Spirit (#6, 1992)

Nirvana was to grunge what the Ramones were to punk. The only difference is that Nirvana was commercially successful. Emerging out of a trailer park in the Seattle, Washington, area (Aberdeen, to be precise), the original members of what would be Nirvana successfully encapsulated the rage and alienation of the youth of their generation (X, to be precise). They merged hard rock and angst with pop sensibilities, making their music accessible to radio and MTV.

In its early days, the band worked to come up with a name. Up for discussion (some of which were actually used from time to time) were Skid Row (before Sebastian Bach's crew was on the scene), Ted Ed Fred, Bliss, Throat Oyster, Pen Cap Chew, Fecal Matter, and Windowpane. However, Cobain had discovered Buddhism after watching a TV show about Eastern religions and, according to Kurt, "I wanted a name that was kind of beautiful or nice and pretty instead of a mean, raunchy punk-rock name like the Angry Samoans." He settled on Nirvana, the Buddhist concept of ultimate enlightenment.

Unbeknownst to the group, a quartet out of Los Angeles had been using the same name and sought an injunction against using Nirvana and the playing of "Smells Like Teen Spirit." To settle the lawsuit, Cobain's outfit purchased the trademark from the LA group, although both groups agreed to allow joint usage of the name.

St. Thomas, Kurt, with Troy Smith. Nirvana: The Chosen Rejects. New York: St. Martin's Griffin, 2004; Wallace, Max, and Ian Halperin. Love & Death. New York: Atria Books, 2004.

No Doubt

GROUP FORMED IN: 1986
ORIGINAL MEMBERS: John Spence, Eric
Stefani, Gwen Stefani, Tony Kanal
LATER MEMBERS OF NOTE: Tom Dumont, Adrian
Young, Alan Meade, Jerry McMahon, Chris Webb
BEST KNOWN SONG: Don't Speak (#1, 1997)

When most people think of No Doubt they think of Gwen Stefani strutting the stage with her white hair and perfect abs. But when the group was formed she was merely a background singer in the band of her big brother, Eric. Together with initial lead singer John Spence, Eric Stefani organized a ska band after falling in love with the genre while listening to the album *Baggy Trousers* by Madness. For years Eric played the album's songs on the family piano and, eventually, began writing reggae-tinged original songs with Spence. Gwen adopted the retro styles common among fans of ska, known as "rudies."

When Eric and John formed the group they struggled to choose a name. The first suggested by Eric was Apple Core, which was a catch phrase from a Warner Bros. cartoon. The name No Doubt was used instead, simply because it was John's favorite expression.

Their band initially included numerous peripheral musicians in a brass section. The personnel changed many times in the early years. John Spence committed suicide in 1987, which led to Gwen becoming lead vocalist. Eric Stefani left the band in 1994 for a career in cartoon animation on the TV series *The Simpsons.*

By the time of the band's breakthrough album, *Tragic Kingdom* (which was released in 1995), the group consisted of just Gwen Stefani, Tony Kanal, Adrian Young, and Tom Dumont. Gwen's on-stage persona, a mixture of innocent little girl and in-your-face feminism, helped propel the album's third single, "Don't Speak," to number one for an incredible sixteen weeks.

Blankstein, Amy. Gwen Stefani. London: Omnibus Press, 2005; www.nduniverse.com.

Oasis

GROUP FORMED IN: 1991

ORIGINAL MEMBERS: Liam Gallagher, Paul "Bonehead"
Arthurs, Paul McGuigan, Tony McCarroll
LATER MEMBERS OF NOTE: Noel Gallagher, Gem Arthur,
Alan White, Andy Bell, Zak Starkey
BEST KNOWN SONG: Wonderwall (#8, 1996)

Noel Gallagher was a guitar technician for the Inspiral Carpets on tour in the United States when he heard his brother Liam was about to give his initial performance at the Boardwalk club as a member of the group he had formed in Manchester, England. Three of the four members were drawn from a group formerly called The Rain. Now Liam's group was called Oasis, so-named for a poster from the very same Inspiral Carpets. Noel had one of the Carpets's promotional posters tacked to the wall of his bedroom. One of the venues on it was the Oasis Leisure Centre in Swindon.

The Boardwalk show, attended by Noel, was met with muted appreciation. But Noel saw something in the band and himself that made him think that with his input they could create something special. The songs he had been scribbling down needed an outlet, he needed to be more than a roadie, and Oasis needed a more powerful sound.

So Noel approached Liam and offered his services if, and only if, he could have complete artistic control of all aspects of the band. The group surprisingly voiced no objections, perhaps recognizing that Noel's swagger and attitude was what the band lacked. "When he walked in, we were a band making a racket with four tunes," said Paul Arthurs. "All of a sudden, there were loads of ideas. Very quickly, you could hear it: something'll happen with this." Oasis quickly became the biggest band in England and has been one of the most written-about bands in the world, known as much for their songs as for the highly public feuds of the Gallagher brothers.

Harris, John. Britpop! New York: Da Capo Press, 2004.

Ohio Players

GROUP FORMED IN: 1959
ORIGINAL MEMBERS: Robert Ward, Clarence
"Satch" Satchel, Ralph "Pee Wee" Middlebrooks,
Marshall "Rock" Jones, Cornelius Johnson
LATER MEMBERS OF NOTE: Leroy "Sugarfoot" Bonner,
Greg Webster, Dale Allen, Walter "Junie" Morrison,
Marvin "Merv" Pierce, William "Billy" Beck, James

"Diamond" Williams, Clarence "Chet" Willis,
Robert "Kuumba" Jones, Darwin Dortch, Ronald
Nooks, and many more
BEST KNOWN SONG: Love Rollercoaster (#1, 1976)

Many groups claim to be funk, but outside of George Clinton/Bootsy Collins entities, the Ohio Players most personify the genre. Unfortunately, their legacy is best remembered for two things that don't have much to do with their music, namely, the barely-this-side-of-pornographic album covers and the rumored murder that occurred during the recording of "Love Rollercoaster" (which was, of course, unfounded but not denied by the band when sales of the record were still relevant).

The band began way back in 1959 out of Dayton, Ohio, as the Ohio Untouchables. This band broke up in 1963 but the core members added new members and re-formed as a house band for New York City-based Compass Records until 1970 when they broke up again. The group got together again, adding a keyboard player and another guitarist to go with the horn-driven bottom-heavy sound they were developing and refining thanks to influential acts such as James Brown and Sly and the Family Stone.

The name chosen for the newest incarnation was the Ohio Players. Leroy Bonner explains the name this way, "Well, in Ohio they sort of got a thing about players, sort of like playboy and I guess the name stuck with us because we were always considered to be the playboys around the area. And we were some of the best musicians that there were in the area — we were the best players."

www.wfnk.com.

Oingo Boingo

GROUP FORMED IN: 1977
ORIGINAL MEMBERS: Richard Elfman, Danny Elfman,
Marie-Pascale Elfman, Gene Cunningham, Matthew Bright,
Steve Bartek, Johnny "Vatos" Hernandez, Sam "Sluggo" Phipps,
Leon Schneiderman, Dale Turner, Billy Superball, Josh Gordon,
Ernie Fosselius, Miriam Cutler, Brad Kay
LATER MEMBERS OF NOTE: John Avila,
Kerry Hatch, Richard "Ribbs" Gibbs, David Eagle,
Paul Fox, Mike Bacich, Carl Graves, Warren Fitzgerald,
Doug Legacy, Marc Mann, Bruce Fowler
BEST KNOWN SONG: Weird Science (#45, 1985)

Oingo Boingo was neither the group's first nor its last name. The group began as "The Mystic Knights of the Oingo Boingo" and ended as simply "Boingo." Although Danny Elfman is the most well known member of the many incarnations of the group, his older brother Richard actually formed the group in 1972 before Danny was involved in the project.

The Mystic Knights of the Oingo Boingo was Richard's musical theater troupe, which performed a wide variety of musical styles ranging from big band to ballet. Richard would eventually leave the band to Danny to become a filmmaker. When asked about the meaning of the group name Richard said, "It really just popped into my head. The only things I might have been unconsciously exposed to were the 'Mystic Knights of the Sea,' which was the lodge hall that Amos and Andy belonged to, and 'Boingy Baxter,' an R. Crumb character."

Amos 'n' Andy was a radio program started in 1929, played by its creators, Freeman Gosden and Charles Correll, in blackface. It later became one of the first television sitcoms, this time played by a black cast (a first on television). The television show ran through 1960.

R. Crumb is actually Robert Crumb, a comic book writer and artist. His off-color comics included a variety of unusual characters, including a dapper man named Boingy Baxter, who bounced up and down all the time. Artwork from this comic series comprises treasured memorabilia from the genre.

www.answers.com; www.greencine.com.

The O'Jays

GROUP FORMED IN: 1958
ORIGINAL MEMBERS: Walter Williams, Bill Isles,
Bobby Massey, William Powell, Eddie Levert
LATER MEMBERS OF NOTE: Sammy Strain, Nathaniel Best
BEST KNOWN SONG: Love Train (#1, 1973)

While attending school together at McKinley High School, Eddie Levert, Walter Williams, William Powell, Bobby Massey, and Bill Isles formed a group they called, in succession, The Emeralds, The Triumphs, and The Mascots. Early performance venues included YMCAs, birthday parties, and talent shows. They were paid more in youthful adulation than money. The group's fortunes took a turn for the better when it hired Cleveland disc jockey Eddie O'Jay as its manager.

Another group with the name of The Mascots was discovered, so a fourth name change was in order. In an effort to bolster the career of his protégés, Eddie O'Jay arranged for Daco Records cofounder Don Davis to listen to the group while he was in Cleveland. Davis liked what he heard and suggested they relocate to Detroit, the burgeoning soul music capital of the world.

After coaxing the group to Detroit, Davis recalled years later a conversation he had with the group's manager, "We recorded this record — *Miracles* — and we sit there and ponder about what the name of the group was gonna be. I said, 'Why don't we just call them The O'Jays, right after you?' And that's how they got their name."

Finally armed with a moniker all its own, The O'Jays reigned among the top soul vocal groups of the 1970s. The group's presence was felt on the pop charts with 30 top-100 hits over a 34-year span, bringing symmetry to a career that started in Canton, Ohio, home of the Football Hall of Fame, and ended in Cleveland, home of the Rock and Roll Hall of Fame.

www.soulfuldetroit.com; www.soul-patrol.com.

Orchestral Manoeuvres in the Dark

GROUP FORMED IN: 1978
ORIGINAL MEMBERS: Paul Humphreys, Andy McCluskey
LATER MEMBERS OF NOTE: David Hughes,
Martin Cooper, Malcolm Holmes
BEST KNOWN SONG: If You Leave (#4, 1986)

This is a really confusing one. Before we get to that, a little background first. The band was essentially a duo of Paul Humphreys and Andy McCluskey with backing musicians. The main pair had previously been in groups named The Id and Hitlerz Underpants. McCluskey had also been a member of Pegasus.

Orchestral Manoeuvres in the Dark (commonly abbreviated as OMD) became one of the great synth-pop bands of the New Romantic era, drawing on a love of Kraftwerk not only for their music but also for their name. As is common, they became big hits in their native England before breaking through in America, but ironically, just as their career was taking off in the States it was waning in England. Their commercial apex came with the release of "If You Leave," which was written specifically for the John Hughes movie *Pretty in Pink* and became OMD's only top-10 hit stateside.

Now for the name. Try to keep up. As was mentioned, McCluskey and Humphreys were very keen on Kraftwerk. The back of Kraftwerk's album *Radioactivity* featured a picture of an electronic valve unit and the model number VCL XI. Humphreys and McCluskey took this roman numeral-looking conglomeration of letters as the group's first name.

While working under this unwieldy moniker they wrote a song called "Orchestral Manoeuvres into the Dark." Then they decided the song title would work better as the group name (with slight modification). Then their former group name was used as the title of a song (obviously called "VCL XI"), which appeared on OMD's 1980 album entitled *Organisation*. Got it? Me neither.

www.omd.uk.com; www.link2wales.co.uk.

The Outfield

GROUP FORMED IN: 1984
ORIGINAL MEMBERS: Tony Lewis, John Spinks, Alan Jackman
LATER MEMBERS OF NOTE: Paul Reed, Simon Dawson
BEST KNOWN SONG: Your Love (#6, 1986)

The Outfield is an East End of London group that scored big in the mid 1980s with their debut album called *Play Deep*. Their signature hit is entitled "Your Love" but most people recognize it by "Josie," as in "Josie's on a vacation far away...." The distinctive two-part harmony of Tony Lewis and John Spinks seemed to channel the vocal standouts of the 1960s but their driving rock tunes made them instant favorites in the '80s until the grunge wave washed away most things melodic.

There are two common misconceptions about the Outfield. One is that they are Americans. The other is that they were big baseball fans, resulting in the name of the band and the first album. Although they did little to dispel these notions, the truth is that these Brits actually knew very little about baseball. One night Spinks watched the movie *The Warriors*, about New York street gangs. One of the gangs dressed in New York Yankees pinstripes, painted their faces white, and used baseball bats as their weapons of choice. Spinks liked the tough image of the gang, which reminded him of the movie *A Clockwork Orange*. So they decided their name would be "The Baseball Boys."

This name lasted two years while the group was active on the pub circuit. Their management in America saw the name as somewhat corny but liked the sports theme. Since the group was a trio, the management suggested The Outfield, (that is, three players in the outfield). According to Spinks, "[W]e just agreed, as we weren't baseball knowledgeable at that point. And then came the logo which is obviously the baseball triangle and such." They must have eventually learned more about baseball because their fourth album was entitled *Diamond Days* instead of *Triangle Days*.

www.theoutfield.com; www.annecarlini.com.

Pablo Cruise

GROUP FORMED IN: 1973
ORIGINAL MEMBERS: Bud Cockrell, David
Jenkins, Cory Lerios, Steve Price
LATER MEMBERS OF NOTE: Bruce Day, John Pierce, Angelo
Rossi, David Perper, Stef Birnbaum, George Gabriel
BEST KNOWN SONG: Whatcha Gonna Do? (#6, 1977)

Pablo Cruise, Steely Dan, Lynyrd Skynyrd, Jethro Tull. Four pretty good musicians, right? Don't be ridiculous, you say. Try more like 15 good musicians (give or take, depending on the particular time). But often enough these and other bands are mistaken by the uninitiated as people, not groups. Not that these misconceptions aren't sometimes aided and abetted by the groups themselves.

Take Pablo Cruise, for example. The band originally consisted of four members who find it amusing that people insist "Pablo" is one of the band members. They have the routine down pat. When asked to explain the band's name they respond, "He's the guy in the middle." The company line continues when they describe Pablo as an honest, down to earth individual. Apparently Pablo got his last name of Cruise as a depiction of his "fun-loving and easy-going attitude towards life."

All joking aside, Pablo Cruise is an American soft rock band that found its niche perfectly in the mid to late '70s with such hits as "Whatcha Gonna Do?," "A Place in the Sun," "Love Will Find a Way," and "Cool Love." The new wave movement swept most pop artists away and Pablo Cruise was among the casualties. Although they broke up in 1985, three of the four original members re-formed in 2004 (George Gabriel replacing Bud Cockrell), reviving the band much to the delight of their loyal fans.

www.pablocruiseband.com.

Parliament / Funkadelic

GROUP FORMED IN: 1955
MAIN MEMBERS OF GROUPS: George Clinton, William "Bootsy" Collins, Phelps "Catfish" Collins, Jerome "Bigfoot" Brailey, Ray Davis, Glen Goins, Ramon "Tiki" Fulwood, Michael "Mickey" Hampton, Clarence "Fuzzy" Haskins, Eddie Hazel, Walter "Junie" Morrison, Cordell "Boogie" Mosson, Billy "Bass" Nelson, Garry M. Shider, Calvin Simon, Grady Thomas, Bernie Worrell
BEST KNOWN SONG: Flashlight (#16, 1978)

George Clinton started out as a hair stylist in Plainfield, New Jersey. In 1955, at the age of 15, Clinton formed a doo-wop quartet called the Parliaments with the name taken from Parliament cigarettes. The Parliaments played various talent shows in the area, frequently winning at the Apollo Theater. This group had minor success on the national scene.

In 1964 Clinton added a backing band made up of local talent that often came in to Clinton's barber shop. This band was called The Funkadelics. Clinton traveled to Detroit often with The Parliaments and recorded a few singles for Revilot Records.

Soon after this, Revilot Records folded and took the legal rights to the Parliaments name with it. To maintain continuity, Clinton made The Funkadelics his main band. Soon after this, Clinton regained the rights to use his former band name and made the slight modification by dropping the "s" off the end and calling them simply Parliament.

By now both bands were gaining strength and building on the roots of James Brown and more notably Sly and the Family Stone. The addition of brothers Bootsy and Catfish Collins (William and Phelps, respectively, to their mother) helped move the group in the funky direction that ultimately landed the two groups in the Rock and Roll Hall of Fame. The bands' inductions were due as much to their tremendous influence on black music, particularly hip-hop, as to their relatively modest chart success.

Talevski, Nick. The Unofficial Encyclopedia of the Rock & Roll Hall of Fame. Westport, CT: Greenwood Press, 1988.

Pearl Jam

GROUP FORMED IN: 1990
ORIGINAL MEMBERS: Eddie Vedder, Stone Gossard,
Jeff Ament, Mike McCready, Dave Abbruzzese
LATER MEMBERS OF NOTE: Dave Krusen, Jack Irons,
Matt Cameron, Matt Chamberlain
BEST KNOWN SONG: Last Kiss (#2, 1999)

Now to Pearl Jam. The seminal grunge band whose name origin is both frustrating and yet extremely fun. First a disclaimer — I have no idea what the name Pearl Jam truly means. You will be given the facts and you may decide for yourself.

Start with the premise that Eddie Vedder is a pretty smart guy. He and his bandmates have limited patience for the same interview questions over and over again. So to make things a little more interesting for themselves a few stories have been concocted, which have been repeated with embellishments like your father's old fishing stories.

One fact is that the band was originally named Mookie Blaylock, after the former University of Oklahoma basketball player whose 13-year NBA career took him through New Jersey, Atlanta, and Golden State. The band toured under this name and even named an album for him (*10*, which was Blaylock's jersey number) before deciding to try something different.

Pearl Jam was then chosen. The most common explanation given by Vedder in interviews (often including laughter and interjections from bandmates), is that his great-grandmother *Pearl* made peyote-laced *jams* as part of Indian tribal customs.

Another story is that they wanted to be called simply Pearl, because they compare the way they make music to the way an oyster makes a pearl, wherein it takes waste and creates something beautiful. But after watching Neil Young *jam* for three hours on nine songs they were inspired to lengthen the name.

There is also a story with the obvious sexual innuendo. No elaboration needed there. So there you have it — you make the call.

www.wisegeek.com; www.sonymusic.com.

Pet Shop Boys

GROUP FORMED IN: 1981
ORIGINAL MEMBERS: Neil Tennant, Chris Lowe
LATER MEMBERS OF NOTE: none
BEST KNOWN SONG: West End Girls (#1, 1986)

Neil Tennant and Chris Lowe met while shopping at an electronics store. They instantly discovered their mutual love for dance music; however, Tennant's taste was more to rock and Lowe's was more to disco. Tennant was working at the time for *Smash Hits* magazine as assistant editor. That was 1981.

It was disco producer Bobby Orlando who helped the Boys realize the potential for the type of buoyant and melodic synth-pop dance hits that would make them a staple on the radio and, more importantly, on the dance floors, for many years to come. They developed an interesting idiosyncrasy of giving all their albums one word titles (similar to the group America beginning all their albums with the letter "H"). It is a testament to the Pet Shop Boys that the popularity of their happy dance songs remained high even as depressing grunge and alternative songs were cornering the market in the 1990s.

Three years would pass before they would have their first hit, "West End Girls." A-ha, you say, "West End Girls" was not a hit until early 1986. True. However, the song was a low level hit in France and Belgium 2½ years before it was a huge hit in the United States. "Opportunities" was also released a few years before becoming a hit across the pond.

The first group name that was considered was West End. Ultimately the Pet Shop Boys was chosen as an homage to some friends of Chris who worked in a local pet shop. Also, they say it reminded them of the hip-hop groups of the early '80s from America. Many people suspect they were thinking of NYC Peech Boys.

www.xs4all.nl.

Phish

GROUP FORMED IN: 1983
ORIGINAL MEMBERS: Trey Anastasio, Jon Fishman,
Mike Gordon, Jeff Holdsworth

LATER MEMBERS OF NOTE: Marc Daubert,
Page McConnell
BEST KNOWN SONG: Down with Disease
(not released — their only MTV video)

Many people have never heard of this band that *Rolling Stone* magazine called "the most important band of the Nineties." Just who is (was) Phish? Trying to describe the group is like trying to describe a color. Bottom line: Phish was one of a kind.

Phish made its name much the same way as did the Grateful Dead — by playing an extended series of concerts to their loyal, traveling fan base. Each concert was entirely unique in that the band never played the same songs the same way in the same order. Concert songs were played in a free-form style, including folk, jazz, bluegrass, country, and pop. Sometimes games would be played using the audience, including throwing a large beach ball into the crowd and playing a note each time the ball was hit.

Often the group's shows were large-scale festivals drawing well over 60,000 people. They released thirteen studio albums and seven live albums without ever having a top-40 hit. And although they were never a true substitute for the Grateful Dead, they were by far the closest thing to them for gen-X'ers.

An easy assumption of how the group got its name is from the nickname of the drummer, Jon Fishman, aka "Fish," but there is more to it than that. According to Fish himself, "When it was time to decide a name for the band, I suggested the sound of a plane taking off—'phssssh.' But then we thought that we needed a vowel. Imagine people saying 'We're going to see Phssssh tonight.'" To make it a word they simply added the "i" in the middle and removed an "s" or two.

Thompson, Dave. Go Phish. New York: St. Martin's Griffin, 1997.

Pink Floyd

GROUP FORMED IN: 1965
ORIGINAL MEMBERS: Syd Barrett, Roger Waters,
Nick Mason, Rick Wright
LATER MEMBERS OF NOTE: David Gilmour
BEST KNOWN SONG: Another Brick in the Wall (#1, 1980)

That Pink Floyd takes up residence in the Rock and Roll Hall of Fame with merely two top-40 hits to their credit is testimony to their unparalleled album sales success. *Dark Side of the Moon* is one of the most successful albums of all time, charting for a record 741 weeks (that's over *fourteen* years). Other albums including *Wish You Were Here, Animals,* and *Another Brick in the Wall* helped punch Pink Floyd's ticket into the Hall of Fame.

Led initially by Syd Barrett, until his LSD-induced mental flameout required his replacement with David Gilmour, the group was originally called Tea Set. Once they were scheduled to play a gig at an RAF base only to discover another group with the same name on the same bill. Barrett made the hasty decision to rename the band The Pink Floyd Sound, using the first names of two venerable blues musicians, Pink Anderson and Floyd Council. The other members of the band were not particularly well acquainted with the namesakes but acquiesced to Barrett's suggestion.

For a while the group oscillated between the two names, but eventually the new name won out. In time the name was shortened to today's version. Ultimately the other band members grew fond of the moniker because of its vaguely psychedelic suggestiveness. Somehow Tea Set doesn't evoke those same mental images.

Mason, Nick. Inside Out: A Personal History of Pink Floyd. *San Francisco: Chronicle Books,* 2004.

Poco

GROUP FORMED IN: 1968
ORIGINAL MEMBERS: Richie Furay, Jim Messina,
Rusty Young, George Grantham, Randy Meisner
LATER MEMBERS OF NOTE: Timothy B. Schmidt, Paul Cotton,
Charlie Harrison, Kim Bullard, Steve Chapman
BEST KNOWN SONG: Crazy Love (#17, 1979)

Poco is known more for the group's members than for the group's music. Richie Furay came from Buffalo Springfield. Jim Messina was also in Buffalo Springfield and later teamed with Kenny Loggins as Loggins and Messina. Randy Meisner left Poco before the first album was recorded to be a founding member of the Eagles. He was replaced in Poco by Timothy B. Schmidt. In an ironic twist of fate, Meisner was also replaced by Schmidt in the Eagles six years later.

This is not to denigrate the contribution made by Poco to the music scene. They carried on the country rock tradition of the Byrds, Buffalo Springfield, and the Flying Burrito Brothers into the 1970s and continued making music for four decades resulting in 13 top-100 hits.

The band made its first appearance at the famed Troubadour Club in West Hollywood in October 1968, billed as Pogo. For the next two gigs they decided to perform as R.F.D. before returning to Pogo. The new/old name was short-lived, however. Walt Kelly, creator of the daily comic strip also called *Pogo,* was not interested in sharing the name he had been using since 1948. Kelly slapped a cease-and-desist order on the group with the threat of a lawsuit if the name was not changed.

Realizing that their legal footing was shaky at best, Pogo capitulated. Not wanting to lose the goodwill created in their short five-month existence, the group made the very slight name amendment, changing Pogo to Poco.

www.noted.blogs.com; www.angelfire.com.

The Pretenders

GROUP FORMED IN: 1978
ORIGINAL MEMBERS: Chrissie Hynde, James
Honeyman-Scott, Pete Farndon, Gary Mackleduff
LATER MEMBERS OF NOTE: Martin Chambers,
Robbie McIntosh, Malcolm Foster, Billy Bremner, Tony
Butler, Blair Cunningham, T. M. Stevens, Johnny Marr
BEST KNOWN SONG: Brass in Pocket (#14, 1980)

Chrissie Hynde is a contradiction in terms. A woman who rocks like a man. An American who has lived abroad for much of her life. An animal über-activist who was a leather queen in her earlier days. An inductee in the Rock and Roll Hall of Fame who would just as soon not have been bothered with the "honor." But there is little evidence to contradict her influence on the rock music scene.

After recruiting the group, which would comprise the classic Pretenders lineup (Martin Chambers would replace Mackleduff after the first recording session), Hynde created a brand of punk/new wave music that was radio-friendly, thus bridging the gap in a way the Sex Pistols were unable to do.

Hynde's original choice for band names was The Rhythm Method, but she decided against using the name as it might prove a hindrance to radio airplay. Hynde confessed, "The important thing to me is songs on AM radio. That's what I was brought up on, that's what I love. I want to make music that's accessible to anybody."

The Pretenders' name is a reference to the Platters' "The Great Pretender." The song has particular meaning to Hynde. "Back before my band had settled on a name, this biker in a white-supremacy-type club took me into his room one day, bolted the door, and said he didn't want his friends to hear the song that meant the most to him," which was Sam Cooke's version of the song. Hynde hoped to affect people with her music on a deep level just as this tough man had been affected by the classic 1955 ballad.

www.pretendersarchives.com.

Procol Harum

GROUP FORMED IN: 1966
ORIGINAL MEMBERS: Gary Brooker, Keith Reid
(lyricist only–did not perform with the band), Matthew
Fisher, Ray Royer, David Knights
LATER MEMBERS OF NOTE: Robin Trower, B. J. Wilson,
Chris Copping, Mick Grabham, Geoff Whitehorn, Matt
Pegg, Mark Brzezicki, Josh Phillips, Geoff Dunn
BEST KNOWN SONG: A Whiter Shade of Pale (#5, 1967)

Procol Harum is one of the more unusual names from the rock era. The legacy of the group's music is much more mundane, including the monster Summer of Love hit "A Whiter Shade of Pale" and little else of note. But back in 1967, the band and its hit song encapsulated the spirit of the times and made them a whiter shade of hot, if only to lose their fire soon after.

Much speculation exists about the origin of the group's name. It was taken from the name of a pedigree Burmese cat belonging to a friend of Guy Stevens, a manager of the band. This begs the question: what in the world does it mean?

It has been suggested that Procol Harum is a Latin phrase translated as "beyond these things." This would make some sense for the name of a progressive rock band in the heyday of the psychedelic era. Unfortunately there is a snag. The actual spelling of the cat's name was Procul Harun. Further clouding the picture is the fact that the precisely accurate translation of "beyond these things" to Latin is "Procul His."

Keith Reid was asked about the name. "There was all this thing about what the name meant.... These were all things that came up after we were successful. We never knew Procol Harum had any Latin derivation or it might mean this or it might mean that. If we'd known about all that we'd been a lot cleverer."

Johansen, Claes. Procol Harum: Beyond the Pale. London: SAF Publishing, 2000.

Psychedelic Furs

GROUP FORMED IN: 1977
ORIGINAL MEMBERS: Richard Butler, Tim Butler,
Roger Morris, John Ashton, Duncan Kilburn
LATER MEMBERS OF NOTE: Vince Ely, Phil Calvert,
Mars Williams, Keith Forsey, Phil Garisto, Don
Yallitch, Frank Ferrer, Ed Buller
BEST KNOWN SONG: Heartbreak Beat (#26, 1987)

The Psychedelic Furs formed during the rise of punk in England and was considered a part of the genre with its droning guitars, saxophone, and Richard Butler's raspy, biting vocals. The group started out with the more punk sounding names of RKO and later Radio. Their style, though, became less punk and more pop with each successive album. Through it all, the Furs had a lengthy career spanning the punk scene to the alternative rock scene, and, in the process, being considered a strong participant in each genre as well as the New Romantic era in between.

For all of the genres the Furs would eventually embrace, the band's heart was in the psychedelic era of the 1960s. Punk rock rejected, among many other things, the psychedelic music movement of the late '60s. While the Furs's music did not bear a strong resemblance to the psychedelic movement, their attitude did. Punk was narrow-minded. The 1960s psychedelia movement was liberal-minded. As such, the Furs wanted a name that captured the wild animal trapped within the punk music framework.

While the group was still going by Radio, a new name was being contemplated — one including the word "psychedelic," according to Richard Butler, to reflect the band's state of mind. Butler felt the word needed to be used as an adjective along with a noun in order to create a descriptive image. He tried several combinations such as Psychedelic Shirts, Psychedelic Shoes, and, finally, Psychedelic Furs.

www.burneddowndays.com; www.last.fm.

Puddle of Mudd

GROUP FORMED IN: 1993

ORIGINAL MEMBERS: Wesley Scantlin, Jimmy Allen,
Kenny Burkett, Sean Samon
LATER MEMBERS OF NOTE: Douglas Ardito,
Paul Phillips, Greg Upchurch, Josh Freese
BEST KNOWN SONG: Blurry (#5, 2002)

Is Puddle of Mudd a group or just Wes Scantlin? It depends on who you ask. Scantlin grew up in Kansas City and had his sights set on rock music stardom from an early age. He was practicing with the original lineup of Jimmy Allen, Kenny Burkett, and Sean Samon in a building they rented for $80 per month near the Missouri River.

A torrential rain storm caused the Missouri River to topple its banks and flood the area, including the building where the new band was holding its practice sessions. Undeterred, the members showed up for practice wearing their grungiest pants and sneakers, waded through the debris downstairs, and got to work. Since the entire area was one big *puddle of mud*, they felt the name was apropos and added one extra "D" for good measure.

This ensemble cut two albums (the second, without Allen), but fame was elusive and the group disbanded. Scantlin continued to push his product and eventually got an audition with Fred Durst's label. He quickly assembled a group, including Burkett. The ad hoc group failed the audition but Durst's A&R man Danny Wimmer saw something he liked and invited Scantlin to disband and re-form the band with new members in Los Angeles. Scantlin took up the offer and left the others behind. The new version of Puddle of Mudd finally hit it big in 2002 with Scantlin and three new musicians and the release of five-time platinum album *Come Clean*. Finally Puddle of Mudd had arrived with Scantlin being the only constant.

www.wesscantlin.net; www.blog.myspace.com; www.pitch.com.

Pure Prairie League

GROUP FORMED IN: 1971
ORIGINAL MEMBERS: Craig Fuller, George Powell,
John Call, Jim Lanham, Tom McGrail, Phill Stokes
LATER MEMBERS OF NOTE: Vince Gill, Michael Connor, Billy Hinds, Mike
Reilly, Patrick Bolin, Curtis Wright, Rick Schell, Fats Kaplin
BEST KNOWN SONG: Amie (#27, 1975)

Pure Prairie League was formed in Ohio when Craig Fuller and George Powell combined their burgeoning songwriting talents. Fuller is self-effacing when describing the band's style. "Our music is an inept mixture of rock 'n' roll and country, just a melange of those two genres—kind of clumsy and thoughtless, actually. We just hope people are discerning enough to weed through it and take away what they like and leave the rest. We've never been too much involved in creation. We just stumble ahead."

For the record, Pure Prairie League is a soft country-rock band that was most successful from 1975 to 1981. Numerous personnel shifts and the changing tastes of the music-buying public kept the band from maintaining its early momentum. The group survived the disco era and made the charts again in 1980–81 with new lead singer Vince Gill, who the band had met when his band opened for them in Oklahoma City. Gill was onboard for only three albums before leaving to start his career as a country music superstar, but he left his legacy with the group by singing lead on their biggest hit, "Let Me Love You Tonight."

The name of the group comes from the movie *Dodge City*, starring Errol Flynn and Olivia de Havilland. It is the story of a lawless town in the old west. A group of elderly women, who are strongly associated with the temperance movement (dedicated to the modification or elimination of alcohol consumption), form an organization they call the Pure Prairie League. Original group drummer Tom McGrail was watching the movie and he receives credit for culling the name.

www.profile.myspace.com; www.classicrock.about.com.

Quarterflash

GROUP FORMED IN: 1980
ORIGINAL MEMBERS: Rindy Ross, Marv Ross,
Jack Charles, Rick DiGiallonardo, Rich
Gooch, Brian David Willis
LATER MEMBERS OF NOTE: none
BEST KNOWN SONG: Harden My Heart (#3, 1982)

Sax-heavy pop band Quarterflash represented the merger of two Portland, Oregon, bands, Pilot and Seafood Mama. The group continued under the latter name for a time with smooth-singing Rindy Ross fronting the band when not contributing the sax solos that became the group's trademark on such hits as "Harden My Heart," "Find Another Fool," and "Take Me to Heart."

This was very much a self-made band that benefited from the good fortune of being in the forefront of the MTV explosion. While still Seafood Mama, they recorded a four-song demo with a single microphone in the basement of Rindy and (husband and guitarist) Marv Ross's home. That demo included an early version of "Harden My Heart" for which 1,000 copies were pressed as a single to distribute to local radio stations and sell at gigs. The local demand for the single far exceeded the supply. Eventually it spread from Portland to Seattle radio stations and then across the country. Geffen records heard the song and presented Seafood Mama with a record deal.

Clearly the name had to go. The name Quarterflash was suggested by the group's producer, who had just returned from Australia and heard a popular Australian phrase that referred to newcomers to the country as "one-quarter flash and three-parts foolish." With the advent of MTV, the saying held even more significance, since music videos required groups to not only sound good but look good as well. The formula of adding a quarter-flash (visual image) to three-quarters substance (song) worked for many groups, including Quarterflash, with Rindy Ross to catch the eye.

www.classicrockrevisited.com.

Queen / Freddie Mercury

GROUP FORMED IN: 1971
ORIGINAL MEMBERS: Freddie Mercury
(born Farrokh Bulsara), Brian May,
Roger Taylor, John Deacon
LATER MEMBERS OF NOTE: Paul Rodgers
(Queen + Paul Rodgers)
BEST KNOWN SONG: Bohemian Rhapsody
(#9, 1976 and #2, 1992)

Headed by Freddie Mercury, one of the most flamboyant front men in rock music history (with perhaps the greatest pop music voice ever), Queen was the ultimate stadium rock band. They created the operatic/rock masterpiece "Bohemian Rhapsody," the double-sided anthem "We Will Rock You / We Are the Champions" (either one of which is played at almost every sporting event), and numerous other much-sampled tunes ("Under Pressure,"

"Another One Bites the Dust," and so forth). In 2001, Queen was inducted into the Rock and Roll Hall of Fame.

Freddie Mercury was born Farrokh Bulsara in Zanzibar, off the east coast of Africa. At St. Peter's boarding school he started his first band, the Hectics, which was named for his piano-playing style. At that time he began answering to the first name of Freddie. When Freddie was 16 his family moved to England, where he later studied graphic illustration at Ealing Art College. It was at this point that Freddie met Brian May, who was playing in a band called Smile with his roommate, Roger Taylor.

When Smile broke up, Freddie persuaded May and Taylor to join him in the creation of a new band. Freddie then changed his last name to Mercury, which was his astrological ruling planet. Mercury had already decided on the name for the new group, for which John Deacon was recruited to play bass. The name would be Queen. Many assume Queen is a reference to Mercury's homosexuality, and it may have been, although Mercury never directly admitted such. He simply said, "The concept of Queen is to be regal and majestic. Glamour is a part of us and we want to be dandy. We want to shock and be outrageous."

www.queenarchives.com; www.geocities.com.

? & The Mysterians

GROUP FORMED IN: 1962
ORIGINAL MEMBERS: ? (born Rudy Martinez
but aka Reeto Rodriguez), Larry Borjas, Robert
"Bobby" Balderrama, Robert Martinez
LATER MEMBERS OF NOTE: Frank Rodriguez, Frank
Lugo, Eddie Serrato, Rudy Rodriguez, Mel Schacher
BEST KNOWN SONG: 96 Tears (#1, 1966)

This Mexican-American band is considered by many to be the first punk rock band and one of the legendary garage bands, though they only mustered one top-40 hit after their anthemic hit, "96 Tears." Eccentric front man Rudy Martinez legally changed his name to the question mark symbol and has answered to it ever since. The group's signature song was written by him but was originally entitled "Too Many Teardrops" and later to the slightly risqué "69 Tears" before he changed the name to its current title in order to deflect any controversy that might limit its airplay.

The band was originally called simply The Mysterians. The name came

from the 1957 science fiction Japanese film of the same name. ? explained later
how the band finally came upon the name. "We played around the Flint, Saginaw, Bay City area. Never Detroit. We were called 'The Mysterians, X, Y, Z'
and I was Question Mark. I thought the three letters were mysterious letters
of the alphabet and my thing was 'Why can't those letters start the alphabet?
Is there any reason why ABC has to be there and not XYZ?'"

"The DJ at one radio station kept saying Question Mark and The Mysterians. People thought it was two groups... Question Mark and the other group
was The Mysterians. Nobody told people there's only one band. So, before "96
Tears," we had to go on the radio and say, 'When you hear Question Mark and
The Mysterians, it's gonna be one group, not two groups.' So that's how it got
from The Mysterians to ? & the Mysterians."

www.classicbands.com.

Radiohead

GROUP FORMED IN: 1989
ORIGINAL MEMBERS: Thom Yorke, Jonny Greenwood,
Colin Greenwood, Ed O'Brien, Phil Selway
LATER MEMBERS OF NOTE: none
BEST KNOWN SONG: Creep (#34, 1993)

Radiohead is a British band that came to the fore in the Britpop era but
is known for more of an alternative sound from its three guitar lineup and
chip-on-the-shoulder lyrics. Originally calling themselves On a Friday (referring to the day the band met for practice), the quintet formed at Abingdon
School just outside of Oxford in 1986. For a time the band members decided
to concentrate more on university studies, but when On a Friday rejoined in
earnest four years later they signed a record deal with the EMI-owned Par-
lophone label. Early on they met with some criticism of the group name from
NME, which called it a "beer swilling Friday night moniker."

The names first considered were Gravitate, Music, and Jude, the latter
taken from a Thomas Hardy novel called *Jude The Obscure*, about a man vainly
trying to get into Oxford University and driving himself insane in the process.

The group ultimately looked across the pond and took the name Radiohead from a track on the Talking Heads album *True Stories* (the song was technically called "Radio Head"—two words). Thom Yorke later explained,
"Radiohead was cool and it is still cool because it just sums up all these things

about receiving stuff and ... all these people in America have these teeth you can pick up radio on. They have this sort of metal in their teeth and some of them can pick up radio with it. I think that is very cool."

Jonny Greenwood views things in a more cynical light. "The radio is everywhere ... I really hate the idea of radio waves being inescapable. Wherever you go, they're going through you. It's horrible."

Clarke, Martin. Hysterical and Useless. *Medford, NJ: Plexus, 1999.*

Rage Against the Machine

GROUP FORMED IN: 1991
ORIGINAL MEMBERS: Zach de la Rocha, Tom Morello,
Brad Wilk, Tim Commerford ("Timmy C")
LATER MEMBERS OF NOTE: None
BEST KNOWN SONG: Bulls on Parade
(#62-airplay chart, 1996)

Agree with them or not, Rage Against the Machine (RATM) is a group with principles. Espousing hard-line leftist beliefs, they are America's 1990s version of the Sex Pistols insofar as what was said was more important than how it was presented. It's the aesthetic of lyrics over music. And few have come across espousing such fierce polemics since the Pistols as has RATM.

The group has not been beyond the reach of criticism. They have been accused of hypocrisy for supporting the machinery of media conglomerate Sony Records, of which Epic Records (their label) was a subsidiary. The group defended themselves by claiming the alliance with the major label was a necessity in order to facilitate their communication with the masses through the best means available.

The group name was originally slated as the title for an album of Zach de la Rocha's former group, Inside Out. The phrase was coined by Ebullition Records founder Kent McLard in his zine *No Answers.* The album was never released, leaving the powerful phrase in need of usage. According to de la Rocha, "I wanted to think of something metaphorical that described my frustrations living in a political and economic system which fuels itself off the blood of oppressed people all over the world for the last five centuries. A machine doesn't

have any humane understanding. To me, it was the perfect metaphor to describe
the structure of the establishment."

Devenish, Colin. Rage against the Machine. *New York: St. Martin's Griffin, 2001.*

Ramones

GROUP FORMED IN: 1974
ORIGINAL MEMBERS: Johnny Cummings
("Johnny Ramone"), Jeff Human ("Joey Ramone"),
Douglas Colvin ("Dee Dee Ramone"), Tommy
Erdelyi ("Tommy Ramone")
LATER MEMBERS OF NOTE: Marc Bell
("Marky Ramone"), Richard Beau ("Richie
Ramone"), Chris Ward ("CJ Ramone"),
Clem Burke ("Elvis Ramone")
BEST KNOWN SONG: Rock and Roll High
School (unreleased, 1979)

According to *The Rock Snob*s Dictionary*, the word "seminal" describes
any group in on a trend too early to sell any records. To no act does this term
apply more than the Ramones. They were *the* seminal punk rock group.
Although punk was perfected and mostly appreciated in England, the Clash,
Buzzcocks, and Sex Pistols all owe a tip of the cap to their American "forefathers." The Ramones captured the punk ideals better than their CBGBs contemporaries by putting less thought and more energy into the group's music
and performances.

There was no member of the band originally named Ramone. In fact, Paul
McCartney was technically the first Ramone. In the early Beatle days, when
that group was still the Silver Beatles, the fabs enjoyed nicknames such as
Johnny Silver (Lennon), George Perkins (Harrison), and Paul Ramone
(McCartney).

Douglas Colvin "thought it was pretty outrageous to change your name
to a made-up one, but I liked the idea. I was lost in another fantasy, and changed
from Douglas Colvin to Dee Dee Ramone." The others followed suit, as did all
future members. Several changed or varied their first names as well. But Ramone
was not just a name, it was an attitude, just like the music they played.

Ramone, Dee Dee, with Veronica Kofman. Poison Heart: Surviving the Ramones. *Richmond
Hill, Ontario: Fire Fly, 1997; Kamp, David, and Steven Daly.* The Rock Snob*s Dictionary. *New
York: Broadway Books, 2005.*

Red Hot
Chili Peppers

GROUP FORMED IN: 1983
ORIGINAL MEMBERS: Anthony Kiedis,
Hillel Slovak, Flea (born Michael Balzary), Jack Irons
LATER MEMBERS OF NOTE: John Frusciante,
Chad Smith, Zander Schloss, Arik Marshall,
Dave Navarro, Jack Sherman, Dwayne
"Blackbyrd" McKnight, Jesse Tobias,
Cliff Martinez, D.H. Peligro
BEST KNOWN SONG: Under the Bridge (#2, 1992)

This groundbreaking group was the first to fuse punk, funk, metal, and rap, thus opening the door for such later acts as Living Colour and Faith No More. The Peppers started out as Tony Flow and the Miraculously Majestic Masters of Mayhem until they secured a record deal with EMI. At that time it became obvious the existing name would not suffice.

According to Anthony Kiedis in his biography *Scar Tissue,* "We started going through these huge laundry lists of idiotic, meaningless, boring names." Though several people claim creating the name Red Hot Chili Peppers, Kiedis knows how it was derived: "It's a derivation of a classic old-school Americana blues or jazz name. There was Louis Armstrong with his Hot Five, and other bands that has 'Red Hot' this or 'Chili' that. There was even an English band that was called Chilli Willi and the Red Hot Peppers, who later thought we had stolen their name."

"No one had ever been the Red Hot Chili Peppers, a name that would forever be a blessing and a curse. If you think of Red Hot Chili Peppers in terms of a feeling, a sensation, or an energy, it makes perfect sense for our band, but if you think of it in terms of a vegetable, it takes on all these hokey connotations. There's a restaurant chain named after the vegetable, and chili peppers have been merchandised in everything from home-decoration hangings to Christmas tree ornaments. Suffice to say we were wierded out when people started bringing chili peppers to our shows as some kind of offering."

Kiedis, Anthony. Scar Tissue. *New York: Hyperion, 2004.*

R.E.M.

GROUP FORMED IN: 1980
ORIGINAL MEMBERS: Michael Stipe, Peter
Buck, Mike Mills, Bill Berry
LATER MEMBERS OF NOTE: Bill Rieflin
BEST KNOWN SONG: Losing My Religion (#4, 1991)

Michael Stipe and Peter Buck began working together while both were at the University of Georgia in 1980. Not long after, they added fellow Bulldogs Mike Mills and Bill Berry with limited expectations of success. But with practice came gigs, and the momentum built upon itself, ultimately resulting in R.E.M. becoming the hardest working band in the 1980s with their album-per-year output and relentless touring. More importantly, they were at the wheel as post-punk was transformed to alternative during this time frame, making it one of the most influential bands of the past 25 years.

Although success came slowly, the group didn't put much initial thought into its name. Going by the Twisted Kites, they played birthday parties and small venues at first, rehearsing in a converted Episcopalian church. As they became better known a change of name was considered. To offend people the group considered the name "Can of Piss," but, according to Buck, "we didn't want to be called something that we couldn't tell our parents or have to mumble. R.E.M. just popped out of the dictionary one night. We needed something that wouldn't typecast us because, hell, we didn't even know what we were gonna do. So R.E.M. was nice — it didn't lock us into anything."

R.E.M. refers to the stage of sleep characterized by rapid movement of the eyes, ergo rapid eye movement or R.E.M. The ambiguity was initially attractive to Buck and the rest of the guys but, thanks to the guys from Athens, Georgia, the term has since become more synonymous with edgy, smart guitar-driven rock than with sleeping.

Sullivan, Denise. R.E.M. Talk about the Passion: An Oral History. Grass Valley, CA: Underwood-Miller, 1994.

REO Speedwagon

GROUP FORMED IN: 1971

ORIGINAL MEMBERS: Terry Luttrell, Gary Richrath, Gregg Philbin, Neal Doughty, Alan Gratzer
LATER MEMBERS OF NOTE: Kevin Cronin, Mike Murphy, Bruce Hall, Miles Joseph, Graham Lear, Dave Amato, Jesse Harms, Bryan Hitt
BEST KNOWN SONG: Keep on Loving You (#1, 1981)

REO Speedwagon is widely considered, along with Styx and Journey, as one of the big-3 American arena rock bands from 1978 to 1985. However, their history goes back many years before and it continued with very few lineup changes well beyond.

Neal Doughty and Alan Gratzer were students at the University of Illinois in 1968. They were in the same dorm and became friends. Gratzer was in a local campus band and Doughty went to watch them play. Doughty was not in the band but played with them on keyboards from time to time. Although the band was not happy with their keyboard player, he was the band's leader. Rather than fire the keyboard player, the other members quit and formed a new band with Doughty. This band mostly dispersed upon graduation so Gratzer, Doughty, and Gregg Philbin added Gary Richrath and Terry Lutrell. Kevin Cronin joined the next year.

When asked about the group's name, Doughty recounts, "I sometimes say that's the only thing I learned in college. I was in a class which studied the history of transportation and one day I walked in and 'REO Speedwagon' was written across the blackboard. It was the first high-speed, heavy-duty truck and was considered a milestone in automotive history. The R-E-O stood for Ransom Eli Olds, the man who later started Oldsmobile. We had just started to look for a name that very day and the other guys liked it immediately. We've never been known by anything else."

www.classicrockrevisited.com; www.speedwagon.uk.com.

Paul Revere & the Raiders

GROUP FORMED IN: 1960
ORIGINAL MEMBERS: Paul Revere (born Paul Revere Dick), Mark Lindsay, "Mooney" White, Dick White, Jerry Labrum

LATER MEMBERS OF NOTE: Jim "Harpo" Valley,
Phil "Fang" Volk, Mike "Smitty" Smith, Drake Levin,
Freddie Weller, Charlie Coe, Joe Correro, Jr., Keith
Allison, Darrin Medley, Daniel Krause,
Doug Heath, Ron Foos
BEST KNOWN SONG: Indian Reservation (#1, 1971)

You may be surprised to know that Paul Revere was not the lead singer of the group that bears his name. You may not care. Either way, it's a fact. The lead singer for most of the group's hits was Mark Lindsay. He and Paul met at the bakery where Lindsay worked. Together they formed a group called The Downbeats, which Lindsay christened after seeing the name on a magazine on his saxophone instructor's coffee table.

Revere was a keyboard player who was born with the name of Paul Revere Dick, as an homage to the Revolutionary War hero. During this time he was going by the name of Revere Dick (no joke). After forming The Downbeats, Revere drove to California to secure a record deal, which he did with Gardena Records.

Revere recalls, "When they found out my real name was Paul Revere, they said, 'you gotta use that as a gimmick.' And so they came up with Paul Revere and The Raiders." Under this new name the group took full advantage of the gimmick by dressing in American Revolutionary War uniforms, which they first used at a fraternity party gig.

In 1970 the group decided to shorten the name to just The Raiders in order to "hip it up" but, as Revere said, "it confused people, 'cause they didn't know if 'The Raiders' and 'Paul Revere and The Raiders' were the same group. They thought maybe I'd left the group. So that was a stupid idea. So we went back to Paul Revere and The Raiders."

www.marklindsay.com; www.classicbands.com.

The Righteous Brothers

GROUP FORMED IN: 1962
ORIGINAL MEMBERS: Bill Medley, Bobby Hatfield
LATER MEMBERS OF NOTE: none
BEST KNOWN SONG: You've Lost That
Lovin' Feelin' (#1, 1965)

The Righteous Brothers were the personification of "blue-eyed soul," a term that followed Bill Medley and Bobby Hatfield throughout their long, illustrious career together. The term is something of a misnomer since it technically refers to white artists (not just blue-eyed artists) who perform soul and rhythm and blues music. Many of the artists so labeled were unwittingly believed to be black, and the Righteous Brothers certainly fooled a few radio listeners in their early days.

Medley and Hatfield began singing together as members of a five-piece group called The Paramours. Hatfield recounts how he and Medley came up with the name for their duo, "Well, we got our name working in a little club in Orange County, California. We were doing a lot of rhythm and blues at the time. And the longer we worked together we started doing more and more duets. On this one particular evening there were several black Marines in there and when Bill and I finished doing a duet, one of them yelled out 'That's righteous, brothers.' Later on, after we dropped the name The Paramours, we started thinking about a name and I don't know which one of us it was but one of us said, 'How about The Righteous Brothers?' And there it is."

The duo came to national prominence when they hooked up with Phil Spector and released their signature song, "You've Lost That Lovin' Feelin'," in late 1964. The two remained together (with the exception of 1968–74 when Medley went solo) until Hatfield's death just before a performance in 2003, the same year they were inducted into the Rock and Roll Hall of Fame.

www.righteousbrothers.com.

Smokey Robinson & the Miracles

GROUP FORMED IN: 1955
ORIGINAL MEMBERS: William "Smokey"
Robinson, Emerson Rogers, Bobby Rogers,
Ronnie White, Warren "Pete" Moore
LATER MEMBERS OF NOTE: Claudette Rogers,
Dave Finley, Tee Turner, Mark Scott, Clarence
Dawson, James Grice, Billy Griffin, Sidney Justin
BEST KNOWN SONG: The Tears
of a Clown (#1, 1970)

Little William Robinson grew up in the ghetto of Detroit listening to and

emulating Jackie Wilson and others. It is no wonder that Motown was successful, considering Aretha Franklin, Diana Ross, the Temptations, and the Four
Tops all came from the area as well. As a child, his uncle nicknamed him
"Smokey Joe" Robinson because the youngster loved going to see westerns on
the big screen. Smokey stuck as a lifetime moniker.

Smokey and four school friends formed a doo-wop group called The Five
Chimes in 1955 at Northern High School. Two members left and were replaced
by brothers Emerson and Bobby Rogers. At this point the group name was
changed a second time, this time to The Matadors.

When Emerson went into the military, his sister Claudette took his place.
She and Smokey harmonized so well that they ended up getting married in
1959. The Matadors came to the attention of Berry Gordy, who was a manager
and the primary songwriter for Jackie Wilson. The Matadors auditioned for Wilson's managers who were scouting talent. Gordy met with Robinson later and
that meeting led to a record deal.

Since The Matadors had added a woman, it was felt the name was no longer
appropriate. A new name was suggested: The Miracles. By 1967 they became
Smokey Robinson & the Miracles until Robinson left to pursue a solo career
in 1971 and the Miracles continued on without him.

www.history-of-rock.com; www.rockstar.ning.com; www.songwritershalloffame.org.

The Rolling Stones

GROUP FORMED IN: 1963
ORIGINAL MEMBERS: Mick Jagger, Keith Richards,
Brian Jones, Bill Wyman, Charlie Watts
LATER MEMBERS OF NOTE: Mick Taylor,
Ron Wood, Darryl Jones
BEST KNOWN SONG: (I Can't Get No)
Satisfaction (#1, 1965)

The Rolling Stones are rock's ultimate cats. They have managed to easily and almost seamlessly jump between different musical trends and styles,
exhibiting numerous "lives" along the way. From the blues-influenced early
sounds to British psychedelia of the late '60s to songs with a social conscience
to disco in the '70s to straight-ahead stripped down rock in the '80s and
beyond, the Stones have brought legions of fans into the fold with each incarnation without alienating their fan base. When combined with the reputation
as one of the premier live bands and their solid 40-plus years in the business,

the Stones can lay strong claim to the title of greatest rock and roll band of all time.

Funny, then, that the origin of the group name should be so mundane. According to Keith Richards, Brian Jones was on the phone to a local paper (*Jazz News*) to advertise the group. When the newspaper representative asked the name he was momentarily stumped for an answer, since the band had never formally agreed on one. The phone call was long distance and every second was costing precious money, so the guys were pressing Jones to wrap up the call as soon as possible. In his haste, Jones spied a record by Muddy Waters face down in front of him. The first song on the album was "Rollin' Stone Blues" and he blurted out, "I don't know ... the Rollin' Stones."

Mick confirmed the story, though he was under the impression *he* came up with the name. "We advertised for gigs—I don't think we got anything from the ad." Au contraire. A legendary name was born for a legendary rock band.

Holland, Jools, and Dora Loewenstein. The Rolling Stones: A Life on the Road. *New York: Penguin Studio, 1998.*

Roxette

GROUP FORMED IN: 1986
ORIGINAL MEMBERS: Per Gessle, Marie Fredriksson
LATER MEMBERS OF NOTE: none
BEST KNOWN SONG: The Look (#1, 1989)

Most casual music fans are not aware that six of Roxette's first seven American hits went to the top two, with four going all the way to number one. Then, just as suddenly as Roxette burst onto the music scene, the duo lost the secret formula and were unable to score any further top-30 hits in the United States. As a result, most dismiss the group as a flash-in-the-pan, which, while somewhat appropriate, diminishes their tremendous early accomplishments. They are a close second to ABBA as the most successful Swedish band on the American pop charts, and they accomplished the feat in six fewer productive years.

Roxette is the Swedish duo of Per Gessle and Marie Fredriksson. Not romantically linked, the two got together in 1986 while Per was a member of the group Gyllene Tider (Swedish for "golden times") and Marie had a burgeoning solo career. When they first met they disliked each other — she thought he was a yuppie mama's boy and he thought she was a wild hippie. Their paths had crossed several times in the recording studio and Marie actually ended up singing backing vocals on occasion for Gyllene Tider.

When the two combined their respective talents they chose the name Rox-ette, taken from a song of the same name by British pub rock band Dr. Feel-good. This band happened to be a particular favorite of Per, having a higher profile in Europe than America. The Dr. Feelgood song "Roxette" was never a hit in the United States and Dr. Feelgood was never able to place a song in the U.S. top-100. Gyllene Tider had actually used the name Roxette in 1984 when being marketed in the United States, but this usage ceased when the duo took over the moniker.

www.mariefredriksson.com; www.faqs.org.

Roxy Music

GROUP FORMED IN: 1971
ORIGINAL MEMBERS: Bryan Ferry, Andy Mackay,
Graham Simpson, Brian Eno, Phil
Manzanera, Paul Thompson
LATER MEMBERS OF NOTE: Eddie Jobson, Rik Kenton,
John Porter, John Wetton, John Gustafson
BEST KNOWN SONG: Love Is the Drug (#30, 1976)

Too prog for glam, too glam for prog, the early version of Roxy Music walked that tightrope, denying the critics the ability to neatly categorize its style or music. The group was heavily influenced by pop art, since Bryan Ferry had studied in Newcastle under one of the genre's innovators, Richard Hamil-ton, who was to Roxy Music what Andy Warhol was to the Velvet Underground. Their style and sense of fashion, together with the quintet's smooth lead singer and androgynous keyboard/synth player, Brian Eno, in many ways presaged Duran Duran.

Drawing on Ferry's art school background, the band considered names drawn from a list of cinemas, including Odeon, Gaumont, and Essoldo. These were in the running, but, according to Ferry, "they didn't really mean anything except that they were a place you went to escape everyday life." Roxy was the one name that really struck a responsive chord. It was both mundane and evoca-tive at the same time. It stood for glamour, excitement, and decadence.

At first the group called itself simply Roxy, but later discovered an Amer-ican band had beaten them to the punch and had even released an album the year before. When the group expanded the name to 'Roxy Music' (originally *with* single quotation marks as part of the name), they soon decided this was an improvement inasmuch as it portrayed their own way of viewing the pop scene, as if Roxy Music was a genre all unto itself. In a sense, it was. Just ask the frustrated critics.

Buckley, David. The Thrill of It All: The Story of Bryan Ferry & Roxy Music. *Chicago: Chicago Review Press, 2004.*

Rush

GROUP FORMED IN: 1968
ORIGINAL MEMBERS: Alex Lifeson (born Alex Zivojinovich), Jeff Jones, John Rutsey
LATER MEMBERS OF NOTE: Geddy Lee (born Gary Lee Weinrib), Neil Peart, Lindy Young, Joe Perna
BEST KNOWN SONG: Tom Sawyer (#44, 1981)

Rush is one of the most musically gifted groups in rock history, yet they have received their share of critics over the years. Most criticisms appear petty, such as (1) their prog-rock beginnings, (2) Geddy Lee's high-pitched vocals, or (3) their series of science fiction album themes. Those who are not troubled by these issues recognize the virtuosity of the players, particularly Peart, who many consider to be the greatest drummer in rock history.

The earliest form of the band was created in Canada in 1968 by John Rutsey and Alex Lifeson, who had changed his name from Zivojinovich ("Lifeson" is the literal translation from Serbo-Croatian). The duo called their group Projection. By September of that year they added Jeff Jones for bass and lead vocals. The first gig came at a local coffee shop call the Coff-In, which was located in the basement of an old Anglican church. The trio was attempting to make a frantic last-minute name change but was having trouble coming up with anything in their rushed condition. John's older brother Bill thought Rush would be appropriate under the situation and the others agreed.

Rush soon replaced Jones with Geddy Lee, whose real name was Gary Lee Weinrib. His stage name came compliments of his Jewish mother who pronounced Gary with such a harsh accent it always sounded like she was saying "Geddy." Various personnel changes took place including Lee leaving (while gone, the band became Hadrian). Lee returned, the band became Rush again, and Peart joined in 1974. Since then the lineup has not changed from the Canadian trio we know today.

www.nimitz.net; www.rush.robpagano.com.

Savage Garden

GROUP FORMED IN: 1994
ORIGINAL MEMBERS: Darren Hayes, Daniel Jones
LATER MEMBERS OF NOTE: none
BEST KNOWN HIT: Truly Madly Deeply (#1, 1998)

In 1993 Daniel Jones, a member and producer of the group Red Edge, placed an advertisement in the Brisbane, Australia, newspaper *Time Off* seeking a new vocalist for the band. Darren Hayes answered the ad and got the job despite a shaky audition. The Red Edge split after failed record contract negotiations, allowing Hayes and Jones to establish a group of their own.

The duo searched for a name for their new endeavor. Their first choice was Crush, which was being used by another Australian band. In order to use the name they purchased the rights, however, not before discovering a band in England was using the name and rising to prominence, thus ending Crush as an option.

Next Hayes and Jones made a list of new name possibilities. Among them were Dante's Inferno and Bliss, but the name selected was Savage Garden. Hayes is a fan of author Anne Rice, who penned *The Vampire Chronicles,* a series of novels revolving around Lestat de Lioncourt, a French nobleman made into a vampire. The second novel was entitled *The Vampire Lestat* from which the group drew its name. A line taken from the book begins "The mind of each man is a savage garden...."

Hayes explained the allure of the phrase. "Anne talks about the world as a savage garden. There are two levels. One is beautiful but in the other, underneath, we're all savage beasts. We thought that was quite fitting — but we don't want to sound too poncy. It's all just pop music."

Rice, Anne. The Vampire Lestat: The Second Book in the Chronicle of the Vampires. *New York: Ballantine, 1985; www.home.swipnet.se; www.arts.enotes.com.*

Scorpions

GROUP FORMED IN: 1969
ORIGINAL MEMBERS: Rudolf Schenker,
Klaus Meine, Michael Schenker, Lothar
Heimberg, Wolfgang Dziony

LATER MEMBERS OF NOTE: Ulrich Roth, Francis
Buchholz, Jurgen Rosenthal, Rudy Lenners, Matthias
Jabs, Herman Rarebell, Ralph Rieckermann,
Curt Cress, James Kottak, Pawel Maciwoda
BEST KNOWN SONG: Rock You Like
a Hurricane (#25, 1984)

Many would be surprised that the earliest stirrings of the band that became the Scorpions occurred just one year after The Beatles' coming out party in America. More than four decades later, the heavy metal band from Hannover, Germany, is still rocking like a hurricane.

Rudolf Schenker spoke about his early years. "Initially I chose football (soccer) because guitar playing was a bit too complicated. But after I came across bands like The Beatles, The Rolling Stones, and The Kinks, I told myself, 'This is what I want to do—play in a rock band.' The first incarnation of Scorpions was ... not known as Scorpions then. We were known as the 'Nameless.' Why? Because we couldn't decide on what to name the band."

Germany has never been known as a hotbed for heavy metal. The members of Scorpions do not betray their German heritage but feel they were born in the wrong country for their musical tastes. Despite toiling in virtual anonymity from the American music fans during their first 13 years as a full-fledged band, they built a following in Europe until their breakthrough in the United States in 1982 with "No One Like You."

The Scorpions's sound dovetailed perfectly into the heavy metal scene of the early 1980s when AC/DC, Iron Maiden, and Judas Priest were banging heads. However, Scorpions always evinced a melodic quality to their songs not always present in the genre, making the band more mainstream radio friendly, and leading to total record sales of over 22 million worldwide.

www.anwarbizri.tripod.com/scorpions.htm; www.diamonddavidleeroth.com.

Scritti Politti

GROUP FORMED IN: 1977
ORIGINAL MEMBERS: Green Gartside
(born Paul Julian Strohmeyer), Nial Jinks,
Tom Morley, Matthew Kay
LATER MEMBERS OF NOTE: Marcus Miller,
David Gamson, Fred Maher
BEST KNOWN SONG: Perfect Way (#11, 1985)

Scritti Politti is the vehicle of Green Gartside, a Welsh singer-songwriter who grew up with strong communist leanings. He changed his name from Paul Julian Strohmeyer by pairing his step-father's surname with a first name taken from the color of the Welsh countryside. While in college at Leeds Polytechnic, Gartside enlisted his childhood friends Nial Jinks and Tom Morley together with Matthew Kay and, heavily influenced by the Sex Pistols, set out to make a name in the punk revolution.

Before any significant success was achieved, Gartside suffered serious heart problems, which required his convalescence for nearly a year. When his health permitted a return to the band, Gartside had changed musical direction to a more synth-pop style, which moved the group to the vanguard of the 1980s music scene instead of following and copying the punk scene of the 1970s. The breakthrough American hit, "Perfect Way," did not come until 1985, but it remains one of the most recognized songs of the New Romantic era.

The name of the band was chosen as an homage to Italian Marxist theorist Antonio Gramsci (1891–1937). *Scritti Politici*, written while Gramsci was in prison, translates from Italian to mean "political writings." Gartside decided to change the spelling slightly in order to give the name a more accessible sound, not unlike Tutti Frutti. Also, Gartside says "politti" was an English word that stood for "any group of individuals who get together for the purpose of working towards a set of aims."

www.everything2.com; www.dosswerks.com.

Sex Pistols

GROUP FORMED IN: 1975
ORIGINAL MEMBERS: Steve Jones, Paul Cook,
Glen Matlock, John Lyndon ("Johnny Rotten")
LATER MEMBERS OF NOTE: John Ritchie
("Sid Vicious")
BEST KNOWN SONG: God Save the
Queen (uncharted in U.S., 1977)

Known more for what they said and how they presented it, rather than how it sounded, the Sex Pistols were certainly one of a kind. As opposed to the innumerable posers since, this group truly disdained the pop music and fashion scenes, but they saved their most angry nihilism for the British establishment. The Pistols were the greatest force among the progenitors of punk rock and eventually grunge. Like them or hate them (you can't be on the fence), it is impossible to deny their impact on pop culture.

The Sex Pistols were largely the creation of their manager, Malcolm McLaren, general huckster and owner of a clothes shop called "Sex." Although the group members had known Johnny Lyndon for three months, he was so secretive and mistrustful he hadn't told them his surname. He was always spitting, blowing his nose, and inspecting his rotting teeth. Steve Jones once said to Lyndon, in all sincerity, "You're fucking rotten!" partly because of his attitude and partly because of his hygiene. Johnny Lyndon *was* Johnny Rotten.

Some of the names considered for the band were Le Bomb, Subterraneans, Beyond, and Teenage Novel. McLaren wanted the name of his shop in the group name. He suggested (demanded?) the group be named the Sex Pistols, with the obvious connotation of sex and violence. Jones favored the name, while Rotten and Matlock were looking for something even more offensive. Cook preferred something more reasonable. McLaren didn't care as long as it would make him some money.

Lyndon, John, with Keith Zimmerman and Kent Zimmerman. Rotten: No Irish — No Blacks — No Dogs. *New York: Picador USA, 1994; Savage, Jon.* England's Dreaming: Anarchy, Sex Pistols, Punk Rock & Beyond. *New York: St. Martin's Griffin, 2002.*

Simple Minds

GROUP FORMED IN: 1978
ORIGINAL MEMBERS: Jim Kerr, Alan McNeil,
Charlie Burchill, Brian McGee, Tony Donald, John Milarky
LATER MEMBERS OF NOTE: Duncan Barnwell, Michael
"Mick" MacNeil, Derek Forbes, Paul Wishart, Kenny
Hyslop, Mike Ogletree, Mel Gaynor, John Giblin, Robin
Clarke, Sue Hadjopoulous, Malcolm Foster, Lisa Germano,
Annie McCaig, Andy Duncan, Peter Vettese, Mark Taylor,
Mark Schulman, Eddie Duffy, Mark Kerr, Kevin
Hunter, Gordon Goudie, Andy Gillespie
BEST KNOWN SONG: Don't You
(Forget about Me) (#1, 1985)

The three-decades-long career of Simple Minds started as Johnny & the Self Abusers in Glasgow, Scotland. The band was influenced in its early days by American punk (Lou Reed, Iggy Pop, The Stooges) and later by the glam-rock and prog-rock forces of England, most notably David Bowie, Peter Gabriel's Genesis, and Roxy Music.

When Johnny & the Self Abusers split into two factions, the Jim Kerr/Charlie Burchill group decided to call itself Simple Minds from a line in the Bowie song called "The Jean Genie." The phrase is taken from the line "He's so simple minded, he can't drive his module." It was speculated Bowie was referring to his friend Iggy Pop in this lyric, but he demurs that it is rather "an Iggy-type character ... it wasn't *actually* Iggy."

Bowie was the catalyst for Kerr's musical direction, "when Bowie and the rest of these people wheeled into town, it is not an exaggeration to say that my life changed. I knew that there was something else out there. I was just a part of that generation of kids that went on to have bands ... so much of it leads to Bowie, Roxy, Iggy, and the Velvet Underground. It was through people like David Bowie — his charisma, the songs, the atmosphere, that propelled us to even dare to write songs of our own."

www.simple-minds.demon.co.uk; www.simpleminds.org.uk.

Siouxsie & the Banshees

GROUP FORMED IN: 1976
ORIGINAL MEMBERS: Siouxsie Sioux (born
Susan Dallion), Steven Severin (born Steven Bailey,
a/k/a Steve Spunker), John McKay, Kenny Morris
LATER MEMBERS OF NOTE: Budgie (born Peter Clark),
Sid Vicious, Billy Idol, Robert Smith, Marco Pirroni,
Peter Fenton, John McGeogh, John Valentine
Carruthers, Martin McCarrick
BEST KNOWN SONG: Kiss Them
for Me (#23, 1991)

Casual music fans have heard of Siouxsie & the Banshees but consider them a one-hit wonder, if they consider them at all. Nothing could be further from the truth. They actually had *two* U.S. top-100 hits (and *18* in the United Kingdom). Of course, the band's pop chart output doesn't begin to reflect its importance to the history of rock music. Such diverse acts as Jane's Addiction, The Jesus and Mary Chain, Garbage and The Cure have all professed to having been influenced by Siouxsie & the Banshees.

Siouxsie Sioux is one of the seminal female punk rock icons, with cultural status up along with Patti Smith and Deborah Harry. In the punk scene from its inception, Sioux could be as shocking and abrasive as Smith, but as seductive and sexual as Harry. Her authenticity came from being unaffected by either persona. Her band's initial run of over two decades is a testimony to its ability to evolve with the music scene while maintaining and even broadening its fan base.

Sioux chose her stage name in support of the Sioux Indian tribe, or more correctly, from her dislike of cowboys. The group's name came from the 1970 Vincent Price horror film *Cry of the Banshee*, which the band viewed just before making their debut at the Punk Festival held at London's 100 Club in 1976. The dark movie was loosely based on some themes of Edgar Allen Poe from his work of the same name.

www.thebansheesandothercreatures.co.uk; www.news.bbc.co.uk

Sixpence None the Richer

GROUP FORMED IN: 1992
ORIGINAL MEMBERS: Leigh Nash,
Matt Slocum, T. J. Behling,
LATER MEMBERS OF NOTE: Tess Wiley, J. J. Plasencio,
Dale Baker, Sean Kelly, Justin Carry, Jerry Dale
McFadden, Rob Mitchell
BEST KNOWN SONG: Kiss Me (#2, 1999)

Sixpence None the Richer was born out of the Contemporary Christian music scene and crossed over to the pop music charts on the strength of its infectious hit "Kiss Me," which featured the sweet, wispy vocals of Leigh Nash. While the "sixpence" part of the name implies that the group is of English heritage, it is actually an American band from Texas, which relocated to Nashville, Tennessee.

The name was taken from a story in the C. S. Lewis book entitled *Mere Christianity*, wherein Lewis adapted a series of BBC radio chats during World War II to explain his religious philosophies and chronicle his conversion from atheism to Christianity. Although written with an aim to avoid controversy, *Mere Christianity* was not entirely accepted on its face. In one such passage Lewis argues Jesus must be considered either the son of God or a lunatic, but not just a great moral teacher, for any mere mortal who spoke as Jesus spoke would have to be considered crazy.

Nash explained the story that begat the group name's origin as follows: "A little boy asks his father if he can get a sixpence — a very small amount of English currency — to go and get a gift for his father. The father gladly accepts the gift and he's really happy with it, but he also realizes that he's not any richer for the transaction. C. S. Lewis was comparing that to his belief that God has given him, and us, the gifts that we possess, and to serve Him the way we should, we should do it humbly ... realizing how we got the gifts in the first place."

www.sixpence-ntr.com.

Skid Row

GROUP FORMED IN: 1986
ORIGINAL MEMBERS: Rachel Bolan, Dave "The Snake"
Sabo, Matt Fallon, Rob Affuso, Scotti Hill
LATER MEMBERS OF NOTE: Sebastian Bach (born Sebastian
Bierk), Jonnny Solinger, Phil Vaorne, Dave Gara
BEST KNOWN SONG: I Remember You (#6, 1990)

If you go way back, you may be aware of two bands called "Skid Row," the heavy metal hair band from the late 1980s and early 1990s featured here, and the Irish band of the late 1960s and early 1970s headed by Gary Moore. They are obviously two entirely separate bands, but there is only one "Skid Row" name. An explanation will follow.

The timing of the heavy metal band's formation was not good. The grunge scene began to overrun the hair band scene within a few years after Skid Row started realizing commercial success, thus shortening their shelf life, despite the highly publicized antics of their lead singer, Sebastian Bach. Bach was a double-edged sword, for it may be fairly argued that the "negative" press he garnered contributed to the group's bad boy image, thus gaining them the credibility that other "softer" hair bands lacked.

Bach explains the interesting way they obtained the name: "Back in 1987 when I joined the band, yes, it was already called Skid Row. I did not think up the name. But the fact is we bought the name Skid Row from legendary British guitar hero Gary Moore. His band Skid Row was around in the early seventies and Gary Moore owned the name when we started in 1987 [sic]. Gary Moore ... said we could have the name for $35,000 ... so we, as a band, did buy the name from Gary Moore. I remember looking at Scotti [Hill] & Rob [Affuso] saying, 'Wow, that's a lot of money but we gotta do it!' We were all glad to do it because it is a great name for a band."

www.sebastianbach.com.

Smash Mouth

GROUP FORMED IN: 1994
ORIGINAL MEMBERS: Steven Harwell, Greg Camp,
Paul De Lisle, Kevin Coleman
LATER MEMBERS OF NOTE: Mitch Marine, Michael
Urbano, Jason Sutter, Michael "Hippy" Klooster
BEST KNOWN SONG: All Star (#4, 1999)

Smash Mouth has worked hard at making music of varying styles, drawing from their numerous influences. The group's catalogue of hits certainly attests to this fact, starting with its breakthrough hit "Walking on the Sun," which channels the organ-heavy sound of the late 1960s. Smash Mouth's biggest hit, "All Star," is straight-ahead alternative rock. The 2001 single "Pacific Coast Party" sounds as if it came right out of the disco era of the 1970s. The band is also proficient at covering former hits, such as the Monkees' "I'm a Believer" (which was on the soundtrack to the movie *Shrek*), as well as hits by such diverse artists as Frank Sinatra, the Beatles, J. Geils Band, and War.

The group of Steven Harwell, Greg Camp, and Paul De Lisle formed in San Jose, California. They have had drummer woes of Spinal Tap proportions, having gone through four since their inception. Through it all, Smash Mouth has built a strong following using Harwell's gravelly lead vocal and a garage and ska-punk aesthetic to give all its songs a post-grunge feel.

As for the group name, credit is given to original drummer Kevin Coleman. He was fond of the phrase, "smash mouth football" coined by Chicago Bears coach Mike Ditka, meaning a style of rugged, in-your-face play that epitomized the new "Monsters of the Midway" teams coached by Iron Mike. Coleman originally wanted to call the band Smash Mouth au GoGo, but this was quickly vetoed by the rest of the band members. They actually decided to go with Smashmouth as one word, but it was later made into two words when the band signed with Interscope Records.

www.smashmouth.com.

Smashing Pumpkins

GROUP FORMED IN: 1988
ORIGINAL MEMBERS: Billy Corgan, D'Arcy
Wretzky, James Iha, Jimmy Chamberlin
LATER MEMBERS OF NOTE: Matt Walker,
Melissa Auf der Maur
BEST KNOWN SONG: 1979 (#12, 1996)

Smashing Pumpkins is considered by many as the most successful alternative band of the early '90s. While its album sales have been impressive, the band has failed to crack the top-10 with any of its singles. Regardless, there is no doubting that Smashing Pumpkins set the curve for any alternative band willing to embrace commercial success.

The Pumpkins have been very difficult to categorize. The band was initially seen as a grunge offshoot, but this classification misses the mark. With elements of psychedelic rock, dream pop, goth-rock, and a little heavy metal mixed in for good measure, the group is a moving target for the critics, which may explain why it has taken few direct hits.

One formula the Pumpkins have followed is to choose an obscure band name and then never fully or honestly explain its meaning. In an interview with Tom Snyder, Billy Corgan said that for the 1,000 times they have been asked about the band name they have given 999 false answers. When this is the case, the truth behind the group name is usually so mundane and pointless that fiction is better than fact.

According to D'Arcy Wretzky, such is the case here. In a *Washington Post* interview she came clean, "The name of the band is a stupid name, a dumb bad joke and a bad idea, OK? 'Smashing' is not a verb, it's an adjective. It's not like we like to smash pumpkins or anything. And we are not amused by pumpkin jokes anymore. People bring us pumpkins, they have pumpkin motifs in our dressing rooms. I mean, this one girl actually asked us if we change our name for every holiday — like we'd be the Smashing Turkeys or the Smashing Santa Clauses. The Smashing Christopher Columbuses. And she was serious."

www.starla.org; www.spfc.org.

Soundgarden

GROUP FORMED IN: 1984
ORIGINAL MEMBERS: Chris Cornell, Kim Thayil,
Hiro Yamamoto, Matt Cameron
LATER MEMBERS OF NOTE: Hunter "Ben" Shepherd,
Scott Sundquist, Jason Everman
BEST KNOWN SONG: Black Hole Sun
(#24 airplay, 1994)

Soundgarden was considered one of the progenitors of grunge and, along with Nirvana, Pearl Jam, and Alice in Chains, was one of the big four Seattle-based bands in the early 1990s. Its heavier sound gave the grunge movement more teeth and made Soundgarden a force to be reckoned with until the band broke up in 1997.

The band members' home town of Seattle can take credit for contributing to the group's name. High on a hill overlooking Lake Washington in Magnuson Park stands a group of twelve silver towers, each holding a vertical organ pipe topped by a wind vane. This "sculpture," erected in 1982, is known as the Sound Garden. When the wind blows through the pipes a series of eerie sounds are emanated. These sounds conjure up images of anything from whales to UFOs, limited only by the listener's imagination. Oddly enough, following the events of September 11, 2001, public access to the structure is restricted for some unknown national security reason.

The band felt a connection to the physical Sound Garden structure, but the members also took a more metaphorical view of the name. According to Kim Thayil, "It's a name that conjures up powerful visual images, although at one point we thought it might be too soft. But there was something about the name we liked. One of our hopes is that people come to see us thinking they're gonna get something pretty, and then get their heads blown off...."

How nice.

www.seattlepi.nwsource.com (article by Rachel Joy Larris, July 22, 2000); www.stargate.net.

Spice Girls

GROUP FORMED IN: 1994
ORIGINAL MEMBERS: Victoria Adams (Posh Spice),

Melanie Brown (Scary Spice), Melanie Chisholm
(Sporty Spice), Geri Halliwell (Sexy Spice, later changed
to Ginger Spice), Michelle Stephenson
LATER MEMBERS OF NOTE: Abigail Kis, Emma Bunton (Baby Spice)
BEST KNOWN SONG: Say You'll Be There (#3, 1997)

Spice Girls was formed from a newspaper ad as in *The Stage* asking "R U 18–23 with the ability to sing/dance? R U streetwise, ambitious, outgoing and determined?" The original lineup, including Michelle Stephenson, was called "Touch." Her early departure led to the addition of Abigail Kis, and then to Emma Bunton. The girls lived together in a small house in Maidenhead, England, while they worked up their songs and dances.

The formula followed was a 1990s version of the girl groups of the 1960s, like the Supremes, but with a fiercely independent feminism attitude borrowed from Madonna. Sex appeal and a sense of humor kept the feeling light and enjoyable for pop music fans of all ages and both genders.

The girls soon fell out of "Touch" and, for a time, were simply called The Girls. Exhibiting their collective independence, The Girls replaced its original management team and worked on an image overhaul, including another change of name. Some of the candidates were Take Five, Plus Five, and Five Alive. They had written a song called "Sugar 'n' Spice," and it occurred to Geri Halliwell one day at her aerobics class that *Spice* could be the short, hot, and edgy name they were looking for, since the girls "were different flavors in the same recipe," as Geri put it.

As so often happens, the name was already being used in the industry, this time by an American rapper. So the name was changed to Spice Girls, and their stage identities were soon developed, based on the girls respective personalities. Geri was originally tabbed as "Sexy Spice" but changed to "Ginger Spice" shortly thereafter. The others became Posh Spice (Victoria), Baby Spice (Emma), Sporty Spice (Melanie C), and Scary Spice (Melanie B).

Golden, Anna Louise. The Spice Girls: The Uncensored Story behind Pop's Biggest Phenomenon. New York: Ballantine Books, 1997; Halliwell, Geri. Only If. New York: Delacorte Press, 1999.

Spin Doctors

GROUP FORMED IN: 1988
ORIGINAL MEMBERS: Chris Barron (born Chris Gross),
Eric Schenkman, Mark White, Aaron Comess

LATER MEMBERS OF NOTE: Anthony Krizan,
Eran Tabib, Ivan Neville
BEST KNOWN SONG: Little Miss Can't Be Wrong (#17, 1993)

Spin Doctors came to the forefront of the pop music scene in 1991, but they couldn't have been farther and further away from the Seattle grunge music explosion happening at the same time. Geographically, they formed on the East Coast as students in New York's New School of Jazz. Musically, they produced a jam-oriented blues rock that lifted peoples' hopes instead of diminishing their prospects.

Lead singer Chris Barron was born Chris Gross in Australia but moved many times in his youth due to his father's naval career before ending up in Princeton, New Jersey. In high school, Barron sang with John Popper, later of Blues Traveler. According to Barron, he was kicked out of the band for "being a pain in the ass." He changed his last name to Barron before teaming up with Eric Schenkman and Aaron Comess at the college.

Once Barron, Schenkman, and Comess got together and recruited Mark White to play bass, the group needed a name. Barron gave Schenkman the credit (or blame) when he explained, "[Eric said], 'I've got the perfect name for the band ... Spin Doctors.' I was like, 'I don't like it.' He said, 'Do you know what it is? It's a guy in a political campaign that tries to make a candidate look good.'"

Barron still wasn't buying. He admitted it was a "kind of cool meaning" but still didn't want to use it for the band. Schenkman challenged Barron to come up with a better name, but Barron admitted defeat and accepted the moniker. After several years, Barron finally came around, "It's a great name. Once it stuck and wore in."

www.members.aol.com; www.musicpix.net.

Spinners

GROUP FORMED IN: 1961
ORIGINAL MEMBERS: Pervis Jackson, Billy Henderson,
Henry Fambrough, Bobbie Smith, George Dixon
LATER MEMBERS OF NOTE: G. C. Cameron, Philippe Wynne,
John Edwards, Edgar "Chico" Edwards, Joe Stubbs,
Frank Washington, Harold "Spike" Bonhart
BEST KNOWN SONG: The Rubberband Man (#2, 1976)

The Spinners hailed from Detroit in the 1960s but they did not ride the coattails of the Motown express, much to their chagrin. Initially signed to Motown Records, they never found much success or support from the label and were dropped in 1972. The group's fame came upon moving to Philadelphia and, with the recommendation of Aretha Franklin, they were signed to Atlantic Records. With new lead vocalist Philippe Wynne and producer Thom Bell, the Spinners began its most productive ten-year period. All but five of its 29 hits came between 1972 and 1982, including all seven top-5 hits.

Originally the Spinners was a doo-wop group called The Domingoes, including Billy Henderson, Henry Fambrough, Pervis Jackson, C. P. Spencer, and James Edwards. Edwards was soon replaced by Bobbie Smith, who sang lead on the group's earliest songs. Spencer soon left as well, replaced by George Dixon.

Because The Domingoes was sometimes confused with The Flamingoes and The Dominoes, the members decided to change to something different and unique. Bobbie Smith supplied the group with its new name, explaining, "I'm a car buff. Back in the Fifties, all the kids had the hot rod cars with big wide skirts and great big Cadillac hubcaps that they called 'spinners.'" When the Spinners released albums in England, however, they went by the name of The Detroit Spinners in order to avoid confusion with a Liverpool-based folk band also called The Spinners.

www.condordmusicgroup.com; www.onlineseats.com.

Steely Dan

GROUP FORMED IN: 1972
ORIGINAL MEMBERS: Donald Fagen, Walter Becker
LATER MEMBERS OF NOTE: Denny Dias, Jeff "Skunk"
Baxter, David Palmer, Jim Hodder
BEST KNOWN SONG: Reeling in the Years (#11, 1973)

If ever a band were inclined to list "brain" as a musical instrument in its credits, Steely Dan would be entitled. The duo's brand of smart, almost impenetrable lyrics took pop/rock music in an entirely different direction in the early 1970s. Just as well documented was their impeccable musicianship and painfully meticulous mixing and re-re-re-re-mixing of songs. They were the painters who could never seem to be able to put down the brush and say "finito."

Fagen and Becker probably laugh at how uneducated the rest of us are.

I'm sure they would not be surprised if you haven't read *Naked Lunch* by William S. Burroughs. If not, you may not be aware that the group's name was drawn from that 1959 book.

But there's more to it than just that. Burroughs was under the influence of what he termed "the sickness" when he wrote *Naked Lunch*, which is translated to mean numerous mind-altering drugs. This was one raunchy book. In one of the last major literary censorship battles in the United States, it was banned by Boston courts in 1962 due to obscenity, child murder, and pedophilic sodomy acts. The ban was overturned by the U.S. Court of Appeals following testimony in favor of the book by Allen Ginsberg and Norman Mailer.

So what exactly was a "Steely Dan" in the book? How about this excerpt from the text: "Mary is strapping on a rubber penis: 'Steely Dan III from Yokohama,' she says...." The dildo was fictional, the book repugnant to many, and the group name a one-of-a-kind original, quite like the band.

Burroughs, William. Naked Lunch. *New York: Grove Press, 1959; www.steelydan.com; www. sfreader.com.*

Steppenwolf

GROUP FORMED IN: 1967
ORIGINALS MEMBERS: John Kay (born Joachim Krauledat),
John "Goldy McJohn" Goadsby, Michael Monarch,
Jerry "Edmonton" McCrohan, Rushton Moreve
LATER MEMBERS OF NOTE: Andy Chapin, Wayne Cook,
Brett Tuggle, Michael Wilk, Larry Byrom, Kent Henry,
Bobby Cochran, Michael Palmer, Rocket Ritchotte,
Danny Johnson, Steve Palmer, Ron Hurst, Nick
St. Nicholas, George Biondo, Chad
Peery, Wilton Gite, Gary Link
BEST KNOWN SONG: Born to Be Wild (#2, 1968)

A benefit of being in a group for 40 years is having the chance to play with several people. Steppenwolf has taken this to the extreme. The one constant has been John Kay, with whom Steppenwolf has been rocking practically nonstop since 1967. Kay emigrated with his mother from East Germany to Canada in 1958. He (born Joachim Krauledat) changed his name and formed the group The Sparrows, which became Sparrow. The group took its mix of blues, psychedelic, and folk rock to San Francisco in 1967 and the name was changed to Steppenwolf at the suggestion of ABC-Dunhill producer Gabriel Mekler, who had read the 1928 novel of the same name by Swiss author Hermann Hesse.

The story of the name is told this way by Kay, "When it came time to put a name on the demo box that was going to go to the first label, ... aside from the obvious joke names and other obscene suggestions which were not marketable [Mekler] finally said, 'Well, look, how about Steppenwolf? I think it's a word that looks good in print, and it denotes a certain degree of mystery and power and you guys are kind of rough and ready types.'

Everybody said that sounds pretty interesting and if we don't get a deal we can always scrawl another name on the box and send it to somebody else, so let's go with that for now. Well that's what it's been now for many years and, to be honest, it's been a very good name."

www.steppenwolf.com; www.kirjasto.sci.fi.

Cat Stevens

BORN: Steven Demetre Georgiou on
July 21, 1948, in London, England
LATER BECAME: Yusuf Islam
BEST KNOWN SONG: Morning
Has Broken (#6, 1972)

Cat Stevens was not this artist's given name nor his current name, but since his music career was under the name of Cat Stevens, this is how I will refer to him. Stevens is many things: Greek-Cypriot (from his father), Swedish (from his mother), Catholic (from his youth), and Muslim (from his later life religious conversion).

He was also something else — a world famous multi-platinum musician. His eight-year run on the pop charts yielded eleven top-40 hits and two triple platinum albums. Ultimately Stevens forsook his music career in exchange for philanthropic and educational causes in the Muslim community as a convert to the Islam religion.

Before he was Cat Stevens he was Steven Demetre Georgiou. In an interview with Larry King, he explained, "That was too longwinded (for a stage name), so Cat was something which, I mean, a lot of people love cats, so I was— I was hoping they were going to end up loving me."

In 1968 he faced a life or death situation when he contracted tuberculosis. His interest in religion as an adult began during his year-long convalescence. In 1975 he nearly drowned off the coast of Malibu, California. Obviously this Cat seemed to be quickly using his nine lives. The second near-death experience intensified his spiritual quest, ultimately leading to his conversion to Islam.

When asked by King for the source of his Islamic name, Stevens said, "The reason I chose Yusuf was because I always loved the name Joseph. And the chapter of the Quran that really moved me was the story of Joseph, the son of Jacob, son of Isaac, son of Abraham."

www.transcripts.cnn.com.

Sting / The Police

BORN: Gordon Sumner on
October 2, 1951, in Wallsend, England
BEST KNOWN SONG: If You Love
Somebody Set Them Free (#3, 1985)
GROUP FORMED IN: 1977
ORIGINAL MEMBERS: Gordon "Sting" Sumner,
Stewart Copeland, Andy Summers
BEST KNOWN SONG: Every Breath
You Take (#1, 1983)

Gordon Matthew Thomas Sumner wanted to be a musician from an early age, even while he was working as a bus conductor, construction worker, tax officer, and, most notably, an English teacher. He was nicknamed Sting when he was playing bass for the Phoenix Jazzmen. The band leader, Gordon Solomon, made a casual reference to Sumner using the nickname of "Sting" from a black and yellow sweater jersey with hooped stripes that Sting had worn a time or two. Reluctantly Sting later had to admit the sweater *did* make him look like a bumblebee.

He now goes by the nickname almost exclusively, except on official documents. Even his children call him Sting; however, his wife still calls him Gordon.

After Sting's time in the Jazzmen, he joined forces with American drummer Stewart Copeland. The trio was completed with Henry Padovani, who was later replaced by accomplished guitarist Andy Summers. The group formed was called The Police. Copeland was the early driving force behind the band and decided to give the band its name. Sting initially hated the name but deferred to Copeland.

Reportedly, Copeland desired a name of this nature because of his family history. His father, Miles, was cofounder of the U.S. Central Intelligence Agency (CIA). One of Copeland's brothers was a founding partner of the record label known as IRS, or International Recording Syndicate (although the same initials stand for the taxing agency Internal Revenue Service). Another brother, Ian, was a partner of the talent agency called Frontier Booking International (FBI), not to be confused with the Federal Bureau of Investigation. With these various bureaucratic-sounding names, The Police was so named to carry on the family tradition.

Sting. Broken Music. *New York: The Dial Press, 2003; www.amiright.com/artists.police.shtml*

Stone Temple Pilots

GROUP FORMED IN: 1990
ORIGINAL MEMBERS: Scott Weiland,
Robert DeLeo, Eric Ketz
LATER MEMBERS OF NOTE: Dean DeLeo
BEST KNOWN SONG: Interstate Love
Song (#18 airplay chart, 1994)

Stone Temple Pilots began as a clash of musical influences. Scott Weiland of post-punk influence and Robert DeLeo of hard rock influence married their styles after the girl they were both dating moved away. While the Pilots were criticized early on for a lack of originality, revisionist history has been kinder with most critics respecting the Pilots's for their tight song structure and melodic riffs, which gave the alternative music scene of the early 1990s a radio-friendly option beyond Soundgarden and Alice in Chains. Throughout the band's tenure, the Pilots were continually dealing with Weiland's drug and legal troubles, which made recording and touring difficult but kept the band in the news, thereby extending their shelf life during the intervals between albums.

Initially the group decided to call itself Mighty Joe Young. They soon recruited Eric Kretz on the skins and Robert's brother Dean on lead guitar. The name was changed when they discovered the existence of a blues performer named Mighty Joe Young. Weiland was fond of the initials STP, reportedly from the initials of the motor oil company. The first incarnation under these initials was the controversial Shirley Temple's Pussy, under which they actually performed in San Diego.

Understanding they could not carry this name to national acclaim (and under pressure from the record label), the name was amended again, this time to Stereo Temple Pirates. This name was short-lived as well. Just before cutting its first album, the group went to the third variation on the STP theme, finally settling on the Stone Temple Pilots on the suggestion of producer Brendan O'Brien. His reasoning was simple: "It sounded cool."

www.mmguide.musicmatch.com.

Styx

BAND FORMED IN: 1970
ORIGINAL MEMBERS: John Panozzo, Chuck Panozzo,
Dennis DeYoung, John Curulewski, James "JY" Young
LATER MEMBERS OF NOTE: Tommy Shaw, Glen
Burtnick, Todd Sucherman, Lawrence Gowan
BEST KNOWN SONG: Babe (#1, 1979)

The origins of Styx go way back to 1960, when grade-schooler Dennis DeYoung invited himself to play his accordion with the Panozzo brothers in their Chicago neighborhood, forming a band called the Trade Winds. As the decade progressed, the band (with fourth member Tom Nardini) made the circuit on the south side of the town in their black suits and long ties, until 1965 when they were forced to change their name because of another group also called Trade Winds, which had a national top-40 hit. So the Chicago group became TW4, standing for "There Were Four."

After John Curulewski and James Young joined, the band started to hit its stride. Its big break came with a record deal with Wooden Nickel Records. One problem: the group name. So the group put its collective effort into renaming itself. Many names were considered including Torch, Kelp, and Styx. Styx was chosen because mystical names were in vogue, especially for bands with prog-rock leanings and, more importantly, it "was the one name no one actively hated," according to Chuck Panozzo.

Styx is the name of a river of Greek mythology that formed the boundary between Earth and the underworld. The river Styx was thought to have miraculous powers and could make men immortal. The mother of Achilles submerged him in the river, holding him by his heel, which was the only part that was not submerged and, of course, became his undoing as his only point of vulnerability. Although the band Styx had a tremendous run of eight top-10 songs over 16 years, it was not immortal either. Styx has not had a hit since 1991 and efforts to reunite the band after DeYoung's departure have proven to be Styx's Achilles' heel.

*Panozzo, Chuck and Michele Skettino. The Grand Illusion. New York: AMACON, 2007;
www.members.aol.com/boardwalk7/Styx.*

Sugar Ray

GROUP FORMED IN: 1992
ORIGINAL MEMBERS: Rodney Sheppard,
Murphy Karges, Stan Frazier
LATER MEMBERS OF NOTE: Mark McGrath,
Craig Bullock (DJ Homicide)
BEST KNOWN SONG: Fly (#1 airplay, 1997)

Sugar Ray is an Orange County, California, band that began as a 1980s cover band calling itself Shrinky Dinx. The band was playing a fraternity party when a friend of the band members, Mark McGrath, jumped on stage and became their lead singer from that night on.

While performing as the Shrinky Dinx, the band members even assumed individual nicknames such as Papa Smear, Romero Dinero, Ajax Babymake, and Hemorrhoid Shaker Face. Soon the frivolity came to an end when the band was threatened with a lawsuit by Hasbro for continued use of the name. The company had marketed a toy called Shrinky Dinks, which were thin, plastic sheets that children could color with felt-tip pens and cut into shapes. When heated in the oven the forms would shrink into smaller, thicker shapes while retaining the colored design.

The group then changed its name to Sugar Ray, a reference to famous boxer Sugar Ray Leonard, who was a favorite of McGrath. Leonard has not threatened to sue the band, but, ironically, another musical artist has.

Raymond Alan Norcia had been going by the stage name of Sugar Ray for almost 30 years when he received an offer of $1,000 from the group's lawyers to waive his rights to sue the group for their use of the name. He countered with $1,500 but never heard back from the group. When the group became nationally known, the solo singer made another play for a payoff but was rebuffed.

By this time the group had decided to risk legal action on the basis that no reasonable person would confuse the two artists. The same logic was obviously not used when the band was the Shrinky Dinx, unless there was a Shrinky Dink named Hemorrhoid Shaker Face.

www.answers.com; www.hardrock.com; www.rollingstone.com.

Supertramp

GROUP FORMED IN: 1969
ORIGINAL MEMBERS: Rick Davies, Roger Hodgson,
Richard Palmer, Robert Miller
LATER MEMBERS OF NOTE: Frank Farrell, Kevin Currie,
Dave Winthrop, Dougie Thompson, Bob Siebenberg
(aka Bob C. Benberg), John Helliwell, Mark Hart, Cliff Hugo,
Lee Thornburg, Carl Verheyen, Tom Walsh, Jesse Siebenberg
BEST KNOWN SONG: Give a Little Bit (#15, 1977)

Originally slated to be called Daddy, the original members of the group, most notably Rick Davies and Roger Hodgson, ultimately settled on Supertramp, naming the band after a 1908 book by tramp poet and writer W. H. Davies entitled *The Autobiography of a Super-Tramp*. The book is the story of the author's early life as a vagabond and vagrant, which turned fruitful only after the author lost a leg under a train leading him to turn to a highly successful writing career. Lessons to be gleaned from the book include that success often requires much trial and error, and perseverance can lead to great things.

The group Supertramp could hardly have been more aptly named. Despite being bankrolled by Dutch millionaire Stanley August Miesegaes and signed to a recording contract with A&M Records, Supertramp was unable to develop a fan base or sell any significant numbers of their first two records. The albums were long-winded progressive rock efforts that did not resonate with the record-buying public as did those of genre bedfellows Pink Floyd, ELP, and Yes. Miesegaes lost interest and withdrew his financial support.

Like Rick Davies's namesake W. H. Davies, Supertramp overcame obstacles to success. The group changed personnel, and slowly morphed into more of a radio-friendly pop outfit. By the time their album *Breakfast in America* was released in 1979 the transformation was complete. The album went on to sell in excess of 18 million units worldwide. Old W. H. would be proud.

Davies, W. H. Autobiography of a Super-Tramp. *London: Cape, 1908; www.classicbands.com; www.bbc.co.uk.*

The Supremes

GROUP FORMED IN: 1959

ORIGINAL MEMBERS: Diana Ross, Mary Wilson,
Florence Ballard, Betty Travis
LATER MEMBERS OF NOTE: Barbara Martin, Cindy Birdsong,
Jean Terrell, Scherrie Payne, Lynda Laurence, Susaye
Greene, Karen Ragland, Karen Jackson
BEST KNOWN SONG: Stop! In the
Name of Love (#1, 1965)

The Temptations were originally called The Primes. The Supremes often performed with them and began as The Primettes. This was when Mary Wilson, Florence Ballard and uber-diva Diana Ross were in high school. The money in those early years was not much, and Berry Gordy (that's Mr. Motown to you and me) even hired Ross as a secretary to help her earn extra money. According to Ross, "All I remember is clearing off his desk several times a day, awed by the important-looking papers that he handled and so wishing to have my name on some of them."

When the Primettes were signed to a record contract in early 1961, Gordy told the girls to change their group's name. After much discussion and soul searching (no pun intended), they reviewed a list of suggestions handed to them by Janie Bradford, a songwriter who was working at the Motown switchboard as another member of Gordy's musically talented secretarial pool.

Among the finalists were The Darleens, the Sweet Ps, the Melodees, the Royaltones, the Jewelettes and The Supremes. Ballard indicated her preference for The Supremes, which Ross initially hated. Wilson still wanted something that ended in "ette." However, by the time the group arrived in the studio the new name was already on the contracts so it was settled, whether they liked it or not.

The rest, of course, is history. The Supremes rocketed to stardom, and they helped Motown influence pop and soul music from then on. They also became the first all-female group to dominate the pop charts, laying the foundation for many who have followed in their footsteps.

Ross, Diana. Secrets of a Sparrow. New York: Villard Books, 1993; Wilson, Mary. Dreamgirl & Supreme Faith: My Life as a Supreme. New York: Cooper Square Press, 1999.

Survivor

GROUP FORMED IN: 1977
ORIGINAL MEMBERS: Jim Peterik, Frankie Sullivan,
Dave Bickler, Gary Smith, Dennis Johnson

LATER MEMBERS OF NOTE: Robin McAuley, Chris Grove,
Billy Ozzello, Marc Droubay, Stephen Ellis,
Jimi Jamison, Barry Dunaway
BEST KNOWN SONG: Eye of the Tiger (#1, 1982)

Jim Peterik is a survivor. He started out as a fourteen-year-old in the band The Ides of March. The group survived for six years before its only hit, but that song entitled "Vehicle" was a number two smash in 1970. The original Ides of March, both with and without Peterik, have survived for over 40 years.

Fast forward to 1977. Peterik has recorded a solo album called *Don't Fight the Feeling* and at one time resorted to singing jingles to, as Peterik put it, "support my expensive recording habit." It was at one of these sessions he met Dave Bickler whose "range was incredible and had an interesting voice." Bickler sang on the solo album and was asked to join Peterik in the new band he was forming. This band also included Frankie Sullivan, Gary Smith, and Dennis Johnson. Peterik originally planned on this being essentially his band and he initially named it The Jim Peterik Band.

Realizing this was more than just himself and a backing band, Peterik decided to give them a more proper name. He drew the name from the liner notes of *Don't Fight the Feeling* where the "Jim Peterik is a survivor" sentence was first uttered. Even though Survivor really hadn't survived anything yet, Peterik was really drawing on his own past.

Survivor survived the ups and downs of the early years and finally struck gold when asked to record "Eye of the Tiger," the main theme song to the third *Rocky* movie, which spent six weeks at #1. This success led to five top-10 hits, making Survivor one of the biggest album-oriented rock bands of the 1980s.

www.geocities.com; www.jimpeterik.com.

(The) Sweet

GROUP FORMED IN: 1968
ORIGINAL MEMBERS: Brian Connolly, Mick Tucker,
Steve Priest, Gordon Fairminer
LATER MEMBERS OF NOTE: Frank Torpy,
Mick Stewart, Andy Scott
BEST KNOWN SONG: Ballroom Blitz (#5, 1975)

Sweet is a conundrum. A paradox. Were they bubblegum, glam or a hard rock hair band? Answer: all of the above. Starting out as a bubblegum outfit under the thumb of U.K. hitmakers Nicky Chinn and Mike Chapman, Sweet eventually found their way to more musical freedom and respect with progressively less success in their later years.

Sweet was formed from the remnants of Wainwright's Gentlemen, which included Mick Tucker and Brian Connolly. In 1968 they left to form a new band with vocalist Steve Priest, who had been with The Countdowns. The new band they formed was originally called The Sweetshop. This name was appropriate because of the bubblegum music that became a staple during their early years.

When Andy Scott joined, the name was shortened to The Sweet. The band continued its not-so-veiled attempt to market to the teeny-bop crowd with such hits as "Lollipop Man,"" Funny Funny," "Co-Co," "Poppa Joe," and "Little Willy," the latter of which became the group's biggest hit in the United States in 1973.

By this time the group was losing interest in the lightweight fare and its androgynous glam stage image. The members officially shortened the group name for the last time, dropping the "The" and simply calling themselves Sweet. Later hits such as "Ballroom Blitz," "Fox on the Run," "Action," and "Love Is Like Oxygen" gave the band more rock cache but diminishing sales. Sweet failed to survive commercially past the late '70s.

www.sweetlife.dk.

Talk Talk

GROUP FORMED IN: 1981
ORIGINAL MEMBERS: Mark Hollis, Lee Harris,
Paul Webb, Simon Brenner
LATER MEMBERS OF NOTE: Tim Friese-Greene
(unofficial member, studio only)
BEST KNOWN SONG: Talk Talk (#75, 1982)

Talk Talk was often compared to Duran Duran, having arrived on the scene at approximately the same time (and having similar repeat names), much to the ire of lead singer Mark Hollis. Early on, many of the comparisons were accurate. But whereas Duran Duran stuck close to the formula that worked, mining the gold (and platinum) for all it was worth, Talk Talk hit the formula and then quit it. As a result, Talk Talk never achieved the same commercial success as Duran Duran, but they were critically more appreciated.

The band was intended to be a vehicle for Hollis to procure a songwriting publishing deal. According to Hollis, "Within a couple of days of working a bit on the stuff I'd done, we actually started writing things together as a band, and although all of us were from very different musical backgrounds in terms of taste, there was a definite unity of directions. After the first week we stopped thinking in terms of me getting a publishing deal and said, 'Let's call this a band.'"

But what to call themselves? Although they had been practicing a song entitled "Talk Talk," it was not the first thought for the name. "We went through the dictionary," Hollis recalls, "had all the novels out like William Burroughs and things, and finally ended up with Talk Talk because, partly, I like the idea of a track with the same name as the band, and I think it's really instant in terms of memorizing it, plus it didn't in any way categorize us. The third reason was from a graphic point of view it would look good, the fourth one, purely from a personal hang-up I've got, is that I don't really like it when people abbreviate it, like The Stones."

www.users.cybercity.dk (Sounds Magazine).

Talking Heads

GROUP FORMED IN: 1977
ORIGINAL MEMBERS: David Byrne,
Tina Weymouth, Chris Frantz
LATER MEMBERS OF NOTE: Jerry Harrison
BEST KNOWN SONG: Burning Down
the House (#9, 1983)

Some two years before Jerry Harrison brought his keyboard and guitar skills to complete the Talking Heads lineup, David Byrne, Tina Weymouth, and Chris Frantz were honing their skills supporting the Ramones at CBGBs. The three art school friends from the Rhode Island School of Design had formed what would become one of the most influential, hippest, and successful bands of the new wave era.

In the days leading up to the band's stage debut several names were suggested by Byrne. He would write on scratch paper such names as Vogue Dots, Tunnel Tones, The World of Love, or The Portable Crushers and attach them to Frantz's bass drum. An art school friend was rummaging through a *TV Guide* and found the term "talking head," which was a technical term for a head-and-shoulder shot of an interviewer or interviewee on television. Considering the influence that Tom Verlaine and his group, Television, had on the band and the entire early days of the American punk rock scene, perhaps selection of the name Talking Heads served as a tacit homage.

Another story is that Weymouth and Frantz were walking down the street wearing matching T-shirts that said Talking Heads. Someone stopped them and asked, "Is that the name of a band? That's a terrible name." Just before their opening number at CBGBs on June 5, 1975, in front of a small crowd of 20-some people, Byrne uttered, "We're Talking Heads," and the name became official.

Bowman, David. this must be the place: The Adventures of Talking Heads in the 20th Century. New York: HarperCollins, 2001.

Tears for Fears

GROUP FORMED IN: 1981
ORIGINAL MEMBERS: Roland Orzabal, Curt Smith
LATER MEMBERS OF NOTE: Ian Stanley, Manny Elias
BEST KNOWN SONG: Shout (#1, 1985)

Ever ambitious and well read, Tears for Fears were the thinking (and feeling) man's synth-pop band. Although Roland Orzabal came from a broken home, he focused his energies on books at an early age, at which time he met Curt Smith, also the product of an unstable upbringing. Together they joined a ska-revival band called Graduate. After being involved in this band long enough to release one album, the two departed and spent time in the band Neon before forming The History of Headaches.

During this time (1981), Orzabal was exploring a theory popularized by Dr. Arthur Janov called Primal Therapy, a trauma-based psychotherapy, which holds that therapeutic progress can be made only through direct emotional experience, which allows access to the source of psychological pain in the lower brain and nervous system. Patients are commonly encouraged to scream or cry for cathartic purposes. John Lennon had helped popularize primal therapy during his Plastic Ono Band phase some ten years earlier.

Orzabal introduced Smith to this treatment and the two changed the name of the band to Tears for Fears in homage to Dr. Janov's contribution to the field of psychology. Their first Tears for Fears album, *The Hurting*, was practically a concept album with primal therapy as the central theme. Such songs as "Mad World" and "Watch Me Bleed" elicited much more raw emotion than much of the New Romantic music of the time, and presaged the more tumultuous alternative music era. The lyrics of their most well known

song, "Shout," sound as if Janov himself is encouraging the listener to partic-
ipate in a session.

www.napster.com; www.stylusmagazine.com.

The Temptations

GROUP FORMED IN: 1960
ORIGINAL MEMBERS: Elbridge "Al" Bryant,
Eddie Kendricks, Otis Williams, Paul
Williams, Melvin Franklin
LATER MEMBERS OF NOTE: David Ruffin, Dennis
Edwards, Ricky Owens, Richard Street, Damon Harris,
Glenn Leonard, Louis Price, Ali-Ollie Woodson, Ron Tyson,
Harry McGilberry, Terry Weeks, Barrington Henderson,
Theo Peoples, G.C. Cameron
BEST KNOWN SONG: My Girl (#1, 1965)

Truly one of the greatest vocal groups of all time, the Temptations have
weathered changing lineups and music trends for five decades. Known for their
tight, smooth harmonies, their impeccable choreography, and their identical
on-stage suits, the Temps (or Tempts, to some) were vocally versatile enough
to roll out a romantic ballad or hit you with souped-up funk. During the group's
tenure, they even handled doo-wop, psychedelia, disco, and adult contemporary with equal aplomb.

The Temps have had almost as many early group names as members, or
so it would seem. In the earliest stages they started as The Primes, during which
time their association with the Supremes (formerly the Primettes) came into
being. When Melvin Franklin came onboard the name changed to The Distants,
and later to Otis Williams & the Distants.

When the lineup of original members was in place for the first time the
group was changed to The Elgins. Just a few days before signing with Motown
Records the group discovered another act was calling itself the Elgins, so the
soon-to-be Motowners determined to settle on a usable name once and for all.
They ruled out anything that was too long, hard to remember, meaningless, or
silly, like the El Domingos or Siberians. Otis Williams blurted out "Temptations" and the rest of the group cracked up, dressed as they were in raggedy,
long winter coats. Per Otis, "We knew we weren't likely to tempt anyone or
anything, but what the hell, it was as good a name as any." Later they all agreed
it was the perfect name, evoking style, elegance, romance, and, in a subtler way
than other groups, sex appeal.

Williams, Otis, with Patricia Romanowski. Temptations. Boulder, CO: Cooper Square Press, 2002.

10cc

GROUP FORMED IN: 1972
ORIGINAL MEMBERS: Graham Gouldman,
Eric Stewart, Kevin Godley, Lol Creme
LATER MEMBERS OF NOTE: Paul Burgess, Rick Fenn,
Stuart Tosh, Duncan MacKay, Tony O'Malley
BEST KNOWN SONG: The Things We
Do for Love (#5, 1977)

A group with the (brief) resume of 10cc would hardly merit a mention in this book but for one thing: the pervasive urban legend about the meaning and origin of the group's name. Despite releasing nine songs that reached the top 100 of the American charts, only two climbed beyond number 40, although those were significant hits, namely, the eerie number 2 smash "I'm Not in Love" of 1975 and the pop anthem "The Things We Do for Love."

The members of 10cc were probably too clever for their own good. In a decade when "smart" songs were rarely hits (the Eagles, Steely Dan and Billy Joel being the exceptions here), 10cc's style of reclaiming songs of genres past and stamping them with their own ironic twist did not prove as successful in the United States than in their native England.

The widely reported explanation for the group's name (with slight variations) is that it denotes slightly more sperm than the average male ejaculates. By extension (pardon the pun), the group was to have used 10cc instead of the true average amount to reflect their prowess.

The truth lies in the words of Jonathan King, who signed the group to UK Records and is universally credited for devising the name. "I had to give them a name ... because I'd signed the record, and I went to sleep that night and had this dream that a band of mine on my label made number one on the album and singles charts simultaneously in America, and the band was 10cc. So I gave them that name the next morning. (The sperm story) was absolutely far from the truth.... There's a lot of apocryphal stories about names, and unfortunately, most of them are much more amusing that the ugly reality, which in this case is that the name came to me in a dream."

www.snopes.com.

10,000 Maniacs

GROUP FORMED IN: 1981
ORIGINAL MEMBERS: Steven Gustafson, Dennis Drew,
Robert Buck, Terry Newhouse, Chet Cardinale
LATER MEMBERS OF NOTE: Natalie Merchant,
John Lombardo, Oskar Saville, Jerry Augustyniak,
Jeff Erickson, Mary Ramsey, Tim Edborg, Bob
"Bob O Matic" Wachter, Jim Foti
BEST KNOWN SONG: Because
the Night (#11, 1994)

Few groups have ever had a more misleading name than the 10,000 Maniacs. Not that people expected to see 10,000 extremely crazy people playing on
stage together. Rather, the name leads most to expect a band something more
akin to AC/DC than to Peter, Paul & Mary.

The group was formed at Jamestown Community College in New York
State by Steven Gustafson, Robert Buck, and Dennis Drew (who were disc jockeys at the school's radio station), along with Terry Newhouse and Chet Cardinale. The group initially called itself Still Life. They were befriended by young
Natalie Merchant (only 17 at the time) who was already enrolled in college
classes. After she sang with the band on stage in an impromptu performance,
Natalie was asked to join. John Lombardo, another key member, joined at that
time and the band changed its name to Burn Victims.

Merchant was not in favor of the new name. The band considered other
options such as Christian Burial, Dick Turpin's Ride to New York, and Merchant's suggestion of Tundra Bunnies. The ultimate choice would be loosely
taken from the 1964 low budget horror film *Two Thousand Maniacs!* The cult
movie was one of the earliest slasher films, noted for its extreme gore and violence as well as for its deficient acting and directing.

The group intended to call the band the exact title of the movie but mis-
heard the title. In retrospect, they have lived to regret the choice of monikers,
but by the time they saw the misleading effects of the name, the group had
become too well known to make a change.

www.natalie-merchant.online.com; www.windspring.com.

Tesla

GROUP FORMED IN: 1984
ORIGINAL MEMBERS: Jeff Keith, Frank Hannon,
Tommy Skeoch, Brian Wheat, Troy Luccketta
LATER MEMBERS OF NOTE: Dave Rude
BEST KNOWN SONG: Signs (#8, 1991)

Tesla was a late comer in the hair metal/heavy metal band scene, entering the fray on the national level in 1987 but not managing their first top-40 hit until 1989, by which time the genre was losing steam. Still, the band persevered into the '90s and managed its biggest hit in 1991 with a live remake of "Signs," the 1971 song by the Five Man Electrical Band.

Since Tesla's music was grounded in gritty blues, the group's expiration date came later than most other hair bands. In all, Tesla had managed five studio albums as of 2004, with estimated sales exceeding 14 million. Not bad for the band that was formed in Sacramento, California, originally called City Kidd. While the band was recording its debut album on Geffen Records, *Mechanical Resonance*, the label felt a better name was needed. Guitarist Frank Hannon admits as much, "I knew we had to change it, but finding a name for the band is the hardest thing to do."

Tom Zutaut of Geffen suggested naming the band after Serbian-American inventor Nikola Tesla. Tesla is generally considered to be the true father of the radio, although the issue was not resolved until 1943 (just after Tesla's death), when the U.S. Supreme Court ruled his patents were superior to those of Guglielmo Marconi.

"At first I wasn't too keen on the name 'Tesla' because I wasn't really familiar with the whole story behind it and initially the sound of it wasn't really rock and roll enough," said Hannon. "Once I got used to the sound of it and really got into reading the stories on Tesla's passion for electricity, his innovative mind and then being screwed in the end, then I thought it was a brilliant idea. I'm glad we used it and I would have to say that I was wrong and everyone else was right."

www.teslatheband.com.

Thin Lizzy

GROUP FORMED IN: 1969

ORIGINAL MEMBERS: Phil Lynott, Eric Bell,
Eric Wrixon, Brian Downey
LATER MEMBERS OF NOTE: Gary Moore, Scott Gorham,
Brian Robertson, Midge Ure, Snowy White, Darren
Wharton, Tommy Aldridge, Randy Gregg, John Sykes,
Marco Mendoza, Michael Lee
BEST KNOWN SONG: The Boys Are
Back in Town (#12, 1976)

Dublin's Thin Lizzy was led by schoolmates Brian Downey and Phil Lynott, the latter of whom was one of the first black men to achieve significant success in the hard rock genre. Like Jimi Hendrix before him, Lynott met with a premature demise at the hands of drugs and alcohol.

Thin Lizzy is well known in the United States even among casual rock music fans. This is somewhat perplexing because the group only had one top-40 hit, "The Boys Are Back in Town." Perhaps the extended popularity of the song is the reason for the bands high profile. Perhaps it was Lynott. Most likely, however, the reason many people remember the group is its name.

There has been speculation over the years as to the meaning of the group's name. Many simply assumed they were named after the Ford Model T car manufactured between 1908 and 1927 called "Tin Lizzie." This is not directly true and has never been cited by the band as the inspiration for the name. It is quite likely, though, that the automobile inspired the cartoon character by the same name from the British children's comic book series entitled *The Dandy*. Tin Lizzie was a robot featured in many of the comic's issues, and *this* was the inspiration for the band name.

Upon its formation, the band struggled with the issue of a group name. Gulliver's Travels was considered and rejected. Eric Bell picked Tin Lizzie out of a *Dandy* comic and offered it up to the group. Downey and Lynott ruled it out initially, but after some thought, Lynott suggested altering the name somewhat to Thin Lizzy, and the band had its name.

www.northernshow.biz/eric_bell.htm.

Third Eye Blind (3eb)

GROUP FORMED IN: 1993

ORIGINAL MEMBERS: Stephan Jenkins, Arion Salazar,
Tony Fredianelli, Kevin Cadogan
LATER MEMBERS OF NOTE: Brad Hargreaves
BEST KNOWN SONG: Semi-Charmed Life (#4, 1997)

Third Eye Blind (often abbreviated 3eb) is a San Francisco band formed in the image of lead singer Stephan Jenkins. As an unsigned band paying their dues in the Bay area, Jenkins bluffed his band's way into opening for Oasis at a sold-out show. The show was a success and served as a springboard for the group to sign with a record label of their choice.

The group's first two hit singles, "Semi-Charmed Life" and "How's It Going to Be" each made the top 10. Although they "only" peaked at #4 and #9, respectively, they spent an unbelievable 43 and 52 weeks in the top-100. As a result, 3eb quickly became one of the foremost post-grunge bands of the new millennium.

The band's name has been subject to much speculation, due to its numerous possible connotations and the band's propensity to give ever-changing explanations (a tactic employed by Pearl Jam and used with increasing frequency by subsequent bands). Jenkins has been a big fan of Camper Van Beethoven, particularly the song "Eye of Fatima." This has been suggested as a possible source of the word "eye" in the name.

The "third eye" is a mystical concept espoused by certain cultures in referring to spiritual enlightenment or clairvoyance. Jenkins has stated his interest in names of a magical nature. 3eb came on to the pop music landscape at a time when, according to Jenkins, there existed a lack of vision or magic. Third Eye Blind is a jab at the circumstances created by other bands, indicating their inner third eye was blind to possibilities that lay in front of them. Conversely, 3eb has tried to recapture the magic and reflect it in their songs.

www.delafont.com; www.anecdotage.com.

.38 Special

GROUP FORMED IN: 1975
ORIGINAL MEMBERS: Don Barnes, Steve Brookins,
Jack Grondin, Ken Lyons, Donnie Van Zant, Jeff Carlisi
LATER MEMBERS OF NOTE: Bobby Capps, Max Carl, Larry
"LJ" Junstrom, Danny Chauncey, Scott Hoffman, Gary Moffatt
BEST KNOWN SONG: Hold on Loosely (#27, 1981)

Formed by Donnie Van Zant, .38 Special is America's most successful band formed in the southern rock vein, with apologies to Lynyrd Skynyrd and the Allman Brothers. .38 Special has more top-40 hits than the other two groups combined and has stayed together for over 30 years.

The group went through many early names, according to Donnie Van Zant, including The Other Side and Standard Production. When he and Don Barnes got .38 Special together, Van Zant was giving serious thought to quitting the music business altogether. He had opportunities with railroad companies and was beginning to appreciate the security of a "regular job." His older brother, Ronnie (founder of Lynyrd Skynyrd), convinced Donnie to give .38 Special his complete attention, which has turned into a lifetime gig.

Barnes recounts the story of the band's name. He and Donnie rented a barn in which to rehearse. "There was manure, and we had to shovel it out of there and then get some pallets to stand on for a floor. We had the place fortified and had it vaulted up with 2 x 4's and a big motorcycle chain that went through the hole in the door to lock it with this old rusty lock. Then we had to climb in a window to get in and out.

"One night we were rehearsing and heard someone banging on the door and when we looked, there were 12 constables banging on the door to get in. We were yelling and telling them we couldn't open the door and one of them yelled that he had a *.38 Special* (gun) to use on the door if we wouldn't let him in. So when we had our first show, we had not thought of a name so we decided to use that name."

www.gritz.net; www.classicrockrevisited.com

Thompson Twins

Group Formed In: 1977
Original Members: Tom Bailey, Peter Dodd,
John Roog, Chris Bell,
Later Members of Note: Joe Leeway, Allanah
Currie, Jane Shorter, Matthew Seligman,
Andrew Edge, Jon "Pod" Podgorski
Best Known Song: Hold Me Now (#3, 1984)

The Thompson Twins stood among the forefathers of the New Romantic era, capturing the essence of synth-pop music. If you were at all conscious in the 1980s you know that none of the members of the Thompson Twins are twins. Or related. Or named Thompson. In fact they were formed as a quartet and were never as few as two members until 1986 when only Tom Bailey and Allanah Currie remained. Those two ultimately married, so it would be illogical to assume they would be twins because of moral and legal constraints.

Formed in England, the band emigrated to Egypt, the Bahamas, back to England, and ultimately to New Zealand. Thomas Dolby played with the band in the studio and on tour in the early years but was never made a full-fledged member. After the extended group realized some early success, Bailey, Currie, and Joe Leeway broke away from the band and formed their own band. The first name considered was The Bermuda Triangle, but the trio ultimately bought the Thompson Twins name from their former bandmates.

The group took its name from a cartoon by Belgian comics writer Herge. The strip was called *The Adventures of Tintin*. The cartoon includes two unrelated bumbling detectives named Dupond and Dupont in the Belgian version. The English version refers to them as Thomson and Thompson. The pair wear identical clothes and bowler hats and can be told apart only by the shape of their moustaches. The detective with a flared moustache describes himself as "Thomson, without a 'p,' as in Venezuela!" The original members colloquially referred to the detectives as the Thompson Twins and decided to use the name for their band.

www.eightiesclub.tripod.com.

Three Dog Night

GROUP FORMED IN: 1968
ORIGINAL MEMBERS: Danny Hutton,
Cory Wells, Chuck Negron
LATER MEMBERS OF NOTE: None
BEST KNOWN SONG: Joy to the World (#1, 1971)

Danny Hutton, Cory Wells, and Chuck Negron, three singers with distinctive voices, came together in Los Angeles in 1968. Each had his own style, but together they created lush harmonies while covering numbers written by others, such as Hoyt Axton, Randy Newman, Nilsson, Laura Nyro, and Leo Sayer. They scored a phenomenal 21 consecutive top-40 hits, largely on the strength of the diversity of the songs, therefore never creating a sound within which to be pigeonholed. Every one of their singles reached the top 40, which is an unmatched feat by so prolific a group.

While the members of the newly formed group were sitting in Hutton's living room trying to come up with a name, Hutton's live-in girlfriend, actress

June Fairchild, walked in with an article from *Mankind* magazine about Australian aborigines from certain tribes in the outback who dug holes in the ground and slept with their dogs for warmth in the winter. The coldest weather was described as a "three dog night."

When the group's manager prodded them to settle on a name they spouted off those under consideration. He exhibited a visceral reaction to the suggestion of Three Dog Night and asked the guys if they were nuts. They figured if a 40-year-old conservative business type hated it so much, kids their age would love it. So defiance won out and Three Dog Night it was.

Negron, Chuck, with Chris Blatchford. Three Dog Nightmare. *Northampton, MA: Renaissance Books, 1999.*

Toad the
Wet Sprocket

GROUP FORMED IN: 1986
ORIGINAL MEMBERS: Glen Phillips, Todd
Nichols, Dean Dinning, Randy Guss
LATER MEMBERS OF NOTE: none
BEST KNOWN SONG: All I Want (#15, 1992)

This group with a name that could not be excluded from this book was formed in 1986 at San Marcos High School just outside of Santa Barbara, California. At the time of the group's formation, lead singer Phillips was only 14 years old and the others were 17, but their literate and complex songs (especially by their third album *Fear*) belied their youth.

Now to the name! So you think you know this one, do you? The common wisdom is that the name came from a skit by Monty Python. If that was your understanding you get only partial credit. That explanation is at best an oversimplification and at worst technically incorrect.

There was a British TV show that ran from 1971 to 1987 called the *Old Grey Whistle Test* but later abridged to just *Whistle Test*. This show featured musical acts performing their songs on spartan sets. A parody of this show was run on a show entitled *Rutland Weekend Television* in 1975, which featured Monty Python's Eric Idle lampooning *Whistle Test's* host Bob Harris in a skit wherein he mentioned a fictional band, "Toad the Wet Sprocket."

Five years later, Monty Python released an album entitled *Monty Python's*

Contractual Obligation Album. On the album are several skits, songs, and vignettes including a 2:11 number called "Rock Notes" in which Idle narrates a series of fictitious news items regarding equally fictitious rock bands and personalities. The first item involves Rex Stardust, lead electric triangle for Toad the Wet Sprocket. So now you know the *real* story behind one of the most unusual band names in rock music history.

Toto

GROUP FORMED IN: 1978
ORIGINAL MEMBERS: Bobby Kimball, Steve Lukather,
David Paich, Steve Porcaro, David Hungate, Jeff Porcaro
LATER MEMBERS OF NOTE: Simon Phillips, Mike Porcaro,
Dennis "Fergie" Fredericksen, Joseph Williams,
Greg Phillinganes, Jean-Michael Byron
BEST KNOWN SONG: Rosanna (#2, 1982)

Toto was formed by brothers Steve and Jeff Porcaro and high school friends who had become renowned studio musicians in Los Angeles. They decided to form a band while helping Boz Scaggs with his highly acclaimed album *Silk Degrees.* The band has gone on to amass ten top-40 hits over a ten-year period. They started with a hard-rocking number called "Hold the Line," then to mid-tempo pop songs ("Rosanna" and "Africa") and later to ballads ("I Won't Hold You Back" and "I'll Be Over You"). Despite lineup and style changes, Toto is well recognized throughout the world, with as much of an audience in Europe and Japan as in their home country.

Although the group's name was inspired tangentially by *The Wizard of Oz,* it was not necessarily an homage to the famous movie dog. Jeff Porcaro wrote the name on demo tapes for their debut album for identification purposes. When considering the word as a name, the group researched the meaning of "toto" and found a Latin meaning of "all-encompassing." "It's representative of our music," claimed Porcaro, who described the mixture of experience of the group's musicians as "mishmash" and "goulash."

During an early interview, David Hungate jokingly referred to Bobby Kimball (who is from Louisiana) as Robert Toteaux. The name continued to follow Kimball as his credited name on some future songs and albums. However the group name *predated* Kimball's new moniker and the group was not named after him, as some believe.

www.toto99.com.

Traveling Wilburys

GROUP FORMED IN: 1988
ORIGINAL MEMBERS: George Harrison (aka Nelson
Wilbury and Spike Wilbury), Jeff Lynne (aka Otis Wilbury
and Clayton Wilbury), Tom Petty (aka Charlie T. Wilbury,
Jr. and Muddy Wilbury), Bob Dylan (aka Lucky Wilbury
and Boo Wilbury), Roy Orbison (aka Lefty Wilbury)
LATER MEMBERS & BACKING MUSICIANS: Jim Keltner,
Ray Cooper, Jim Horn, Gary Moore
BEST KNOWN SONG: Handle with Care (#45, 1988)

A supergroup if ever there was one, the Wilburys were formed mostly by accident. The five original members were all working with each other on various projects and they came together ostensibly to help Harrison record a song for an album Lynne was producing entitled *Cloud Nine*. As the lineup of rock legends jammed, they decided as a lark to record an album together but under assumed identities.

Lynne and Harrison had coined the term "wilburys" for the "gremlins" in the equipment that seemed to sabotage the recording process. This was the genesis of the fictitious group's last name. Harrison originally suggested the Trembling Wilburys, but when put to a vote Traveling Wilburys won out.

Harrison had the idea that the legends would masquerade as half-brothers all sired by the same father named Charles Truscott Wilbury, Senior. For their first album they posed in costume and all credits were given to their fictitious names, Nelson, Otis, Charlie T., Jr., Lucky, and Lefty.

Shortly after the first album shot to number three, Orbison died of a heart attack. The remaining Wilburys reunited in Orbison's absence for a second album, oddly entitled *Volume 3*, this time with new individual names of Spike, Clayton, Muddy, and Boo. The second album was much less successful and the group was to play no more, a fact assured when Harrison died in 2001.

www.everything2.com; www.sing365.com.

The Troggs

GROUP FORMED IN: 1964
ORIGINAL MEMBERS: Reginald Maurice Ball ("Reg Presley"),
Chris Britton, Pete Staples, Ronnie "Bond" Bullis

LATER MEMBERS OF NOTE: none
BEST KNOWN SONG: Wild Thing (#1, 1966)

The Troggs were a garage band. Not much more or less. But knowing their limits allowed them to maintain a career well beyond their expiration date. Whereas the much-covered "Wild Thing" was not their only hit (they also had a top-10 hit with "Love Is All Around" in 1968), it is certainly their signature song and a cornerstone of every fraternity toga party. According to the outstanding music reference book, *Rock, The Rough Guide,* this classic song "redefined the limits of just how wonderfully dumb rock could be."

In a sense, the Troggs played the grunge of their time. Reg Presley later confided, "We wanted it dirty, grungier, more aggressive — and, without devices that were developed later, we had to get that out of equipment that was available. You could get really weird noises from a bass, for instance, by bending its neck right in front of the amp."

En route to a music shop to help Reg pick out a bass guitar, the group picked up two hitch-hikers. On noticing the dilapidated condition of the bus, the freeloaders referred to the band members as "grotty troggs." Grotty, as in grotesque. Troggs as in troglodytes (prehistoric cave dwellers). This seemed apropos, and (sans the descriptive adjective), the poster outside the next gig proudly displayed the groups new moniker, The Troggs. Since that time, many have referred to the Troggs's style as "caveman rock," a description devised from the name of the band to which it applies.

Clayson, Adam, and Jacqueline Ryan. Rock's Wild Things: The Troggs Files. *London: Helter Skelter Publishing, 2000.*

The Tubes

GROUP FORMED IN: 1972
ORIGINAL MEMBERS: Fee Waybill (born John Waldo
Waybill), Bill "Sputnik" Spooner, Roger Steen, Charles "Prairie"
Prince, Michael Cotton, Vince Welnick, Rick Anderson,
Re Styles (born Shirley Marie MacLeod)
LATER MEMBERS OF NOTE: Mingo Lewis
BEST KNOWN SONG: She's a Beauty (#10, 1983)

If all you know of The Tubes is their top-10 hit "She's a Beauty" and its entertaining video, then you really don't know The Tubes. For over ten years prior to their only significant chart success, The Tubes carved out a niche in the rock music scene through their theatrical and campy concerts, which were as much a part of the entertainment value as was the music. It's no wonder, then, that The Tubes did not cross over to mainstream success until the era of the music video.

The Tubes were led by charismatic and enigmatic lead singer Fee Waybill, who assumed various on-stage personas including Quay Lewd (a burned-out British rock star), Dr. Strangekiss (the crippled Nazi), and Hugh Heifer (country singer). Together with high school friends from Phoenix, Waybill formed the group from the merger of two bands, The Red, White and Blues Band and The Beans, the latter of which was intended to be used for the ongoing concern, but not before considering and rejecting "Radar Men from Uranus."

Waybill tells the story of how they ended up as The Tubes. "We decided the name would be The Beans finally, and then about a month later an album came out on United Artists by a band called Beans. We contacted the record company but they said 'tough shit.' So we changed the name. Some of the suggestions we didn't pick were The Gasmen (and) Larry and Mary." The group decided on the name Tubes Rods and Bulbs, which refers to parts of the eyeball. Later the name was shortened to The Tubes.

www.industrypages.com.

The Turtles

GROUP FORMED IN: 1963
ORIGINAL MEMBERS: Howard Kaylan, Mark Volman,
Chuck Portz, Al Nichol, Don Murray, Jim Tucker
LATER MEMBERS OF NOTE: John Barbata, Chip Douglas
BEST KNOWN SONG: Happy Together (#1, 1967)

Names and name changes. You will find them here with the Turtles and its members. In fact, the first name change came from founding father Howard Kaylan who was originally Howard Kaplan. In 1965 he changed his last name simply because "Kaylan" was how he always wrote it. He started a surf band called the Nightriders, which included future Turtles Chuck Portz and Don Murray. Mark Volman later joined the group and the name of the band was changed to The Crossfires, which played around the Los Angeles area and won several Battle of the Bands competitions.

Despite these local triumphs, there was little money being made and the band was on the verge of breaking up when they were approached by local disc jockey Reb Foster, who wished to be their manager. Foster signed them to a record deal with fledgling label White Whale Records. The group felt this new beginning should be christened with a new group name. The sextet considered descriptive names such as The Half Dozen or Six Pack, but ultimately accepted the suggestion of Foster to name the band something similar to the Byrds. Foster's suggestion was The Tyrtles, which was later amended to the spelling under which the band became famous.

From 1965 to 1969 the Turtles had a string of nine top-40 hits, including the terminally peppy "Happy Together." In 1970 the Turtles folded, and Kaylan and Volman joined Frank Zappa's Mothers of Invention. They later went out as a duo and, due to contract restrictions that prohibited them using the name The Turtles or even their own names commercially, they formed a duo called Phlorescent Leech and Eddie, which was later shortened to Flo and Eddie.

www.theturtles.com; www.classicbands.com.

Shania Twain

BORN: Eilleen Regina Edwards on August 28, 1965,
in Windsor, Ontario, Canada
BEST KNOWN SONG: You're Still the One (#2, 1998)

Shania Twain was born and raised in Timmins, Ontario, about 500 miles north of Toronto, the second oldest of five siblings. When she was just two years old, her parents divorced and her mother subsequently remarried a man named Jerry Twain, a full-blooded member of the Ojibwa First Nation Indian tribe. Jerry adopted young Eilleen and she took his last name.

With her natural beauty and musical talent, she was shunted around to perform just about anywhere in the area there was an audience. This included performing at the tender age of eight in clubs after midnight, when alcohol sales had ended. In 1987, when Eilleen was 21, her parents died in an automobile accident. She cared for her younger siblings with a job at Ontario's Deerhurst Resort while honing her stage talents. Soon she decided to change her first name to Shania, which translates in Ojibwa to "I'm on my way." Rarely has a name been more true. Shania has gone on to make music history when her third album, *Come On Over*, sold over 22 million copies and became the best selling album of the 1990s and one of the top-selling albums of all time.

Shania has been criticized by members of her biological father's family for exploiting or at least exaggerating her Indian heritage to benefit her career. The daughter of Irish and French-Irish parents she has little or no discernable Indian blood. However, Shania counters those critics by noting, "I don't know how much Indian blood I actually have in me, but as the adopted daughter of my father Jerry, I became legally registered as 50 percent North American Indian. Being raised by a full-blooded Indian and being part of his family and their culture from a young age is all I've ever known. That heritage is my heart and my soul, and I'm very proud of it."

Auty, Dan, et al. 100 Best Selling Albums of the 90s. *New York: Barnes & Noble Books, 2004; www.cmt.com; www.shania.u-net.com.*

Twisted Sister

GROUP FORMED IN: 1973
ORIGINAL MEMBERS: Jay Jay French (born John Segall),
Michael Valentine, Billy Diamond, Mell Starr (born Mell Anderson)
LATER MEMBERS OF NOTE: Kevin John Grace, Eddie "Fingers" Ojeda,
Daniel David "Dee" Snyder, Kenny Neill, Tony Petri, Mark
"The Animal" Mendoza, A.J. Pero, Joe Franco, Ronni Le Tekro
BEST KNOWN SONG: We're Not Gonna Take It (#21, 1984)

It took Twisted Sister eleven years of paying dues before finally mining MTV video gold and, in the process, bridging androgynous heavy metal from Kiss to the hair band explosion of the late 1980s. In short order the star of this group burned white-hot and then burned out, a victim of overexposure. Eventually tension between Jay Jay French and Dee Snyder led to the band's demise at a point when practically nobody noticed.

In 1973, French, who had almost become a member of Kiss, joined a New Jersey-based band called Silverstar. The group planned to wear dresses and play hard rock. One of the first orders of business once French was onboard was to change the name. Michael Valentine, the first of the group's four lead vocalists, came upon the name Twisted Sister during a drinking binge. Nobody, Valentine included, can attest as to how he stumbled upon the name or its origins. According to French, "It would've been easy for me to take the credit. Michael was a full-throttle drinker, and he rang from a bar saying he'd come up with this great name. But when he came home he'd completely forgotten making the call. Thank God ... if I hadn't picked up the phone, we may never have called ourselves Twisted Sister."

The newly christened band struggled to find its sound until Dee Snyder joined in 1976 and took the band in a heavier direction, à la Alice Cooper. The band has consistently disdained "glam rock" as a description of their music. Snyder has said "I don't think Twisted Sister is 'glam' because that implies glamour, and we're not glamorous. We should be called 'hid' because we're hideous."

www.daveling.co.uk; www.kochdistribution.com.

U2 / Bono / The Edge

GROUP FORMED IN: 1976
ORIGINAL MEMBERS: Paul Hewson ("Bono"), Dave Evans
("The Edge"), Adam Clayton, Larry Mullen
BONO BORN: May 10, 1960, in Glasnevin, Ireland
THE EDGE BORN: August 16, 1961, in Barking,
East London, England
BEST KNOWN SONG: With or Without You (#1, 1987)

The band that turned out to be the world's most important band of the late 1980s and spawned one of the most relevant political activists of the early twenty-first century, was formed in Dublin, Ireland. Paul Hewson obtained his nickname of "Bono" as a child, from a sign in a hearing aid store in Dublin advertising Bono Vox of O'Connell Street. His nickname came compliments of a friend who claimed Bono sung so loudly it was if he was singing for the deaf. Bono Vox means "good voice" in cockeyed Latin, but the nickname was shortened before he learned this fact.

Dave Evans's (The Edge) nickname is more cryptic. Growing up, he was never at the center of activity, always hanging around the edges. Bono came up with the name, claiming, "*The edge* is the border between something and nothing." Some have also claimed the nickname came from the sharp profile of his face and nose. Others say it comes from the edgy sound his guitar playing makes, as if he were playing with the edge of a knife.

The group name of U2 was first suggested to Adam Clayton by Steve Averill (who would later be involved in designing the cover of almost every one of U2's albums). The band was ultimately sold on the name by the ambiguity created by the numerous potential meanings. On the one hand, it borrows from the reconnaissance spy plane of the same name. U2 is also a name for a brand of batteries. Other meanings derive from the play on the phrase "you too" or "you two."

Bordowitz, Hank. The U2 Reader: A Quarter Century of Commentary, Criticism, & Reviews. *Milwaukee, WI: Hal Leonard, 2003; Chatteron, Mark.* U2: The Complete Encyclopedia. *Richmond Hill, Ontario: Fire Fly, 2001.*

Uriah Heep

GROUP FORMED IN: 1969
ORIGINAL MEMBERS: Mick Box, Dave Byron,
Tony Newton, Ken Hensley, Alex Napier
LATER MEMBERS OF NOTE: Nigel Olsson, Keith Baker, Iain
Clarke, Mark Clarke, Lee Kerslake, Gary Thain, John Wetton,
John Lawton, Trevor Bolder, John Sloman, Chris Slade, Gregg
Dechert, Peter Goalby, John Sinclair, Bob Daisley, Steff
Fontaine, Phil Lanzon, Bernie Shaw and others
BEST KNOWN SONG: Easy Livin (#39, 1972)

If you think being in a heavy metal band gives you immediate street cred, consider the case of Uriah Heep, then think again. However, despite being the recipients of ridicule from the heavy metal press, Heep has thumbed their collective noses at the critics and survived nearly 30 different musicians to release 43 albums since their very 'umble beginnings in 1969.

Uriah Heep's output derives from a strong mixture of heavy metal, prog-rock, and blues influences. The main character in this group's story is guitarist Mick Box, who has been with the group throughout its entire history. His goal of being a rock musician was set at an early age, "Straight from school I took a job in the city in London at an export firm. This was purely to pay the payments on my Les Paul guitar! To save money, I cycled 20 miles a day so that I could pay the guitar off quickly, thereby not having to pay the train fare. On the last payment, I handed in my notice and I was gone!"

Box and vocalist David Byron had been in a band called Spice. When keyboardist Ken Hensley joined, they changed musical direction and name. "We were formed on the 100th anniversary of Charles Dickens, the great English novelist," recounted Box. "There was publicity all over London to celebrate his birthday and there was a film made of one of his novels, *David Copperfield* on release. Gerry Brown, our manager, took his son to see the film and came back and suggested one of the characters, Uriah Heep for the name of the band. We liked it and the rest is history!"

www.classicrockrevisited.com.

The Velvet Underground

GROUP FORMED IN: 1965
ORIGINAL MEMBERS: Lou Reed, John Cale, Maureen
"Moe" Tucker, Sterling Morrison
LATER MEMBERS OF NOTE: Nico, Doug Yule,
Walter Powers, Willie Alexander
BEST KNOWN SONG: Sweet Jane
(unreleased as single, 1971)

The Velvet Underground is the most groundbreaking and respected band in the history of rock music with so little commercial success to show for it. Even the Grateful Dead had six top 100 songs. There were no top 100 hits for the Velvet Underground, not even "Sweet Jane," which has been covered numerous times. Nor was "Walk on the Wild Side" theirs, it being a Lou Reed solo top-20 hit two years after he left the band.

Despite the poor sales, the Velvets are considered (together with Richard Hell, the Stooges, and the New York Dolls) the godfathers of punk rock. Such a title has guaranteed the group immortality among rock snobs and led to its induction into the Rock and Roll Hall of Fame. Brian Eno put it best when he said that although the Velvet Underground didn't sell many albums, everyone who bought one went on to form a band.

The group began as just Reed and John Cale, calling themselves The Primitives. When Sterling Morrison joined, the band became The Warlocks, then The Falling Spikes. Then Reed came across the 1963 book entitled *The Velvet Underground* by Michael Leigh. It dealt with aberrant sexual practices that eventually contributed to the groundswell for the sexual revolution. Reed considered the book "the funniest dirty book I've ever read. 'Into the murky depths of depravity and debauchery with the Velvet Underground'... this is TOO good,

I mean just the name, I love the ring of it." The other group members found the name evocative of "underground cinema" and they unanimously adopted the book's title as the group's new name.

Heylin, Clinton. All Yesterday's Parties: The Velvet Underground in Print 1966–1971. *New York: Da Capo Press, 2005; Kemp, David, and Steven Daly.* The Rock Snob*s Dictionary. *New York: Broadway Books, 2005; Leigh, Michael.* The Velvet Underground. *New York: McFadden Books, 1963.*

Vertical Horizon

GROUP FORMED IN: 1992
ORIGINAL MEMBERS: Matt Scannell, Keith Kane
LATER MEMBERS OF NOTE: Ed Toth, Craig McIntyre,
Seth Horan, Sean Hurley, Blair Sinta
BEST KNOWN SONG: Everything You Want (#1, 2000)

Vertical Horizon started out as an impromptu pairing of Georgetown University students Matt Scannell and Keith Kane. Keith invited Matt to play an acoustic number on stage, and was so impressed that Keith decided to make his solo act a duo. They graduated and relocated to Matt's hometown of Boston. They recorded their first album in Matt's former high school, playing all the instruments themselves and sharing vocals and songwriting credits.

By the time Matt and Keith were ready to record again, they decided to include guest musicians to help fill out the sound. Eventually permanent band members were added, including Ed Toth (drums) and Sean Hurley (bass). By this time the band was moving away from the acoustic sound and more to the electric guitar sound that was prevalent on their 1999 album *Everything You Want*, which contained the number one hit title track.

The band's name is unusual. In an interview, Toth said, "The name came from Keith. He was at a party one night and needed a name for the band to advertise. He just thought it sounded great for the moment and it would change, but it just stuck. It's funny, everyone likes to think that there's some meaning behind it, and we've had people who have come up with some ideas, but there really isn't any meaning behind the name."

One such idea claims Keith wrote "Vertical" above "Pool" on a child's magic writing slate. When the plastic cover sheet was raised "Pool" was erased along with part of "Vertical," leaving a horizontal line. This was supposedly the inspiration for the oxymoron of Vertical Horizon that became the group's name.

www.verticalhorizonfaq.tripod.com; www2.cedarcrest.edu/crestiad.

Village People

GROUP FORMED IN: 1977
ORIGINAL MEMBERS: Victor Willis (policeman),
Felipe Rose (Indian), Alex Briley (military member),
David "Scar" Hodo (construction worker), Glenn Hughes
(leatherman/biker), Randy Jones (cowboy)
LATER MEMBERS OF NOTE: Eric Anzalone (leatherman/biker),
G. Jeff Olsen (cowboy), Ray Simpson (policeman), Miles
Jaye Davis (policeman), Ray Stephens (policeman),
Mark Lee (construction worker)
BEST KNOWN SONG: YMCA (#2, 1979)

The Village People was a disco act formed by Jacques Morali and Henri Belolo. Belolo recalls it as if it was yesterday, "One day we were walking in the streets of New York. I remember clearly it was down in the Village, and we saw an Indian walking down the street and we heard the bells he was carrying on his feet. We followed him into a bar. He was a bartender, he was serving and also dancing on the bar. And while we were watching him dancing, and sipping our beer, we saw a cowboy watching him dance. And Jacques and I suddenly had the same idea.

"So we started to fantasize on what were the characters of America. And this is how we came with that idea of putting together a group of five males because we discovered these characters in the Village." As a reference to the location, they named their group the Village People.

The Bee Gees and Donna Summer may have sold more records, but no act encapsulated the disco craze like the Village People, bringing together the music, campy act, the gay influence, and the attitude of casual sex. The good-time message the group put forth made theirs the most played music of the disco revival. The extended shelf life of the Village People owes to the nonthreatening way that its blatantly gay act came across to heteros, as if they were a disco version of cirque de soleil. The gay community overlooked the stereotypical way their culture was being portrayed and embraced the Village People as the first big music act they could call their own.

www.disco-disco.com.

The Wallflowers

GROUP FORMED IN: 1990
ORIGINAL MEMBERS: Jakob Dylan, Rami Jaffee,
Barrie Maguire, Peter Yanowitz, Tobi Miller
LATER MEMBERS OF NOTE: Fred Eltringham,
Greg Richling, Mario Calire, Michael Ward
BEST KNOWN SONG: One Headlight
(#2, airplay chart, 1997)

The Wallflowers have been called "the Dire Straits of the Alternative Nation" by *Trouser Press* writer Jason Reeher. This assessment seems to fit the laid-back band based in Los Angeles, headed by Jakob (Jake) Dylan. Just in case you are one of the five people who don't already know this, Jake is the son of Bob Dylan, and he possesses much of his dad's lyric writing ability while improving on his looks and voice. But Jake has always downplayed his famous lineage so that the band would be judged on its own merits and any success would be rightfully earned.

Tobi Miller and Barrie Maguire came from a band called the 45's until they split. Miller and Dylan then played together in a variety of bands, including the Boot Heels. Maguire joined, along with Peter Yanowitz, and the quartet changed the name to The Apples. The final piece to the original puzzle is Rami Jaffee, who Dylan calls "the last available Hammond B3 player that exists who will sit between a piano and organ."

The Apples then become the Wallflowers. So does the name reflect the personality of the band members? Are they painfully shy or unsociable so that they want to avoid being the center of attention? It depends on who you ask. "We're pretty much shy people," says Miller, "so the name just seemed to fit really well."

Dylan refutes this statement somewhat. "The name isn't necessarily a reflection of the band. Every band needs a name and it just has a nice sound. A lot of people seem to think that we've ended up as wallflowers, but that wasn't really part of it."

www.thewallflowers.com; www.trouserpress.com; www.the-wallflowers.net.

Wang Chung

GROUP FORMED IN: 1979

ORIGINAL MEMBERS: Jack Hues, Nick
Feldman, Darren Costin
LATER MEMBERS OF NOTE: none
BEST KNOWN SONG: Everybody Have
Fun Tonight (#2, 1986)

Wang Chung was a new wave dance-pop group that hit its stride during the New Romantic era of the 1980s. The group was originally called Huang Chung, actually recording one album as such before renaming itself Wang Chung.

Huang Chung is translated from Chinese as "yellow bell." The term dates back to the thirteenth century b.c. It refers not just literally to a bell, but to a philosophical idea that music was sacred and served as the metaphoric voice of the emperor. According to Jack Hues, "It's like a Buddhist concept, and it's a bell that rings at the center of the universe and creates a vibration. The job of court composers in China, when this concept was happening, was to write music that harmonized with this vibration. So if the emperor started losing wars and stuff, the first guy to get executed was the composer, because he was obviously writing the wrong kind of music."

The group changed the spelling to Wang Chung before their second album. Per Hues, "when we signed to Geffen they were kinda like 'How do you say it?' So we were like 'Huang Chung' or 'Wang Chung' and they were like 'if it's Wang Chung then spell it Wang Chung' and so we did. It's not like a name where it has to mean what it means, it's just like a label. So we changed the spelling and then everybody Wang Chunged tonight!"

The group has joked in the press that the name represents the sound a guitar makes (Wang on the down stroke and Chung on the up stroke). Since that time the group has defined the name as a feeling, not a word. Nick Feldman says, "It represents an abstract, an escape from pragmatic, complex ideas. Wang Chung means whatever you want it to mean. Have fun with it." Tonight.

www.wangchung.com; www.yellowbellmusic.com.

War

GROUP FORMED IN: 1969
ORIGINAL MEMBERS: Eric Burdon, Lonnie Jordan, Howard
Scott, Charles Miller, Morris "B.B." Dickerson, Harold
Brown, Lee Oskar, Thomas "Papa Dee" Allen
LATER MEMBERS OF NOTE: Alice Tweed Smith,

Luther Rabb, Pat Rizzo, Ronnie Hammond, Rae
Valentine, Charles Green, Kerry Campbell, Tetsuya
Nakamura, Sal Rodriguez
BEST KNOWN SONG: Low Rider (#7, 1975)

Which did War change more, its personnel or style? With no fewer than 17 members, the group's sound morphed from psychedelic blues-jazz to funk to gospel-tinged soul to latin rock to disco. The group started out as The Creators but later became Nightshift, when, believe it or not, they became the backing band for football player and future Hall-of-Famer Deacon Jones (while he was in the middle of his playing days).

One evening while Nightshift was supporting Jones at the Rag Doll club in North Hollywood, a business associate of Eric Burdon's (formerly of the Animals), heard the group and told Burdon to check them out. Burdon had left the Animals several years before and was more excited in pursuing an acting career than reviving his singing career. Yet the idea of this white but soulful Brit fronting an all-black American band was intriguing. Burdon was blown away by Nightshift's talent. Conversely, Nightshift knew its visibility would be enhanced more by teaming up with Eric Burdon than Deacon Jones.

The group's new name, Eric Burdon and War, was an interesting choice. Keep in mind this was in 1969 at the height of opposition to the Vietnam War. Burdon said, "The idea was to take the most negative word we could find and turn it into a positive." Group founder Lonnie Jordan had another spin on the name. "Our mission was to spread a message of brotherhood and harmony. Our instruments and voices became our weapons of choice and the songs our ammunition." Either way, War stood for peace.

Burdon, Eric, with J. Marshall Craig. Don't Let Me Be Misunderstood. New York: Thunders Mouth Press, 2001.

The Who

GROUP FORMED IN: 1964
ORIGINAL MEMBERS OF NOTE: Roger Daltrey, Pete
Townshend, John Entwistle, Keith Moon
LATER MEMBERS OF NOTE: Kenney Jones
BEST KNOWN SONG: Who Are You (#14, 1978)

Known originally as The Detours, these London boys combined a mixture of the Rolling Stones's bravado and the Beatles cheekiness. Soon they had created their own style and reputation, both on and off stage, for loutish behavior and violence, and along the way they managed to create some of the most anthemic songs of the 1960s. At their peak, the Who was one of the most innovative and powerful bands in rock history.

As the band's popularity grew, the members decided a change of name was in order. The band looked for names that created no particular identity, including such offbeat suggestions as No One and Group. Then Pete Townshend offered The Hair, which was a cultural reference in light of the Beatles's mop tops and the Stones's unkempt locks. A completely off-the-wall suggestion was the name British European Airways, which thankfully received little support.

Finally The Who was mentioned. This worked well on several levels. It was sufficiently nondescript but at the same time made people think twice. It was short and therefore would print up big on posters. It was ambiguous and coolly abstract. Roger Daltrey ultimately made the decision for the band ruling in favor of The Who over The Hair and everyone else was in agreement. Or were they?

According to Townshend, "We chose the name The Who a little bit prematurely. It was too weird for a long time. So we used The High Numbers for a bit and then the time came when we were able to use The Who again." The group actually recorded a record called "I'm the Face" during the six-month period in 1964 when The High Numbers was in use, but they reverted to The Who by the time they began charting in the United States.

Giuliano, Geoffrey. Behind Blue Eyes: The Life of Pete Townsend. *New York: Dutton, 1996;* Sound International Magazine, *April 1980. Interview by Steve Rosen.*

Stevie Wonder

BORN: Stevland Hardaway Judkins on
May 13, 1950, in Saginaw, Michigan
BEST KNOWN SONG: Ebony and Ivory (#1, 1982)

This one is tricky, because there are two competing primary sources for information on how Stevie Wonder became Stevie Wonder. Those sources are Stevie and his mother. In his mother's autobiography entitled *Blind Faith: The Miraculous Journey of Lula Hardaway, Stevie Wonder's Mother,* Lula lists Stevie's birth name as Stevland Hardaway Judkins. On his web site, Wonder indicates he was born Steveland Morris (in addition to the different last name, note the extra 'e' in the first name).

It is more likely Lula's account is accurate. She indicates Stevie's middle name is the same as her maiden name. His last name is taken from Stevie's father, Calvin Judkins, who was a mostly absentee father and who was abusive when he *was* around. He was, by some accounts, about 33 years older than Lula.

When Stevie was a child he changed his last name from Judkins to Morris. This has been referred to as an "old family name." Interestingly, all of Stevie's children go by the last name of Morris.

Stevie showed a talent to master multiple musical instruments and developed a tremendous charisma and singing voice, and he was brought to Motown Records at the age of 11. He so impressed CEO Barry Gordy that he was signed to Motown's Tamla label. His name was changed to Little Stevie Wonder due to the boy's wondrous talents, particularly in light of his blindness since infancy.

Stevie's first single, "Fingertips—Pt. 2," was an immediate hit, holding down the number one spot for three weeks during the summer of 1963. The live recording featured Stevie playing harmonica and bongos. Two other top-100 songs were released under the Little Stevie Wonder name before he dropped the "Little" portion of the nickname.

www.who2.com; www.tvguide.com.

XTC

GROUP FORMED IN: 1973
ORIGINAL MEMBERS: Andy Partridge, Barry Andrews,
Colin Moulding, Terry Chambers
LATER MEMBERS OF NOTE: Dave Gregory
BEST KNOWN SONG: Senses Working Overtime
(#10 UK-uncharted in US, 1982)

Define success. If you consider commercial sales and worldwide fame "success," then XTC failed to achieve it. However, if success means recognition by ones peers as an influential force in the field, then XTC most certainly did achieve it. Blatantly and charmingly British, this group actually used intelligence in its lyrics instead of the same cookie-cutter clichés passed down from those who came before. Most often the band's smart songs hit the mark, but their tendency for shooting themselves in the collective foot kept the members of XTC from reaping the commensurate financial rewards.

Formed originally by Andy Partridge as the Helium Kidz, the group was influenced by the New York Dolls, The Stooges, Alice Cooper, and all things glam. The group's first identity came courtesy of the genre, complete with gold fur pants, glitter boots, and bouffant hairdos. But as glam wound down in 1975 and stardom was not yet a bedfellow, they swayed toward the punk aesthetic.

According to Partridge, "About this time we changed our name to XTC, which I thought was great, a little shorthand way of writing 'ecstasy,' with sharp connotations, fast and fun and euphoric. And I got the band dressed in boiler suits, very baggy with huge Chinese characters drawn all over them. We looked pretty fast, sort of pre–Devo."

The silver bullet for the group was a case of stage fright Partridge developed, which was so severe that entire concert legs were cancelled just as the group was gathering momentum. From 1982 on, XTC has been strictly a studio group. While its product has continued to be held in high regard, the lack of touring support has relegated it to underground favorites.

www.artistwd.com.

Yes

GROUP FORMED IN: 1968
ORIGINAL MEMBER: Jon Anderson, Chris Squire,
Bill Bruford, Tony Kaye, Peter Banks
LATER MEMBERS OF NOTE: Steve Howe, Rick Wakeman,
Alan White, Patrick Moraz, Geoff Downes, Trevor
Rabin, Igor Khoroshev, Billy Sherwood
BEST KNOWN SONG: Owner of a Lonely Heart (#1, 1984)

Yes is prog-rock personified. Commercially viable into the twenty-first century, Yes has stayed truer to its roots than other prog ship-jumpers such as Genesis and King Crimson. Although sometimes self-indulgent and pretentious, Yes was also imaginative and skillful. And despite the loss of key members at crucial periods of the band's history, it has continued to attract young fans and build on its following with the MTV generation hits "Owner of a Lonely Heart" and "Leave It."

The earliest formation of the band was called Syn, which included future Yes members Peter Banks and Chris Squire. They later joined forces with Jon Anderson in 1968 in the band Mabel Greer's Toy Shop. Tony Kaye was picked up after his band, Bitter Sweet, disbanded, and, after Bill Bruford joined, the original lineup of Yes was in place.

The new band was in search of a name. The story of the origin of the name is as short as the name itself. Peter Banks made the suggestion to name the band Yes since it was just a few letters, and is a word with an upbeat connotation. As with other names of the era such as The Who and Cream, the group liked the fact that they could make the letters very big on promotional posters as an eye catcher. For a short while, the name included an exclamation point ("Yes!"), which was later dropped, apparently after the initial enthusiasm died down.

Frame, Pete. Rock Family Trees. Vol. 2. London: Omnibus Press, 1983; www.reference.com; www.answers.com; www.m-ideas.com.

ZZ Top

GROUP FORMED IN: 1970
ORIGINAL MEMBERS: Billy Gibbons,
Dusty Hill, Frank Beard
LATER MEMBERS OF NOTE: none
BEST KNOWN SONG: Sharp Dressed Man (#56, 1983)

This group is special if for no other reason than for the ability of the members to put up with each other for almost four decades. The original members of ZZ Top have remained together without a personnel change since the group was formed in 1970. They are also distinguished for the long beards sported by Billy Gibbons and Dusty Hill, which have not been cut since 1979. Ironically, drummer Frank *Beard* is the only member without one. In 1984 the Gillette Company reportedly offered Gibbons and Hill one million dollars to shave their beards for a television commercial but they declined.

Another trademark of the group (Beard included, this time) is the sunglasses they wear on stage and in their videos, which they immortalized in their song "Cheap Sunglasses." They also were among the first of the "old-timers" from the '70s to embrace the MTV video age and exploit it with Playboy centerfolds and a more danceable funky sound to ensure heavy rotation of their songs, particularly "Gimme All Your Lovin'," "Sharp Dressed Man," and "Legs."

The origin of the band name has been subject to unsubstantiated speculation by fans for years. A plausible explanation was that it combined Zig-Zag and Top rolling papers. Some have claimed Gibbons saw the two words running together on a dilapidated billboard. Another less likely source was the Z-shaped barn door braces Gibbons once saw at a farm.

Gibbons claims the name is a tribute to blues legend B.B. King. It may also derive from homage to another blues great, Z.Z. Hill, who, like ZZ Top, hailed from Texas. They were going to call the band Z.Z. King but instead changed King to Top, honoring King as one of the tops in his profession.

Appendix 1:
Previous Names

ABBA	Bjorn & Benny, Agnetha and Anna-Frid; Bjorn & Benny with Svenska Flicka
AC/DC	Third World War
Ace of Base	Tech-Noir
Alice in Chains	Diamond Lie
Ambrosia	Ambergris Might
The Animals	Alan Price Combo; Pagan Jazzmen; Pagans
Badfinger	The Iveys; The Panthers
The Bangles	The Bangs; Colours; The Supersonic Bangs
Bay City Rollers	The Ambassadors; The Longmuir Brothers; The Saxons
The Beach Boys	Carl & the Passions; Kenny & the Cadets; Pendletones
The Beatles	Johnny & the Moondogs; Quarry Men; The Silver Beetles, Beatals
The Black Crowes	Greasy Little Toes; Mr. Crowe's Garden
Black Sabbath	Earth; Polka Tulk Blues Band
Blondie	Angel & the Snakes; Blondie & the Banzai Babies
Blue Öyster Cult	Oaxaca; Soft White Underbelly; Stalk-Forrest Group
Blues Traveler	Blues Band; Blues Entity
Blur	Seymour
The Boomtown Rats	The Nightlife Thugs
The Box Tops	The Rockers; Ronnie & the Devilles
Bush	BushX
The Byrds	The Jet Set
The Cars	Cap'n Swing
Cheap Trick	The Bun Birds; Ozzie & Harriet; Sick Man of Europe; Wham Bam Thank You M'am
Coldplay	Starfish
Counting Crows	Sordid Humor
The Cranberries	The Cranberry Saw Us
Creed	Naked Toddler

Creedence Clearwater Revival	The Golliwogs
Culture Club	Sex Gang Children
The Cure	Easy Cure; Malice
Deep Purple	Roundabout
Def Leppard	Atomic Mass
Devo	Sextet Devo
Dire Straits	Cafe Racers
The Doobie Brothers	Pud
Electric Light Orchestra (ELO)	The Move
Fastball	Magneto USA; Star 69; Starchy
The 5th Dimension	The Versatiles
The Flaming Lips	Chrome Leeches
Foreigner	Nothing; The Romeos; Trigger
Frankie Goes To Hollywood	Hollycaust
Frankie Valli & the 4 Seasons	Four Lovers; Frankie Valle & the Romans; The Wonder Who?
Goo Goo Dolls	Sex Maggots
Grateful Dead	Warlocks
Green Day	Sweet Children
The Guess Who	Chad Allan and the Expressions
Heart	Hocus Pocus; White Heart
Herman's Hermits	The Heartbeats
The Hollies	The Deltas
Icehouse	Flowers
INXS	The Farriss Brothers; The Vegetables
Jethro Tull	Bag o' Blues; Candy Coloured Rain; Ian Henderson's Bag o' Nails; Navy Blue
Journey	Golden Gate Rhythm Section
Keane	Cherry Keane; The Lotus Eaters
The Kinks	Boll Weevils; The Ravens; The Ramrods
Kool & the Gang	The Five Sounds Jr.; The Jazz Birds; The Jazziacs; Kool & the Flames; The Soul Town Band
Lynyrd Skynyrd	The One Percent
Madness	Morris and the Minor; The North London Invaders
Maroon 5	Edible Nuns; Kara's Flowers; Mostly Men
matchbox twenty	Tabitha's Secret
The Mothers of Invention	The Soul Giants
Mott the Hoople	Silence
Mungo Jerry	The Buccaneers; Camino Real; The Conchords; The Good Earth Rock N Roll Band; Memphis Leather; The Sweet and Sour Band; The Tramps
Night Ranger	Stereo
Oingo Boingo	The Mystic Knights of the Oingo Boingo

The O'Jays	The Emeralds; The Mascots; The Triumphs
Orchestral Manoeuvres in the Dark	VCL XI
The Outfield	The Baseball Boys
Pearl Jam	Mookie Blaylock
Pink Floyd	Tea Set
Poco	Pogo; RFD
Psychedelic Furs	Radio; RKO
Quarterflash	Seafood Mama
Radiohead	On A Friday
Red Hot Chili Peppers	Tony Flow & the Miraculously Majestic Masters of Mayhem
R.E.M.	Twisted Kites
Paul Revere & the Raiders	The Downbeats
Smokey Robinson & the Miracles	The Matadors
Roxette	Gyllene Tider
Rush	Hadrian; Projection
Savage Garden	Crush
Scorpions	Nameless
Simple Minds	Johnny & the Self Abusers
Smash Mouth	Smash Mouth au GoGo
Spice Girls	The Girls; Touch
Spinners	The Domingoes
Steppenwolf	Sparrow
Stone Temple Pilots	Mighty Joe Young; Shirley Temple's Pussy; Stereo Temple Pirates
Styx	TW4
Sugar Ray	Shrinky Dinx
The Supremes	The Primettes
Survivor	The Jim Peterik Band
(The) Sweet	The Sweetshop
Tears for Fears	The History of Headaches
The Temptations	The Elgins; Otis Williams & the Distants; The Primes
10,000 Maniacs	Burn Victims; Still Life
Tesla	City Kidd
.38 Special	The Other Side; Standard Production
The Turtles	The Crossfires; The Nightriders
Twisted Sister	Silverstar
Uriah Heep	Spice
The Velvet Underground	The Falling Spikes; The Primitives; The Warlocks
The Wallflowers	The Apples
Wang Chung	Huang Chung
War	The Creators; Nightshift
The Who	The Detours; The High Numbers
XTC	The Helium Kidz
Yes	Mabel Greer's Toy Shop

Appendix 2:
Names Considered
and Rejected

ABBA	Alibaba; Baba; Black Devils; Flower Power; Friends & Neighbours; Golden Diamonds
Aerosmith	Spike Jones & the Hookers
Badfinger	The Glass Onion; Home; The Prix
Bay City Rollers	The Arkansas Rollers
The Black Crowes	Confederate Crowes; The Kobb Kounty Krows; Stone Mountain Crowes
Blind Melon	Brown Cow; Frog; Gristie; Head Train; Mud Bird; Naked Pilgrims
Blur	The Government; Sensitize; The Shining Path; Whirlpool
The Clash	The Mirrors; The Outsiders; The Phones; The Psychotic Negatives; The Weak Heart Drops
Coldplay	Pectoralz
The Cranberries	The Cranberry Doodles; The Crandoodles
Cream	Sweet and Sour Rock 'n' Roll
Creedence Clearwater Revival	Deep Bottle Blue; Gossamer Wump; Muddy Rabbit
Culture Club	Can't Wait Club; Caravan Club
Deep Purple	Concrete God; Fire; Orpheus
Evanescence	Childish Intentions; Stricken
Fastball	Magnetic Heads
The Flaming Lips	Tijuana Toads
Foghat	Concrete Parachute; Titanium Turtle
Genesis	Champagne Meadow; Gabriel's Angels
Grateful Dead	The Hobbits; Mythical Ethical Icicle Tricycle; Vanilla Plumbego
The Human League	ABCD
Icehouse	Industrial Chilli
Journey	Hippie-potamus; Rumpled Foreskin

223

Kiss	Crimson Harpoon
Level 42	88; Kick in the Head; Powerline
The Mamas & the Papas	The Magic Cyrcle
Metallica	Blitzer; Red Veg
Motley Crue	Christmas
Mungo Jerry	The Incredible Shark
New Order	The Eternal; Stevie & the JDs; Sunshine Valley Dance Band
Nirvana	Bliss; Fecal Matter; Pen Cap Chew; Ted Ed Fred; Throat Oyster; Windowpane
No Doubt	Apple Core
The Pretenders	The Rhythm Method
Psychedelic Furs	Psychedelic Shirts; Psychedelic Shoes
Radiohead	Gravitate; Jude; Music
R.E.M.	Cans of Piss
Roxy Music	Essoldo; Gaumont; Odeon
Savage Garden	Bliss; Dante's Inferno
Sex Pistols	Beyond; Le Bomb; Subterraneans; Teenage Novel
Spice Girls	Five Alive; Plus Five; Take Five
Styx	Kelp; Torch
Supertramp	Daddy
The Supremes	The Darleens; Jewelettes; Melodees; Royaltones; Sweet Ps
Talking Heads	The Portable Crushers; Tunnel Tones; Vogue Dots; The World of Love
The Temptations	El Domingos; Siberians
10,000 Maniacs	Christian Burial; Dick Turpin's Ride to New York; Tundra Bunnies
Thin Lizzy	Gulliver's Travels
Thompson Twins	The Bermuda Triangle
Traveling Wilburys	Trembling Wilburys
The Tubes	The Gasmen; Larry and Mary; Radar Men From Uranus
The Turtles	The Half Dozen; The Six Pack
The Who	British European Airways; Group; The Hair; No One

Index

Index